The Politics of Education

Schools in Conflict

by

Frederick M. Wirt
University of Illinois at Champaign-Urbana

Michael W. Kirst
Stanford University

McCutchan Publishing Corporation
2526 Grove Street
Berkeley, California 94704

ISBN 0-8211-2261-4
Library of Congress Catalog Card Number 81-83250
© 1982 by McCutchan Publishing Corporation. All rights reserved
Printed in the United States of America

Cover design by Terry Down, Griffin Graphics
Typesetting composition by Marin Typesetters

For Valerie, Wendy, Chip, and Anne,
  who must endure or enjoy the schools of which we write

I would like to acknowledge the financial support of the Center for Advanced Study in Behavioral Sciences and the Spencer Foundation.

—M.W.K.

Preface

The politics of education has changed dramatically since we closed our first edition in 1970. It is surprising how quickly the political structures, actors, and processes of educational politics have become so fundamentally reorganized. The era of the local superintendent as "administrative chief" was then dawning. We did not, however, anticipate the multitude of actors and the complexity of the governmental patterns nor the large amount of discretion the chief executive would lose. The 1970s will be remembered as an era when the previous hallmark of American education—local control—became fully a myth. The political web surrounding the school district tightened and included many more participants. In this edition, we devote more space to this governmental complexity, so much so that most of the writing in this volume is new.

The 1970s was also a time when state government became ascendant, and teachers' organizations were empowered by state statutes. Consequently, we have expanded our discussion of collective bargaining and have included a separate chapter on state policy innovation. As a result of developments in these areas, the issues of state versus local control intensified, and we treat these issues in depth here. Further, the ability of state government to formulate educational policy was transformed as legislatures and governors acquired the capacity and willingness to intrude on local prerogatives. Too, the loss of public confidence in education is a critical cause of more state intervention, and we expand on this new orientation in several places.

At the outset of the 1980s, the federal role is changing profoundly for the first time since the burst of federal activism during 1958–1965. Federal aid is being slashed and, with this, federal control pruned. At this point, it is unclear whether or not this will result in a renewal of local discretion. It is more likely to reinforce state activism and control. We stress here the gradual evolution of the federal role and demonstrate the incremental impact of federal requirements on local practice. This should serve as a bench mark for measuring the federal deregulation that is likely during the next decade.

Further, we have expanded our earlier treatment of the courts due to the tremendous range of court-supervised educational policies now in effect. For example, as president of the California State Department of Education, one author was a defendant in 108 different lawsuits up to the year 1981. The judiciary has had to develop new roles as a result of such litigation, and the courts now employ a number of administrative devices such as masters or monitors to direct local policies.

We continue to find the conceptual framework of systems analysis useful in organizing and charting the increasingly complex political web of American education. For example, the loss of diffuse support for the political system of American schools illustrates the use of this concept. The current educational atmosphere is characterized by a rising public tide questioning the legitimacy of the public school. Tuition tax credits are one indicator of this loss of broad public support for public education. In another change of the early 1980s, the demands of school officials now center on questions of quality for the typical student, with less demand for radical structural change such as community control. Systems analysis has the scope to encompass this rapidly shifting scene and interpret the threats to the viability of public education as well.

Use of systems analysis reminds us that the study of educational politics has ballooned during the last decade. Schools of education regularly offer this type of analysis to graduate students in educational administration. Panels on the subject are now a regular part of the programs of the American Educational Research Association (AERA) and political scientists' conventions. Only a decade after a few people founded it, the AERA roster of members of the Special Interest Group in Politics of Education numbered well over 400. A new journal, *Education Evaluation and Policy Analysis*, provides a forum for serious analytical work, and for almost a decade, the Lexington and McCutchan series in the politics of education have contributed major analyses of scope and depth.

Education may be a "declining industry," as some claim, but the study of its politics is vigorous in this country. There are also stirrings of interest in the subject elsewhere. Grant Harmin of Australia has chronicled this international development during the 1970s in annotated bibliographies.

As we turn to analysis of the literature since we closed the first edition in 1970, we find a river of writing where before there were only creeks. We are most impressed by its quality and scope. This edition benefits greatly from these writings, though we also suggest potentially fruitful additions for the next decade.

Finally, we are deeply concerned by the uncertainties facing public education in the decade ahead. Loss of funds and support, critical attacks from friends and foes, a changing demography and inflated economy all combine to make the future challenging and exciting. But recall the ancient Chinese *curse*, May you live in exciting times! We first turn to a sketch of the political forces that engendered this contemporary turbulence.

Contents

1

The Political Turbulence of American Schools

The purpose of this book is to trace the ways in which American schools are viewed as political. This perspective arises in part from the school's connection to the recognizable political systems of state and national governments. It also arises from the way in which schools act as miniature political systems. However, many school professional and lay participants regard both of these points as not only untrue but also misleading, if not actually pernicious. Their view is that the institution they know and operate is "apolitical," having nothing to do with politics—for, as everyone knows, politicians are vile folk, somewhat equivalent to used-car salesmen in status. An indirect purpose of this volume is to reveal the extent that politics and education do intersect and to demonstrate that "professional" tasks are highly political and that professionals are politicians.

The differences in interpretation stem from varying conceptions of what constitutes a political act. Traditionally, schools have been characterized as apolitical, which meant that they had nothing to do with political parties, whose usual interactions with the citizenry have been regarded as "dirty"; schools were considered sanitized products, outside the hands of party politics. For political scientists, however, parties represent only one facet of political life. From their perspective, the essence of a political act is the struggle of a group to secure the authoritative support of government for its values. Within this definition, much of what schoolfolk regard as apolitical is highly political indeed.

Let us be clear on our focus. We are not discussing *how* schools should be run nor *what* they should teach and *why*. Rather our focus is on *how the process of policy making in schools has characteristics that can be termed* political. We will show how the policy-making process is becoming increasingly and more openly politicized as a result of major changes in how state and local governments and citizens themselves relate to the school system. New definitions of school purposes, new claims on school resources, new efforts to make the schools responsive to certain groups and their values are all giving rise to a larger, more weblike set of political relationships surrounding the local school. Almost any and every element of school governance could currently be caught up in political controversy. First, however, we will explore the popular notion of a divorce between schools and politics.

THE MYTH OF APOLITICAL EDUCATION

By a mutual but unspoken and long-standing agreement, American citizens and scholars have contended that the world of education is and should be separate from the world of politics. Although *elections* and *referenda* concerning school policies were viewed as political, these words did not connote "politics" in the usual sense when used for educational policy. There were two reasons for attempting to preserve the myth that "politics and education do not mix." The first was the risk to the school professionals who were overt players of politics when they were expected not to be. The second reason was the relative benefits to them —more legitimacy and money— if they preserved the image of the public schools as a uniquely nonpolitical function of government.[1]

At the turn of the century, a nationwide interlocking affiliation of "progressive" university presidents, school superintendents, and nonprofessional allies emerged from urban business and professional elites. One aim of these people was to free the schools from partisan politics and excessive decentralization. They saw political corruption as the prime cause of educational inefficiency in urban schools. Indeed, at that time many politicians did regard the schools as a useful support for their spoils systems, and they awarded school jobs and contracts as political favors.

Municipal corruption was everywhere, and the schools were just as bad as any other city office. Muckrakers exposed textbook publishers and contractors allied with corrupt school trustees for common boodle in the common school. Leaders concerned about these practices in urban education from 1890–1910 reported:

A superintendent in one of the Eastern States writes: "Nearly all the teachers in our schools get their positions by political 'pull.' If they secure a place and are not backed by political influence, they are likely to be turned out. Our drawing teacher recently lost her position for this reason." One writes from the South: "Most places depend on politics. The lowest motives are frequently used to influence ends." A faint wail comes from the far West: "Positions are secured and held by the lowest principles of corrupt politicians." "Politicians wage a war of extermination against all teachers who are not their vassals," comes from the Rocky Mountains.

In Boston, the teachership is still a spoil of office. It is more difficult, at the present time, for a Catholic than for a Protestant young woman to get a place, but, nevertheless, some Catholics secure appointments, for "trading" may always be done, while each side has a wholesome fear of the other assailing it in the open board. A member said one day, in my hearing: "I must have my quota of teachers."

The worst kind of boss rule has prevailed in San Francisco, and the board of education gradually became a place sought by those who wished to use the position for political preferment or for personal ends. Once every six or eight years there would be an effort at reform, and a few good men were elected; but they were usually in a minority, and the majority, held together by "the cohesive force of plunder," ruled things with a high hand.[2]

This situation was reinforced with a vengeance by local control. A decentralized, ward-based committee system for administering the public schools provided opportunities for extensive political influence. In 1905, Philadelphia had forty-three elected district school boards consisting of 559 members. There were only 7 members on the Minneapolis board, while Hartford, with a third as many people, had 39 school visitors and committeepersons.[3] Despite great variations, at the turn of the century sixteen of twenty-eight cities with more than one hundred thousand population had boards of 20 members or more.

Reformers contended that board members elected by wards advanced their own parochial and special interests at the expense of the school district as a whole. What was needed to counter this atomization, they believed, was election at large. A good school system was good for everyone, not just one segment of the community. Professional expertise rested on the assumption that scientific ways to administer schools did exist and were independent of the values of any particular group. This unitary-community idea would help protect schools from local political processes. Reformers also charged that the executive authority of the larger school boards was splintered because they worked through numerous subcommittees. No topic was considered too trivial for a separate subcommittee, ranging from the ways to teach reading to the purchase of doorknobs. At one time, Chicago had seventy-nine subcommittees, and Cincinnati had seventy-four.[4] The primary prerequisite for better management was thought to be centralization of power in a chief executive who would have considerable delegated authority from the school board. Only under such a system could someone make large-scale improvements and be held accountable.

By 1910, a conventional educational wisdom had evolved among the schoolfolk and leading business and professional men who had spearheaded the reforms. Sometimes only a very small group of patricians secured new charters from state legislatures and thereby reorganized the urban schools without any popular vote.[5] The watchwords of reform became *centralization, expertise, professionalism, nonpolitical control,* and *efficiency*—all of these would inspire "the one best system." The governance structure needed to be revised so that school boards would be small, elected at large, and freed from all connections with political parties and regular government officials such as mayors and councilmen.

The most attractive model for this organization and governance was the large-scale industrial bureaucracies that were rapidly emerging in the turn-of-the-century economy. Divorced from the city political leaders, a board elected by the city as a whole would be less susceptible to graft and job favoritism. The centralized power of the superintendent would overcome the bureaucratic tangle and inefficiency of board subcommittees. These reform concepts spread rapidly from the large to small cities and towns, and they found their major forum and vehicle in the National Education Association (NEA).

At the turn of the century, urban school reform was part of a broader pattern of elite municipal change. Public rhetoric of the time pitted the corrupt politician against the community-oriented citizen. However, the underlying motives of the reformers have been questioned by several historians. Hays has emphasized that financial and professional leaders deplored the decentralized ward system largely because it empowered members of the lower and lower-middle classes (many of whom were recent immigrants). Reformers wanted "not simply to replace bad men with good; they proposed to change the occupational and class origins of decision makers."[6] Tyack expresses this viewpoint in stronger language:

Underlying much of the reform movement was an elitist assumption that prosperous, native born Protestant Anglo-Saxons were superior to other groups and thus should determine the curriculum and the allocation of jobs. It was the mission of the schools to imbue children of the immigrants and the poor with uniformly WASP ideals.[7]

After these reforms were enacted, membership on governing agencies did change. Counts' classic study done in 1927 showed that upper-class professionals and business people made up the centralized boards of education.[8] For instance, in Saint Louis, after reforms in 1897, professionals on the board jumped from 4.8 percent to 58.3 percent and big businessmen from 9 percent to 25 percent; small businessmen dropped from 47.6 percent to 16.7 percent, and wage earners from 28.6 percent to none.[9] In turn, these board members delegated many of their formal powers to professionals along with discretion to shape schools to meet the needs of industrial society—but as defined by one segment of that society.

The no-politics ideal of public education has enjoyed impressive and lasting popularity with the general public. There have been hardnosed advantages for the professional in nursing this folklore, as summarized by one school superintendent.

1. The higher social status and salary generally accorded schoolpeople by the public is better maintained and somewhat dependent upon a situation in which the schools are seen as unique rather than as a mere extension of the same local government that provides dog catchers and sanitation departments.
2. In maintaining a tighter control over the public school system, the image of "unique function" allows greater leverage by the professional school administrator than an image acknowledging that schools are "ripe for the picking" by dilettante and professional politicians.
3. The "unique function" image also provides the schools with a stronger competitive position for tax funds wherever voters are allowed to express a choice of priorities among government agencies.[10]

The outcome of this nonpolitical ideology is a massive irony in our political system that is characterized by Martin:

Thus is the circle closed and the paradox completed. Thus does the public school, heralded by its champions as the cornerstone of democracy, reject the political world in which democratic institutions operate. Thus is historical identification with local government accompanied by insistence on complete independence of any agency . . . of local government, lip service to general citizen activity attended by mortal fear of general politics, the logical and legitimate companion of citizen action.[11]

Political Turbulence and School Policy

More recently, several national trends have made the public schools more overtly political, strongly challenging the tenets of turn-of-the-century reformers. In the 1960s, there was a call for "community participation" in all types of public agencies that was widely accepted by social critics and reformers. Proponents contended that citizens have to be more than "involved" or "consulted" if government is to gain their active consent. Rather they have to actually "participate" in democracy, even though this might sometimes involve social conflict, such as picketing and strikes. The federal school-aid legislation of the 1960s encouraged participation by creating a number of watchdog citizens' advisory commissions and requiring consultation by school authorities with community groups.

This recent change in governing style highlights a continuing basic problem in the governance of American schools: the tension between the community's need for school leadership that can lead and be trusted and the same community's desire to have its own will carried out by that leadership. Since its inception with Horace Mann's heresy, American public education has sought responsiveness to public needs with what Raymond Fosdick termed the extraordinary possibilities of ordinary people. The altering focus of American civic education over a century shows this.[12] So does the ongoing search for methods to ensure public responsiveness—from party control of schools through the progressive model of corporate centralization to the contemporary call for "community control." This history shows the truth of Solomon's adjuration that there is nothing new under the sun, for there has been an intriguing repetition of issues in schools over the last century:[13] smaller school systems exhibit tensions of bureaucracy versus participation, superintendents are dependent on southern community power structures, and there are variations in principals' political styles.[14] In large part, we read both the repetition and variety as reflections of the classic political tension between leaders and the led, in this case centered on having school policy work the way each wishes.

This tension between leader and led underlies current conflict brought on as new groups arose during the last two decades to challenge the old power pattern in the schools. New "core constituencies" of the school have emerged. (*Core* indicates that we have separated these groups for analytical purposes although they are not necessarily mutually exclusive in experience.) Each group creates special tensions for the school's political authority as exercised by the board and its administrators because each core constituency challenges the leadership in a special issue that involves reallocation of school resources. These issues and their core constituencies are:

> Parents—shared or community control, advisory input, decentralization, or whatever term is current.
>
> Students—rights of governance, expression, dress, behavior, and so on.
>
> Teachers—organization for collective bargaining (hereafter shortened to "teacher power").
>
> Taxpayers—reform of local financing involving a larger assumption of costs by the state.
>
> Minorities—the issues generated by the *Brown* decision which encompass desegregation and integration.
>
> Federal and state authorities—guidelines, mandates, court orders in matters of discrimination, curriculum, finances, and so forth.

Controversy over such issues may vary from locality to locality, but they do move in response to certain forces. That is, local school conflict is shaped by forces both outside and inside an individual district. The absence of walls around the school districts opens them to public and private influences from the external, multiple centers of decision making that characterize American national life.[15] New concepts about how society should be conducted or life enjoyed, the episodic eruption of national events that crystalize local hopes and fears about school matters, and the immediate transmission by media of such thought and action into every urban crevice are all major extracommunity stimuli of school conflict. When such local conflict mobilizes new groups, when national currents are at work locally, and when the rancor and clamor swells, we reach a level of conflict better termed *turbulence.*

CURRENTS OF TURBULENCE

We will develop a fuller treatment of these new power groups throughout this book, but at this point it will help focus our analysis to briefly review their roles. Figure 1.1 provides an introduction to the concept of turbulence and to these groups.

Parents and Shared Control

The turn-of-the-century triumph of the doctrine of efficiency, which was achieved through centralization and bureaucracy, attenuated the ties between school leadership and its constituents. That was acceptable in the pre-World War II decades when schooling laid minimal claims on district resources and professionals benefited from their own publicity about education as the sovereign key to success. In the two decades after that war, this weakened linkage (as voting studies showed) continued to be acceptable in the rush to obtain schooling for all.[16]

Sometime during the late 1950s, the professionals' aura began to fade. In 1954, the *Brown* decision illustrated the disgraceful failure of southern educators with their Black students for the first time. Other complaints emerged that, regardless of race, Johnny could not read or speak languages or calculate in base ten, and that the Russians were somehow outperforming our school system. Our rivalry with the Russians generated a vast injection of local and federal funds into schools—the National Defense Education Act in the late 1950s, university support in the early 1960s, and finally the Elementary and Secondary Education Act in 1965.

The more voters contributed, however, the more they complained that somehow the educational bureaucracy was not sensitive to parental preferences in schooling their children. Social scientists joined with analyses of the monolithic—that is, unresponsive—nature of the schooling administration, with New York City's central head-quarters at 110 Livingston Street regarded as the prototype rather than exception.[17] Suburbanites maintained that administrators were insensitive to their demands either for richer or plainer curricula,

Figure 1.1

Paradigm of Turbulent School Politics

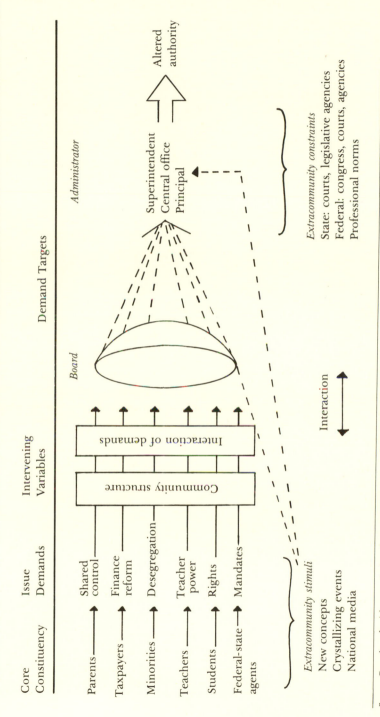

Core Constituency	Issue Demands	Intervening Variables		Demand Targets	Administrator

Parents → Shared control

Taxpayers → Finance reform

Minorities → Desegregation

Teachers → Teacher power

Students → Rights

Federal-state agents → Mandates

Community structure

Interaction of demands

Board

Superintendent
Central office
Principal

Altered authority

Interaction

Extracommunity stimuli
New concepts
Crystallizing events
National media

Extracommunity constraints
State: courts, legislative agencies
Federal: congress, courts, agencies
Professional norms

Source: Reprinted with permission from Frederick M. Wirt, "Political Turbulence and Administrative Authority in the Schools," in Louis H. Masotti and Robert L. Lineberry, eds., *The New Urban Politics*, p. 63. Copyright 1976, Ballinger Publishing Company.

whether in affluent Scarsdale, New York, or working-class Maple Heights, Ohio. In the central cities—particularly in the newly mobilized Black communities—central offices and site principals were increasingly pilloried for their insensitivity, which was easily labeled "racism." Across a surprisingly wide gamut of lifestyles, parents-as-voters came to criticize their lack of connection with school district decision making.

Although reasons for this lack differed with locale and status, clearly the old participatory impulse had increased. Notions of shared control took on different forms during the 1970s. Sometimes participation involved parents having structured input into school decisions. Thus, there were new structures for parental advisory committees at the school site level. In California, for example, community members joined the principal and teachers of the school to set a budget in tune with their own definition of good education. In Chicago, parental committees came to have a large—but not definitive—role in evaluating principals' professional behavior.

Parental input also moved directly to concerns about what was being taught in the classroom. The fear of teaching Communism during the 1950s became in the 1970s the anger at teaching about biological evolution or about children reading fiction with harsh language or critical views of American society. Other parents rose to the defense of these same curriculum subjects. Battles took place in street demonstrations, court suits, state legislative lobbies—accompanied by a steady vilification of professionals and board members. The worst example of this was in Kanawha County, West Virginia, in the mid-1970s, when the school district's central office was dynamited by someone opposed to the teaching of "Man: A Course of Study" (MACOS).

Parental input went even further and challenged the very quality of the school's results, namely, academic achievement. From the earlier concern with whether or not Johnny could read, there have been growing claims—and some supporting data—that schools were not teaching effectively. National news magazines featured articles on school "failures" in this regard during the late seventies and early eighties. Demands arose to hold teachers individually responsible for their pupils' progress, while professionals pointed to numerous factors more potent than teachers in influencing results. By the end of the 1970s, some states had moved to require examination of teachers for effectiveness.

In short, parents became much more than just the old PTA clique, which had unquestioningly supported professionals prior to the mid-1960s. Parental energies and their agendas swelled along with their growing numbers. It no longer worked to keep them busy with a cake sale to raise money for a classroom projector. The traditionally unchallenged use of public authority that had been tendered to school professionals was being reexamined—and the professionals were widely regarded as failing.[18]

Taxpayers and Financial Reform

Demands for more control of schools have not been restricted to parents concerned with what schools were doing to their children; over the last fifteen years, taxpayers have also challenged school financing.[19] A spate of litigation developed from the fusion of the Ford Foundation and university scholars in law and educational finance. It began in California with the famous *Serrano* decision, which found the principle that student expenditures were based on district wealth unconstitutional. The United States Supreme Court's 1973 *Rodriquez* case narrowly prevented this from being elevated into a constitutional principle. Reform efforts continued though, focusing on state legislatures after the abortive attempts at change through the Supreme Court and statewide referenda.

Pressures to redistribute school financial resources are accompanied by pressures to have the state take on a higher share of local school costs. Since 1900 that state share has grown, stabilizing at around 40 percent after World War II (a figure concealing numerous small shifts up and down). By 1970 it was still at that level, but by 1981, it had jumped to over 60 percent because of recent reform movements. Local financial support had also fallen off. The mid-1960s were the peak for support of local bond and tax issues; thereafter the phenomenon of multiple trips to the public well began, each to pass a single issue.

A network of school finance reformers appeared amid this current of protest. Public policy issues emerge on state political agendas for many reasons, but one of the most important and least understood is the role of interstate lobbying networks that sponsor and promote the issues in a wide variety of forums. Elements of the network may be entrepreneurs, private nonprofit advocacy organizations, lawyers, interstate technical assistance groups, and often private foundations. These networks spread ideas and create opportunities for state politicians to champion particular causes or programs. Many of the most interesting educational innovations, such as competency testing, have been promoted by a lobby network.

By 1981, two of the largest networks—those for school finance reform and spending or tax limits—had begun to clash with each other. School finance reformers advocated large increases in state and local spending to meet "equity" criteria and special needs, such as those for bilingual, handicapped, or urban students. Members of the other reform group were crusaders for tax limitation, seeking to stop or reverse the growth in state and local spending. Both networks were spawned by entrepreneurs who generated activity and structured rewards; both drew together members from diverse organizations.

The school finance reform movement for equity can claim impact in about half the states, those twenty to twenty-five states containing about 60 percent of the nation's pupils. Its predominant approach has been to bring up the level of the low-spending districts. Meanwhile, the high-spending districts have lobbied not to be hurt. Those seeking tax limitations have been less immediately successful, but during the 1980s this group will probably gather more support due to the nation's increasingly conservative mood. Both movements represent popular challenges to traditional authority. Local professionals and boards can no longer expect voter support for spending programs based on the old taxing methods. The sources and amounts of school monies have become a very dry well. State legislatures, often under goading from the courts, are scenes of complex formula making for raising and distributing state school funds. And all of this operates within a tide of disenchantment about school results, which further undercuts traditional public support for school finances.

Racial Minorities and Desegregation

The core constituency of racial minorities, so intimately involved in school desegregation, has two purposes. First these groups seek a status goal, recognition that the Constitution's commitment to equal protection of the law applies to them as well, despite centuries of prejudice and discrimination. As such, desegregation is only one aspect of the "politics of deference," the central struggle of American ethnic politics to gain respect for one's importance and value as individuals and as a group.[20] The second goal of minorities in school desegregation is material, namely, the reallocation of school resources to improve life opportunities for their children. Desegregation is therefore one aspect of the concern for redistributive justice sparked in the recent decades by challenges to the standards of urban service provided to America's poor of whatever race.

In this effort, almost nothing has been achieved without external pressure upon the local district. Everywhere the forces of court orders and in the South, prior to the Nixon administration, the threat of fund cutoffs to segregated schools have accounted for whatever has been done. Local protests brought little change in encrusted racial conditions despite nationwide publicity.

Against local racial barriers, a coalition of national and local interest groups, scholars, legal studies centers, and national media arose that interacted with the federal courts to dramatically alter the face of southern education. Between 1962 and 1972, the South dismantled its de jure segregated schools under the combined attack of private groups and federal action. Year after year, the number of all-white schools shrank so abruptly that it amazed many who thought such change was a matter of decades. By 1981, southern desegregation had gone well beyond the publicized stage of parental protest over busing or white supremacists's fears of racial mixing. Now these schools' problems were more educational than political; that is, the problems involved improving the educational services and enhancing the life chances of the poor regardless of race.

The situation in the North during the 1970s looked much like that of the South during the 1950s, with actual segregation taking place. The federal thrust diminished over the years because of presidents with little political will for the issues, Congresses under great pressure from those who saw busing as the special evil of desegregation, and the lack of support from northern whites for a range of special programs that originated in President Johnson's Great Society program. Enormous movements of whites out of central cities, recalcitrant local school boards, aroused local political organizations, and hesitant local press all combined at the district level to slow or block a movement that was simultaneously changing dramatically in the South. But there was continuing litigation in the North, and a rash of federal district judges ordering desegregation planning and busing. Every fall during the 1970s, the opening of northern schools witnessed some big city in turmoil over beginning this task; in 1980 it was Los Angeles and Saint Louis. Yet much desegregation did transpire without publicity, especially in middle-sized places. But for many Americans, the street fighting in Boston was what they associated with such change, although Denver desegregated quietly that same fall. Wherever such turbulence occurs, there is a formal, almost inescapable, drama that must unfold, with each stage set regardless of locale. By 1981, however, there were an impressive number of districts where desegregation had at least extended to the stage at which the outcry dies down, the buses roll regularly, and education begins.

Students and Their Rights

Core constituencies sketched to this point are based outside the school walls, but two groups operate on the inside, that is, students and teachers. Both have known the same remarkably brief and recent period during which novel concepts have suddenly flowered to provide them with new powers formerly controlled by administrators. Considering their position of relative weakness, students have made strides that contrast dramatically with the background of the law's long indifference to them.[21]

For most of our history, the authority of the school administrator over the student's life at school has been almost complete. Legislatures gave the state departments of education broad authority that they in turn passed on to the school professional for daily implementation. The federal Constitution and statutes had no sway here for the idea of student rights rooted in these sources did not yet exist. During this era, an administrator's response to any student even politely questioning why he or she had to dress, walk, eat, speak, and otherwise act in the prescribed manner was much like that of writer Ring Lardner when his children questioned him: " 'Shut up,' I explained."

The seminal United States Court decision in this field, which typified subsequent thinking by other courts, was another of those abrupt changes in the power context of schools—the 1969 decision of *Tinker* v. *the Des Moines School District*. Here, Des Moines students wearing black armbands to protest the Vietnam War had been suspended even though they had created no disruption. The Court's opinion noted that when a basic constitutional right, such as free speech under the First Amendment, was being exercised, and there was no evidence that the student action interfered with school purposes or disrupted schooling, no punishment could be levied. As later cases showed, such an exercise *could* create disruptions and so be prohibited. Thus, southern schools could not restrict the wearing of civil rights buttons if the results were nondisruptive, but they could do so if they caused disturbances.

In a few years, this principle and those of due process and equal protection of the laws have permeated many traditional school practices. Only a brief listing of judicial restraints on once-conventional disciplinary rules and management decisions is possible here, but recall that these have all emerged since 1969. They include rulings in the areas of censorship of student publications; use of athletic symbols, Confederate flags, and school names; regulating hair length; lack of procedures for suspension and expulsion; corporal punishment; use of bulletin boards; use of achievement or aptitude tests; rules for athletic eligibility; preference for male rather than female sports programs, and so on.

As a result, school authorities everywhere drew up lengthly statements of student rights and school authority. Professional associations assisted with model statements relating to different fields. None of this meant that students could not be expelled or suspended, their publications controlled, or their expressions banned. They could, but now only according to set procedures and over a longer period of time. All of this constituted an additional challenge to the once unchallengeable school authority, adding another eddy to school turbulence.

Teachers and Organizational Power

The other core constituency challenging traditional authority from inside the school is teachers—once widely viewed as submissive. It would be hard to find a city superintendent or principal who would regard teachers so today. A change has transpired among teachers in the past twenty years. In part this stems from changes in American education itself and in part from teachers' perceptions of themselves. As with other education groups, things will never be the same here again.

Teachers achieved a potential for power as education became big business.[22] When more parents wanted their children to have more schooling after World War II, and there were also more children to educate, Americans spent more on education. This in turn meant that more teachers were needed. As a proportion of the gross national product (GNP), school expenditures rose during the period 1949 to 1970 from about 3.5 to 8 percent. Where we spent only $2 billion in 1940, we spent $50 billion in 1970 and over $100 billion in 1980. Riding this massive injection of funds into the schools, teachers grew in numbers from just over 1 million in 1940 to almost 3 million in 1971 and to about 3.3 million in 1980. By the mid-1970s teachers were 1 million fewer in number than farmers but substantially more than teamsters, auto workers, steelworkers, and doctors. Not surprisingly, their income also rose. Between 1952 and 1968, teachers' incomes increased by over 125 percent, while personal income and employee average earnings rose nationally by about 94 percent. Their salaries passed the average earnings of industrial workers some time back, and the gap increased even more during the 1960s. Since the middle 1970s, however, teachers' wage increases have lagged behind inflation and private industry.

Concern about wages helped cause teachers' increasingly conscious efforts to organize for collective bargaining on salary and other matters. The cause-and-effect relationship is ambiguous, however. Did bargaining legislation and subsequent organization precede or follow teachers' dissatisfactions? Were boards and legislatures frightened into voluntary improvements in reaction against successful teacher strikes elsewhere? What were the costs incurred with such new power?

There is no question, however, about the growth of teachers in affiliations that have become more insistent on improving working conditions. This insistence was seen in the toughening up of the larger National Education Association (NEA), once passive on these issues, or in the rise of the smaller but more militant American Federation of Teachers (AFT). These groups also became more active in party politics. For the first time, the NEA endorsed a presidential candidate, Carter, in 1976 and 1980. An estimated three hundred members of the Democratic convention delegates in 1980 were NEA members, the largest interest block there; the AFT had another sixty-six but endorsed another candidate. Not surprisingly, President Carter successfully pushed for a new cabinet-level Department of Education in his term, something the NEA had much desired. However, his successful opponent in the 1980 election moved to abolish the department in 1980, and its future is doubtful.

The growth of powerful teacher organizations has been paralleled by the rise of the strike. Despite widely prevalent state laws against public employees' use of this tactic, some form of strike—"withholding of labor"—has developed as the main instrument used to secure teachers' benefits in recent years. Between 1955 and 1965 there were only 35 strikes in all, but during the one year of 1967–1968 there were 114 and 131 the next year. Coincidental or not, during this first period of strike action, 1966–1968, the number of signed contracts increased by almost one-half. By 1980, the strike of teachers was as much a part of autumn as the opening of the football season.

This success has not been without its attendant problems for teachers. As teachers participate more and more in the reallocation of resources at the local, state, and national political level, they lose the aura of being apolitical. It was this mythical quality that enabled them to claim a large share of resources for so long without having to contend with other claimants. Now, in the state legislatures and city councils, where school budgets are sometimes reviewed, teachers are only one more pressure group whose claim to special treatment must be balanced against others' claims. It follows that other pressure groups will increasingly combine against the teachers' claims and draw them even more into open political conflict. The status of teachers may also decrease because they are seen as being "political," with all the opprobrium the term signifies in American culture.

From the big cities, where the AFT has been most active, the teacher movement has spread to the suburbs, although it rarely reaches the small towns outside the metropolis. Sometimes the movement skips these places and blankets them in under state laws providing for negotiation of teacher salaries. However, these laws vary in their elaborateness and the level of their requirements. Some make it optional for the school board to negotiate, and others make it mandatory; some limit negotiation to a few issues, and others provide wider scope. Whatever their form, however, these laws change the traditional interaction between teacher and administrator, adding another constraint to the broad authority officials once had.

Federal and State Authorities

From the perspective of school boards and professionals who watch this turbulence breaking against their walls, probably the most noticed—because most complained of—has been the force of external governments. The movement of core constituencies, demanding new definitions of how schools should be structured, financed, and their services delivered—has often been frustrated by local authorities. The protests have then escalated to higher levels of government within the federal system. This second stage of the conflict resulted in some groups securing state and federal statutes, administrative rulings, or court orders in their favor that then impinged upon the local power structure. This has resulted in great limitations on local authorities' control of the school program.[23]

Each of the constituencies referred to has generated a spate of such external requirements. These cross the desk of local authorities in the forms of mandates, guidelines, orders, suggestions, and reporting forms. Sometimes the source is a funded program to enhance educational services, but it can come in the form of a court injunction not to do something or a court mandate to do something else. These can become enormously detailed in their requirements. In some cases, regulations or suggestions come without the finances necessary to administer them. And always there are multiple forms for demonstrating to a state or federal authority that what was required has in fact been achieved. These add enormously to the volume of services and standards the schools must maintain.

Not surprisingly, many districts found this new volume of demands beyond their capacity, even had they the will for it. The period since the mid-1960s has therefore brought about the curious phenomenon, reportedly widespread, of respectable school authorities evading the law—be it court order, regulation, or statute. The fact that the higher authorities do not always or even often supervise what they have commanded makes these evasions easier for district authorities to adopt as a coping strategy.

Not all of the mandates can be evaded, however. Some work their way into the regular procedures of the district, where they consitute a new force from a new constituency working against the previous professional dominance of schools. The general rule, supported by research, is that what the district favors in this flow of external demands becomes what is most implemented. But where the district neither asks for nor rejects the demands, then studied evasion of the law becomes the norm. It would be a rare district among the sixteen thousand in the nation where this response did not take place, but bit by bit, across two decades, this extramural force has challenged and incrementally altered traditional local control to become another current in the contemporary turbulence of American schools.

Political Forces Outside the Locality

No constituency acts independently; the turbulence of school politics is also affected by extracommunity stimuli. The outside forces noted in figure 1.1 may be the most important factor in all contemporary local politics, whether dealing with schools, high-rise buildings, welfare, ethnic conflict, roads, or other public policies.[24]

There are three broad stimuli that affect the school constituencies. First, the *state of the economy* greatly influences the amount of resources available and their allocation. Many administrators, particularly the older superintendents, have witnessed the two extremes of our national economy—bust and boom. The Great Depression of the 1930s shrank all school budgets, preventing new programs and cutting others. Under such intense constraints from a public sorely pressed, the school boards could listen to few if any claims from core constituencies except the taxpayers.

More recently, an enormous prosperity and then subsequent recession penetrated every school district in the nation. In the resurgence of public support for schools, which began with the post-Sputnik fervor and ended in the late 1960s as a direct consequence of the Vietnam War, booming expenditures were visible in local politics. With ever-expanding resources seemingly available, claimants for new programs and benefits could be satisfied by boards and administrators. When this brief era ended, federal money entered local school districts to support claims from parents of the poor, minorities, and handicapped for compensatory education. By 1981, the recession and inflation of the Carter years penetrated local districts, drying up federal funds and constraining the core constituencies. These economic fluctuations demonstrate how interdependent our economy is.

Another extracommunity stimulus is *the power of new concepts*, particularly those centered on social change. Every change mentioned for a core constituency illustrates this process. In addition, education seems particularly subject to faddishness in curricular matters, such as new math, techniques of language instruction, ethnic studies, career education, and so on. Certainly the new concept of "evaluation," given a powerful initiative by Title I of the 1965 Elementary and

Secondary Education Act (ESEA), has penetrated many elements of school activity wherever federal monies are deposited.

Spawned by some scholarly "scribbler," funded by foundations, transmitted by educators' meetings and journals, researched and certified by schools of education, reform ideas sweep through the American school system in recurring tides. Some are transitory, for example, Nixon's Right to Read program, but others leave a permanent effect on schools, such as desegregation in the South. Behind them all, however small or large, is someone's notion of the preferable, the efficient, the humane, the inexpensive, and the just in matters of schooling.

Another class of extramural stimuli is those highly publicized *crystallizing events* that quickly become visible to core constituencies and dramatically generate new demands on local school authorities, adding even more turbulence to school politics. A successful statewide teachers' strike in Oklahoma and Florida; precedent-shattering judicial decisions in the *Tinker, Brown,* and *Serrano* cases; a clash over community control in New York City—all these illustate the kind of event that no one can ignore.

These extramural events are not totally separable from extramural concepts, for each of the examples noted above emerged from a new full-blown conception about the schools' allocation of resources and values. But a concept that is only circulated among scholars lacks both life and influence until an event embodying it suddenly captures national attention. A concept can also have an effect without the crystallizing event; the dissemination of sex education programs by school administrators illustrates this change-from-within process.[25] But the combination of concept and event creates a very powerful stimulus for change among the core constituencies that make local school politics so turbulent today.

THE IMPACT OF TURBULENCE ON SCHOOL GOVERNANCE

The Era of Nobody in Charge—1960 to 1980

One impact of school turbulence is that the local superintendent has lost his once-preeminent position in setting the district agenda and controlling decision outcomes. The superintendent and school board have become a reactive force, trying to juggle diverse and changing coalitions across different issues. Many school reforms such as new math have disappeared, but some left a deposit of structural changes that could be easily monitored and which created a constituency. Consequently, a partial legacy from the 1960–1980 era was tremendous growth in the specialized functions of the school, including administrative specialists in career education, bilingual education, nutrition, health, remedial reading, and so on. Many of these new structural layers diluted the superintendent's influence because the specialists were paid separately by federal or state categorical programs. Hence they were insulated from the superintendent's influence by separate financing and the requirements of higher levels of government.

The discretionary decision zone of local superintendents and boards has in effect been squeezed progressively into a smaller and smaller area. The superintendent's discretion is squeezed from the top by increasing regulations from the legislative, administrative, and judicial arms of the federal and state governments, as noted. In addition, there has been the expanding influence of private interest groups and professional reformers, such as the Ford Foundation and the Council for Basic Education. Moreover, interstate groups, such as the Education Commission of the States, increased their influence, as did nationally oriented organizations, such as the Council for Exceptional Children. All over the nation, networks of individuals and groups sprang up to spread school finance reform, competency testing, spending limits, and other programs.

Superintendents and local boards also found their decision-making powers squeezed from the bottom by forces such as the growth of local collective bargaining contracts reinforced by national teacher organizations. A recent study documents the incursion of these organizations into educational policy.[26] And, as noted, the last two decades have been a growth period for local interest groups often resulting from national social movements, as our thesis on turbulence proposes and as shown in figure 1.1. A yet-unstudied question is whether these constraints and forces external to the local settings have been more influential and effective than those of the 1920–1950 era, for example, the Progressives and professional societies.

Beleaguered local boards and superintendents found that as the 1970s ended their discretionary authority was further reduced due to other kinds of outside forces, primarily economic and demographic. Student populations declined and there was a spreading resistance to increased school taxes, both highly constraining. The seventies witnessed a disillusionment with professionals in general and educators in particular in many states. Distrust had grown as more actors squabbled at the local level over the decreasing school resource base. All of this is exemplified by the spreading movement of "accountability," largely coming from federal and state sources. Such diverse subjects as due process and competency-based graduation are good examples of this new accountability orientation.

The social movements of this period differ form those of the nineteenth century, exemplified by Horace Mann, which were interested in building up institutions like the schools. Today social movements are interested in challenging these public institutions and trying to make them more responsive to forces outside the local administrative structure. Some would even assert that these movements help fragment school decision making so that schools cannot function effectively. The litany of the media includes violence, vandalism, and declining test scores as the predominant state of public education.

In California, for example, this situation has become so serious that the schools increasingly suffer from shock and overload characterized by loss of morale and too few resources to operate all the programs the society expects schools to offer. The issue then becomes how much change and agitation a public institution can take and still continue to function effectively. Californians are confronted with numerous initiatives such as Proposition 13, vouchers, spending limits, and an extreme version of all the other forces sketched above. Citizens there and elsewhere go to their local school board and superintendent expecting redress of their problems only to find that the decision-making power is at the state or some other nonlocal level. The impression grows that no one is "in charge" of public education.

All of this does not mean that local school authorities are helpless. Rather it means that they cannot control their agenda or shape decision outcomes as they could in the past. The superintendent must deal with shifting and ephemeral coalitions that might yield him some temporary marginal advantages. But many of the policy items on the local agenda arise from external forces, such as state and federal governments, or from the pressures of established local interest groups, including teachers. The earlier—1920–1960—era of the "administrative chief" has passed with profound consequences, as the new school politics is much more complex and less malleable. How can we understand as political the seeming confusion of actors and events, emotion and rationality, conflict and conformity described in this chapter? That is the purpose of this book—to provide an analytical framework for understanding the politics of education.

NOTES

1. The theme was introduced by Thomas H. Eliot, "Toward an Understanding of Public School Politics," *American Political Science Review* 52 (1959): 1032–51.

2. David Tyack, "Needed: The Reform of a Reform," in *New Dimensions of School Board Leadership*, National School Boards Association (Evanston, Ill.: NSBA, 1969), pp. 29–51.

3. Ibid., p. 32.

4. Ibid.

5. Raymond E. Callahan, *Education and the Cult of Efficiency* (Chicago: University of Chicago Press, 1962); David Tyack, *The One Best System* (Cambridge, Mass.: Harvard University Press, 1974).

6. Samuel P. Hays, "The Politics of Reform in Municipal Government in the Progressive Era," *Pacific Northwest Quarterly* 55 (1963): 163.

7. Tyack, "Needed: The Reform," p. 35.

8. George S. Counts, *The Social Composition of Boards of Education* (Chicago: University of Chicago Press, 1927).

9. Elinor M. Gersman, "Progressive Reform of the St. Louis School Board, 1897," *History of Education Quarterly* 10 (1970): 8–15.

10. Lesley H. Browder, "A Suburban School Superintendent Plays Politics," in *The Politics of Education at the Local, State and Federal Levels,* Michael W. Kirst, ed. (Berkeley: McCutchan, 1970), pp. 191–94.

11. Roscoe C. Martin, *Government and the Suburban School* (Syracuse, N.Y.: Syracuse University Press, 1962), p. 89.

12. Gladys A. Wiggin, *Education and Nationalism* (New York: McGraw-Hill, 1962).

13. Michael B. Katz, ed., *School Reform: Past and Present* (Boston: Little, Brown & Co., 1971).

14. The findings stated are drawn, in order, from : Robert R. Alford, *Bureaucracy and Participation* (Chicago: Rand McNally, 1969); Ralph Kimbrough, *Political Power and Educational Decision Making* (Chicago: Rand McNally, 1964); Harry L. Summerfield, *The Neighborhood-based Politics of Education* (Columbus, Ohio: Charles E. Merrill, 1971).

15. Norton Long, *The Unwalled City* (New York: Basic Books, 1972); Frederick M. Wirt, *Power in the City* (Berkeley: University of California Press, 1974).

16. See the survey data in Richard F. Carter and John Sutthoff, *Communities and Their Schools* (Stanford: Institute for Communication Research, 1960).

17. David Rogers, *110 Livingston Street* (New York: Random House, 1968).

18. For a broader perspective on current professional challenge, see Frederick M.

Wirt, "Professionalism and Political Conflict: A Developmental Model," *Journal of Public Policy* 1 (1981), in press.

19. The fullest analysis of the following material is found in Walter Garms, James Guthrie, and Lawrence Pierce, *School Finance: The Economics and Politics of Federalism* (Englewood Cliffs, N.J.: Prentice-Hall, 1978).

20. The ethnic factor is set out in Wirt, *Power in the City*, pt. V. The fullest analysis of events in this section is found in Gary Orfield, *Must We Bus? Segregated Schools and National Policy* (Washington, D. C.: Brookings Institution, 1978).

21. The following material draws upon John C. Hogan, *The Schools, the Courts, and the Public Interest* (Lexington, Mass.: Lexington Books, 1974).

22. Following data are drawn from James W. Guthrie and Patricia A. Craig, *Teachers and Politics* (Bloomington, Ind.: Phi Delta Kappa Educational Foundation, 1973).

23. The fullest review of this current is Tyll van Geel, *Authority to Control the School Program* (Lexington, Mass.: Lexington Books, 1976).

24. See this theme developed in the sources of note 15.

25. Neal Milner and James Hottois, *The Sex Education Controversy* (Lexington, Mass.: Lexington Books, 1975).

26. Lorraine McDonnell and Anthony Pascal, "National Trends in Teacher Collective Bargaining," *Education and Urban Society* (1979): 129–51.

2

Systems Analysis: A Guide to Political Turbulence

Given the turbulence described in the previous chapter, it would seem hard to find patterns in such turmoil, in what Henry James called the "buzzing, booming confusion of reality." The currents discussed operate in roughly sixteen thousand school districts, a truly indecipherable mosaic without some guide for classifying and explaining what transpires. In short, one needs an analytical scheme that can make sense of both the diversity and similarity found in American education. Moreover, one needs a political framework of analysis to understand the political nature of school turbulence.

METHODS OF EDUCATION SYSTEM ANALYSIS

Some of the explanation that follows has been provided by scholars, albeit with different purposes in mind. Educational journals are filled with a type of analysis termed *description*. These are descriptions of the operations of school systems and subsystems, their agents and participants, and their laws and regulations. The description of a purported reality is invariably accompanied by normative *evaluations*. These are value judgments about whether the object described is worthwhile or workable. Description and evaluation further merge indefinably into *prescription*—recommendations for changing the reality to achieve the normative objectives, to close the gap between the real and the ideal. What is least common is *explanation*—suppositions and supporting evidence about the causes, consequences, and interrelationships of objects in reality. Causal theory of this kind is frequently found in the psychology of education and sometimes in the sociology of education but seldom in educational administration before the 1970s.[1]

When we look for causal theory in the study of the politics of education, however, we find very little. The reasons lie in the myth of apolitical schools and the lack of a theory to direct and channel research. This is less true in 1982 than before, as the myth is being discarded and the theory sought. So long as school policy was regarded as "above" politics, its study—using standard, political, analytic frameworks—was regarded as misguided. As a consequence, theoretical statements of explanatory power were unlikely to develop. Accepted theories of one sort make it difficult to entertain opposing explanations. If the stork is said to bring babies, there is not much room for sex education.

Iannaccone has explained how the profession incorporated this orientation by asserting that education is a "closed system," isolated from politics, and its leaders are therefore free from external control. Also, by controlling what comes in from the outside environment, educators could reduce change within their system. Such effort is clearly useful for professional educators, freeing them from many external constraints and the unsettling demands for internal change that characterize other social and "more political" institutions.[2] In the past, educators were so skilled that they moved the community to adopt the apolitical myth. As Eliot wryly noted, a successful super-intendent was one adept in "community relations," but "why not say frankly that he must be a good politician?"[3] Yet most political scientists accepted the educators' closed-system definition unques-tioningly. Only recently—seeing similarities in education to other policies—have they recalled that "Rosy O'Grady and the Colonel's lady are sisters under the skin."

The most significant reason, however, for the once-meager scholar-ly analysis of educational politics is probably the lack of an applicable theoretical orientation and methodology. As Kirst and Mosher have shown, it is clear that no single theory, simple or complex, presently guides such research, nor is there agreement on the appropriate methodology.[4] Political scientists are severely divided between traditional studies of institutional or legal analysis and those who use statistical and other quantitative studies of political behavior. Among the second group, the behavioralists, there are a number of partial theories of political behavior, which is another complication. In short, despite the flood of "politics of education" work done in the 1970s noted in the preface, there is still no overarching general theory that generates hypotheses that could be tested by acceptable methods in the crucible of political experiences. Instead there is a grab bag of partial theories and contrasting methods. That this is typical of the early stages in any scholarship is nonetheless frustrating for those who want to make some order amidst the confusion. The politics of education is certainly not a field for those who prefer scholarship that explicates established truths, but it will be exciting to those who prefer to innovate in the development of theory and hypothesis.

How can we proceed, then, in the absence of an established theory for organizing knowledge? *Theory in its traditional sense is directed toward explanation and prediction* by means of "a set of . . . related propositions which include among them some law-like generalizations, and which can be assigned specific truth value via empirical tests."[5] Because scholarship, like life, is always imperfect and because all research involves some compromise with ideal requirements, we turn instead to another form of theory—heuristic. *Heuristic theory is not so much a predictive scheme as a method of analytically separating and categorizing items in experience.* Much of what parades in political science as theory of the first type—predictive—is actually heuristic, at best providing a "framework for political analysis." We agree with Easton that "the appropriate question to ask about a theoretical analysis today is not: does this fully explain the functioning . . . or does it offer a fireproof set of concepts toward the end? . . . The appropriate question is: does this approach help us to take a small step in the right direction?"[6]

Easton's comment is appropriate, for it is his heuristic scheme or "framework for political analysis" that we employ in organizing the concepts and data of this book. This framework is most often termed *systems analysis*. Easton deemphasizes theory in the classical sense and prefers instead to discuss a "conceptual framework" or "categories for the systems analysis of politics."[7] The utility of systems theory is that, of all heuristic schemes, it enables us at least to order existing information or hunches about reality and thereby to determine what portions of the scheme are clearly untenable in reality, which have some support there, and which need to be further studied. The use of systems analysis has limits, as we shall note later, but presenting the current state of knowledge in the politics of education is our major purpose; for this, systems analysis provides an organizing principle to deal with the current turbulence in school politics. In this fashion only, we believe we can "take a small step in the right direction."

COMPONENTS OF SYSTEMS ANALYSIS

Easton's framework contains the familiar perspective of a society composed of major institutions or "subsystems"—the economy, the school, the church, and so on. Individuals interact with one another and with these institutions in patterned ways of belief and activity that constitute a distinctive culture. One of these institutions is the *political system*. It is different from the others because it alone is the source of "authoritative allocation of values, [i.e.,] those interactions through which values are authoritatively allocated for society." This is the subsystem whose decisions—about how individuals and groups will be allocated the valued but limited objects—are generally accepted as authoritative, that is, *legitimate*. The values allocated by this system may be *material*—a textbook, defense contract, free land for constructing railroads, or "dropout" schools. They may also be *symbolic*, conferring status and deference on favored groups—for example, making Christmas or Martin Luther King's birthday a school holiday. Such an allocative system exists and persists in every society, although its exact form, inherent values, and public politics differ with place and time.

The link between the political system and other subsystems is a key element in this analysis because Easton is reaching for a general statement about the conditions under which other subsystems reciprocally interact with the political system. This interrelationship is one in which *stress* in other subsystems of the social environment generates *inputs* of *demands* on and *supports* of the *political system*. The political system then reduces or *converts* these inputs into public decisions or *outputs*, which in turn *feed back* allocated values into the society whence the process began. Figure 2.1 is a sketch of this set of interactions.[8] These concepts seek to describe components of a dynamic, interactive, political system that may or may not *persist* in the society in which it is embedded. Easton's concern is not merely with how the political system operates, but with how it persists through time by adapting itself to the host of demands made on it.

Figure 2.1
A Simplified Model of a Political System

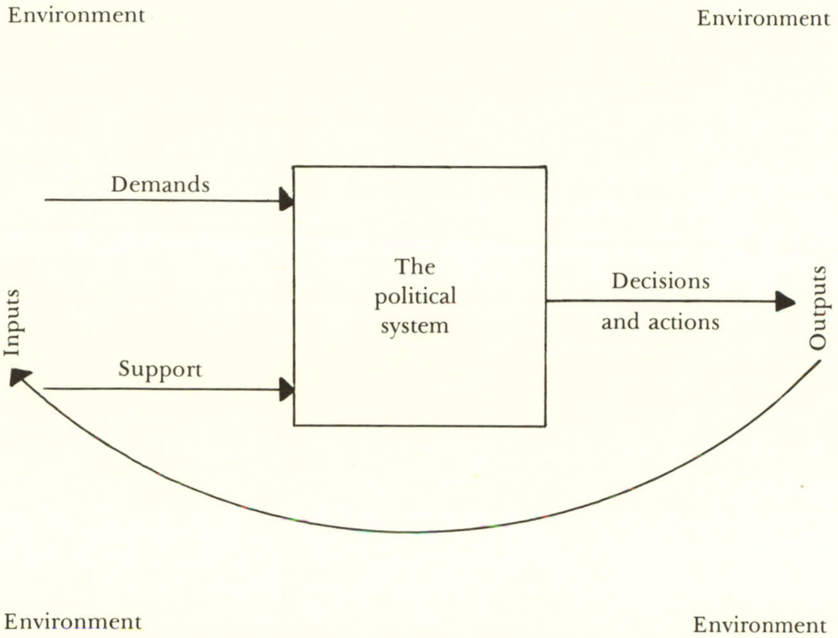

Environment   Environment

Demands

Inputs

The
political
system

Decisions
and actions

Outputs

Support

Environment   Environment

Source: Reprinted from A Systems Analysis of Political Life by David Easton by permission of the University of Chicago Press. © 1965 by the University of Chicago Press.

The Model Illustrated for Schools

What does all this have to do with schools? The rest of this book will answer this question, but we can briefly illustrate the concept now. Schools allocate resources—revenues, programs for educating distinct groups, skilled professionals—and they also allocate values—teaching Americanism or the importance of learning for intrinsic or occupational purposes. If so, then schools are as much political systems as are Congress or the presidency, the state legislature or executive. School systems do this in a society in which other institutions—economic, religious, family, and so on—seek certain valued resources from the schools. This interaction can take two forms. The most obvious are *demands*, such as those set out in the preceding chapter, that characterize the new school politics. For example, a group wants a special curriculum, more parental authority, or more teacher power, and these wants are *articulated* to and *mobilized* toward the school authorities.

A second form of interaction with the schools is *support*; that is, certain groups provide the school with taxes or with intangibles such as a favorable attitude toward the educational function.

The political system of the school that receives demands must deal with them selectively because it lacks sufficient resources to meet them all. The gap between human wants and available resources is a powerful generator of social and political conflict in all times and places. So, school systems act politically because they must choose which group demands will be favored and which will not. The result is an *output*, for example, a state or federal law, a school board resolution, or a superintendent's program. An output could even be a principal's memo to the faculty on how the library budget will be allocated between the science and social studies departments. This may not seem to be choosing among resources and values on a major scale— unless you are affected by that memo. Whatever form an output takes, all are alike in containing a statement of "who gets what, when, and how," the classic definition of politics by Harold Lasswell. More formally stated, all these outputs are alike in authoritatively allocating values and resources.

After this act, as the arrow at the bottom of figure 2.1 implies, the output must be administered in order to deal with the inputs that originally gave rise to it. For example, demand for bilingual education generates a district program, which must then be implemented by organizing the resources of personnel and material that constitute the program. In another example, the lack of popular support for a school program because it is unproductive or biased can generate pressures on the school authorities to alter it in favor of a modified program. In short, schools can be viewed as miniature political systems because they share certain qualities with large-scale political systems. And, as discussed in a later chapter, the school professional must operate within this system in a fashion that shares much with the classical position of the politician. That is, he or she mediates among competing demands from school constituencies organized to seek their share of valued allocations from the school system.

The Concepts Defined

A somewhat fuller statement of systems analysis is appropriate here, beginning with the environment of subsystems outside the political system.[9] This environment is of two parts. The first is that within a nation—such as the economy, culture, social structure, and personalities—which represents potential sources of inputs for the political system. The second part is the environment outside the nation, the international world, a "supra system of which any single society is part." This includes the international, political, economic, and cultural systems of the world.

Within either part of the environment, disturbances arise from changes in existing interactions. Some are in the form of *stress*, something which critically impinges upon the basic capacities of a political system—its ability to allocate values for society and induce most members to accept such decisions as binding. This stress could be a defeat in war, a major depression, or an energy crisis within a nation; or it could be a new consciousness of ethnic frustration within a school district. The Greek city-states and the Roman and Aztec empires, as well as various tribal clusters, may be illustrations of political systems that failed to reduce stress and consequently disappeared. However, so long as the stress is maintained within a critical range, the system as such persists.

At some point, a disturbance becomes a stress that moves from the external environment in the form of *exchanges* or *transactions* which penetrate the political system's *boundaries*. These stress-generated influences, *outputs* of the environment and hence *inputs* to the political system, "concentrate and mirror everything in the environment that is relevant to political stress." The inputs, whether *demands* or *supports*, are "key indicators of the way in which environmental influences and conditions modify and shape the operations of the political system."

Demands are most often associated with pressures upon the government, requests for justice or help, reward or recognition. Behind these diverse demands lies the common presence of wants, the human condition of longing for that which is in short supply. In all societies these wants are never plentiful enough to satisfy all claims—a phenomenon of tremendous importance to all aspects of society. This is particularly the case with the political system, for without such wants there would be no demands; without demands (not all of which can be met), society would not need to authorize an agent to meet them— that is, to "authoritatively allocate resources and values."

Those making demands mobilize resources in order to affect other private groups, hoping to influence the disposition of the political system. The issues that develop and the way in which demands penetrate the political system vary among cultures, economics, and political systems.

Supports, on the other hand, take the form of a willingness to accept the decisions of the system or the system itself. A steady flow of supports is necessary if any political system is to sustain its legitimacy (the accepted sense that the system has the right to do what it is doing). So vital is this input that all societies indoctrinate their young to support their particular system, a task that is part of the school's work but is shared with family and peers.

The whole process of demands and supports can be seen in the issue of school desegregation. Demands for desegregation arose from a racially based stress, long endured—but more lately unendurable—by Blacks. Moving from private rancor across the political boundary to create a public challenge, Blacks mobilized their limited resources, first in demands upon courts and later upon Congress but continually upon local school boards. The counterdemands of segregationists mobilized other resources to block and delay this challenge. During this process, those seeing too much change arising from this specific conflict and those seeing too little both began to decrease support for the Supreme Court's authority to allocate values generally.

The political system *converts* such inputs, sometimes combining or reducing them, sometimes absorbing them without any reaction, but sometimes converting them into public policies or outputs. Clearly not all demands are converted into policy, for the political system is more responsive to certain values, those dominant in the conversion machinery and its personnel (that is, the government) and in the larger society. What gets through depends upon which values the conversion process reinforces and which it frustrates and the values of the political authorities as they operate within this flow of inputs.

For example, some educators insist that maintaining discipline is a prime value of classwork, while others prefer to achieve intellectual excitement. Which of these values gets reinforced by state authority is the end result of a political struggle. That is, one will eventually be "authorized," and the school system and its personnel will allocate their resources toward that value. This struggle to have resources allocated authoritatively for one's own educational value is political, sharing much with the process in other policy fields.

The authorities responsible for the daily running of the political system constantly interact in the conversion process with either those outside or those inside the political system. The pattern of their interactions often stems in part from role definitions imposed by the political system itself. Such interactions generate certain pressures inside the political system—or *withinputs*, which in turn shape the conversion process and its products.

For example, desegregation demands were ignored much longer by Congress and some presidents than by the Supreme Court and other presidents. Border states desegregated more quickly than southern states did, and Mississippi school boards resisted most of all. These differing reactions reflected various combinations of power and values in each political subsystem and the varied role definitions of different political authorities. The role definition of a congressman or a school board member who represented Atlanta, Georgia, or Holmes County, Mississippi, was different from the role definition of an official who spoke for Kentuckians. Each used his or her resources in the political system to advance or impede these demands, and the resulting conflicts generated the conversion process—which still continues.

The outputs of the political subsystem become inputs to the other social subsystems, which had first generated outputs as stresses. The administration or implementation of outputs in the larger community, however, always has a differential impact. Policy implementation acts to enhance the safety, income, and status of some persons or groups while it detracts from others. A resulting profile of public policy, while varying with the culture and times, mirrors the structure of power and privilege and tells us much about the allocation of values by the political system.

Moreover, the authorized purpose of the output gets *meaning* in reality only through the process of *feedback*—the interaction of output with its administration which becomes in time established behavior and its effects—an *outcome*. For example, the Supreme Court required desegregation at "all deliberate speed," but federal district courts defined that output—deliberate speed—differently for innumerable school districts. Congress authorized school aid for poor children, but the *outcome* in the U.S. Office of Education's administration of that law was aid for all schools.

Clearly, the gap between output and outcome is a major stimulus to future policy making. That is, the action of the political system may not conclude with outcomes. Outputs, in influencing the society, can generate another set of inputs to the political system through a *feedback loop*. This term designates one way in which the system copes with stress—that is, (1) dealing with stress causes a response in the system, (2) the response creates new stress, and (3) the new stress is communicated to the political authorities, and a new round begins.

The Concepts Illustrated

The preceding concepts are incorporated in figure 2.2, which uses educational examples for Easton's system analysis. Stresses affect the schools from events as far away as Saudi Arabia or the USSR or as close as meetings of local ministers or teachers. These events crystallize on the school's political system as group demands, such as to cut school costs or institute school prayers. All such demands, whatever their content, seek to reallocate values or resources of the schools. Those in the school political system who are authorized to decide on such reallocations—from formal agencies to the voters—reject some of these demands but convert others into formal outputs, be it an act of Congress or a local referendum. The resulting educational policy is then implemented as an administrative decision—for example, busing plans—which in time has outcomes for particular groups, say academic gains for Blacks. And that particular group generated the environmental stresses in the first place.

Note that this framework presents the political system as something other than just an allocative process. Moreover, this framework is an attempt to address the larger question of how any allocative process persists; or, as Easton notes:

... the processes underlying system persistence through time. And persistence ... is intricately connected with the capacity of a political system, as an open, self-regulating, and goal-setting system, to change itself. The puzzle of how a system manages to persist, through change if necessary, forms a central problem of the analysis of political life.[10]

The belief that schools are embedded in society and responsive to its demands is a truism, perhaps the oldest in the study of education. We believe systems analysis can help the student to see this relationship more clearly through such specific conceptual terms as *wants, demands,* and *supports*. We believe that considerable explanation can result from observing the school systems as converting inputs from subsystems of society and doing so in response to group-defined stresses. Further, it

Figure 2.2

The Flow of Influences and Policy Consequences in the School's Political System

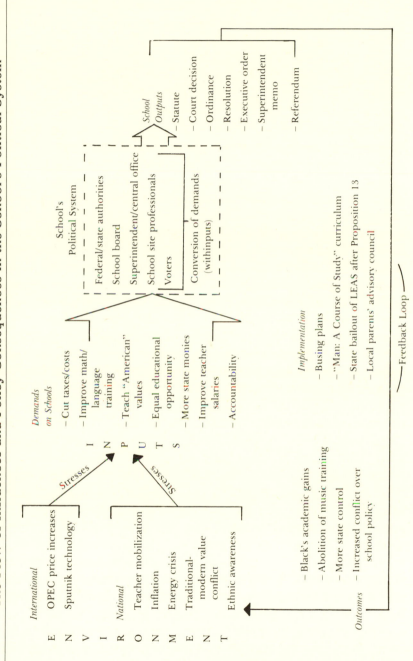

seems to us that schools exhibit conversion processes similar to those in other subsystems that are more clearly recognized as political. That political authorities in schools seek to maximize support through use of appropriate outputs also seems demonstrable. Certainly a central question to be explored in this book is the degree to which the feedback loop operates between schools and society.

In exploring similarities between schools and larger, more recognized political systems, we say with Easton that we are seeking to "elaborate a conceptual structure and suggest, where possible, some theoretical propositions. . . . In the outcome, we shall not have a theory in the full-blown sense of the term [but] a conceptual structure which . . . is the most that we can expect in the area of general theory today."[11]

In this work we seek something more. We want to know how valid such a general concept is in explaining the structure and processes of American public education in this time of increasing stress. As the first chapter noted, old forms and ideas in education are everywhere challenged, and not merely by new interest groups seeking a reallocation of resources. Widespread and increasing resistance to school tax referenda in recent years (about one in three failed during 1969, three in four in 1979) suggests disappointment, frustration, or malaise over what our schools are or are not doing. Stress, then, is not merely an abstract academic concern. It is a characteristic of contemporary education that permeates school boards, classrooms, administrators' offices, and professionals' conventions, as well as the decision-making forums at state and national levels. And, as polls show, the public's disenchantment with schools creates a nationwide condition of stress.

To answer this basic question of the validity of systems analysis, we offer a contour study designed to stimulate thinking and research by scholar and layperson alike. We explore knowledge based on existing research and provide some of our own. This is done not merely to show its relevance to the concepts we use, but to suggest where more needs to be done. We go on to explore major national educational policies, not only because systems analysis seems to explain them well, but also because of what they can suggest about stress adaptation to all those interested in the survival of their schools.

The precise labels used for these concepts are not the important thing, of course. What is relevant is whether the concepts provide an insight into what is happening and some guide to action. If so, then our contribution must ironically be classified as feedback, which Wiener defined as "the property of being able to adjust future conduct by past performances."[12]

Uses of Systems Analysis

The links between politics and education are clearly not new, as chapter 3 explains. However, two disagreements arise over this tie. How are politics and education to be viewed, whether empirically or in the world of values? In other words, how *do* schools and politics relate to one another as a matter of fact, and how *should* they relate as a matter of value? In many respects, this book focuses only on the empirical question. Putting an empirical question to reality, however, is no simple matter, for the effort is subject to fallacies in framing the question—as well as in verifying it and estimating the significance of the facts unearthed.[13] Nor do we stand mute on the value questions at the heart of turbulent issues. But to do all this, we use the systems analysis framework to organize this wealth of experiential data and values.

We must point out, however, that this framework has been criticized. Criticisms have been basically of two kinds. One set argues that such analysis is ineffective, that is, it does not or cannot do what it claims to as an analytical tool. The second set argues that even if it does meet its claims, it is an undesirable way of thinking about schools—or any other segment of social experience—because of what it implies about the values of humans in society. That is, individuals are ignored in such a global concept, and it is a conservative concept for its emphasis on how political systems cope with stress. We have countered these criticisms in detail in the first edition of this book. Documenting the rich pool of research and ideas from the 1970s seems a better use of limited space than repeating our evaluation again, and our subsequent thinking has not changed our view that these two criticisms are not valid.

We continue to find this concept useful in organizing the complex reality that constitutes the politics of education. For this reason, systems analysis frames the rest of this book, in which we attempt to make sense out of the new actors, issues, and resources swirling about the schoolhouse.

NOTES

1. Fred N. Kerlinger, "The Mythology of Educational Research: The Descriptive Approach," *School and Society* 93 (1965): 222–25.

2. Laurence Iannaccone, *Politics in Education* (New York: Center for Applied Research in Education, 1967).

3. Thomas H. Eliot, "Toward an Understanding of Public School Politics," *American Political Science Review* 52 (1959): 1032–51.

4. Michael W. Kirst and Edith K. Mosher, "The Politics of Public Education: A Research Review," *Review of Educational Research* 39 (1969); Frederick M. Wirt, "American Schools as a Political System: A Bibliographic Essay," in *State, School and Politics: Research Directions*, Michael W. Kirst, ed. (Lexington, Mass.: Lexington Books, 1972), pp. 247–81.

5. A. James Gregor, "Political Science and the Uses of Functional Analysis," *American Political Science Review* 62 (1968): 425.

6. David Easton, *A Systems Analysis of Political Life* (New York: Wiley, 1965), p. 490; hereafter referred to as Easton, *Systems Analysis.*

7. David Easton, *A Framework for Political Analysis* (Englewood Cliffs, N.J.: Prentice-Hall, 1965).

8. Easton, *Systems Analysis*, p. 30.

9. Citations for following unnoted quotations are Easton, *Systems Analysis,* pp. 22, 26, 27.

10. Easton, *Systems Analysis*, p. 479.

11. Easton, *Systems Analysis,* pp. vii–viii.

12. Cited in Easton, *Systems Analysis*, p. 368.

13. For the problems involved, see David H. Fischer. *Historians' Fallacies: Toward a Logic of Historical Thought* (New York: Harper & Row, 1970).

3

Schools
and System Support

Current concerns with the tie between the schools and the political system reflect their reciprocal importance. It must be kept clear that we view as political both the larger system, over all of society, and the smaller one of the schools. In this chapter, for clarity, we shall use a shorthand term for each of these political systems: *State* and *School*. We focus in this chapter on one of the links between these two—the child to be educated. Other factors tie State and School, particularly programs of finance and regulation, but these will concern us in later chapters. Before we focus on the child at the intersection of the two systems, however, we must clarify some theoretical problems.

STATE-SCHOOL LINKS IN DEMOCRATIC THOUGHT

The previous delineation of the apolitical myth of the schools needs to be recast from a broader perspective on the State-School relationship. Three views of this interlinking are found in classical political theory, democratic theory, and systems analysis.

The Classical Question: Which Is the Independent Variable?

As Eulau noted, Western political philosophy concerning the State-School relationship centers around one basic query: Should the State shape the School's function and purpose, or should the School shape and guide the State's?[1] During any period of history, much of the controversy over schooling has been rooted in how one answers this question.

The Greek tradition was most explicit on the matter. The two were one, both concerned with producing the good political community (*polis*). Schooling shaped citizens so that they could fulfill themselves in the interests of the *polis*, which in turn ensured that the school did their job well. There is about this something that Eulau termed "the utopian scent—education can create the perfect political order." More important, this orientation assumed that education was subordinate to, indeed the servant of, the political order.

While Plato and Aristotle wrote about a culture now twenty-five centuries dead, in which a good society was sought by the integration of all institutions and values, their insistence on the State-School relationship has echoes today. We hear it from School critics on the right who insist that teacher, student, and curriculum should uphold the ends of the national government. They demand an uncritical acceptance of a patriotic and generalized presentation of history. Individuals must be subordinated to the State and School in order to shape their values. Only by having School support State and State support School can society be preserved. On the left, meanwhile, one hears that the School creates and reinforces the "establishment" that dominates and controls American life. These charges are followed by demands that the School be reformed because its submission to false values is producing a conformist and corrupt population.

These opposing views are alike in many ways, however. Both wish subordination of School to State. Both agree that the State can be upheld only by the School's instruction in a moral life, though there is disagreement about what that is. Both believe that the State can be only what the School supports. In short, the potential independent effect the School can have on the State makes it the potentially dominant institution in society—and therefore it must be controlled. In such a formulation, the collectivity or society as a whole is more important than the individual, and the individual must be shaped to the larger end. The Athenians would agree.

The harnessing of education to shape the political and religious order was a dominant feature of states until quite recently. Education for the pursuit of other than approved ends, political and religious, was unknown. Indeed, the development of private education in this country, with an implied sense of independence from the dictates of the State, originated in the desire to be free—free, that is, to inculcate the right religion. Not even that development, however, was allowed to be unpatriotic or politically heretical.

In the last century, however, another possibility emerged from this State-School union. After all, it would be hard to find, as Eulau has observed, a "political order in the real world which, even if we could agree on its being close to perfection, has been created out of or by an educational system." Might not the reverse be the case, that the condition of the political order shaped the educational system, that the State is the independent variable? If so, political problems are basically traceable not to the School but to the State.

The argument here is something more than that schools have to teach patriotism so as not to undermine the State. It is, rather, that from society to society the basic School philosophy and accompanying practices and structures are shaped by the State more often than the reverse. Note two examples of this. First, conceive of a State whose political premise is exclusive, unchallengeable, and immutable. School philosophy there will take as its first duty the shaping of the child to understand, accept, and glorify that premise. Behind this duty is the belief that when the Truth is known, it is foolish at best and sinful at worst to permit the malleable young equal access to Error. This thinking influenced Plato's classic advice of a strict curriculum to produce different classes of society. All authoritarian societies have since followed the Platonic syllabus.

However, the case is different if the premise of the State is that political Truth is either not known or not knowable, that there is not Truth but truths. Then the School may be more open to instruction admitting of plural truths—from which individuals may choose as befits their individual values.

The second example of the State shaping the School underlies the rise of the liberal democratic state in the Western world. Its pluralist premise doubts a Truth and rejects the absolutism of those who do not question truths. These are familiar elements of English and American thinking in the nineteenth and twentieth centuries. Eulau reminds us that John Stuart Mill's essay *On Liberty* is an expression of this philosophy just as Plato's *Republic* expresses the other. Writing before universal education, Mill argued against "State education" and for "enforcement of education by the State" in a statement that directly urges breaking the State-School pattern from its traditional mold. "A general State education is a mere contrivance for moulding people to be exactly like one another . . . in proportion as it is efficient and successful, it establishes a despotism over the mind, leading by natural tendency to one over body."

The possibility that school systems vary with political systems suggests the independent quality of the latter. A major research question would be to determine whether new School concepts change old State programs or whether State changes School. This question is not only academic. The importance education plays in the development of new states has been closely studied in the post-World War II era. Yet there has not been enough comparative research to determine whether or how school systems are shaped by distinctive elements in new and old political systems.*

In the United States, which of the two institutions is independent and which dependent? Is the union a closed one, wherein Truth is known and each system reinforces the other in its impact on the young? Or is the union an open one, where doubt prompts a search by School and State for answers to fit a varied population? Our necessarily ambiguous answer to such queries points directly to the fact that education is caught in a conflict of values rooted in traditional political thought.

Problems of Education in a Democracy

An additional conflict arises because our study focuses on a democratic system in which the School must manage tensions between opposing values. Two paradoxes underlie these tensions. First, the School must teach not only support of the State but also the virtues of individualism. However, individualism can result in opposition to the State, as our history of civil rights protests and violence attests. The line between support and opposition gets easily blurred. This is the current and yet historic dilemma haunting the sensitive intellect from

*Until recently comparative education as a subdiscipline consisted primarily of country-by-country analyses, in which the potential power of diverse influences in the political order was not completely assessed. However, in the late 1970s, there was a shift to comparing a number of states' school systems or policies within a comparative framework guided by theory. The *Comparative Education Review* led in this change.

Antigone to today's conscientious objector: How far can the State go in commanding my obedience?

A second paradox arises when the breadth of pluralistic values is narrowed by the institutional demands of State and School in order to control the environment in which they exercise authority. An example is seen in the School that praises the American ideal of freedom but seeks to regulate every aspect of the student's life. The familiar ringing of bells in American high schools is a reflection of this trend toward standardization and regularity. We discuss this paradox more fully below.

These conflicting norms of freedom and regulation created a major crisis in the 1960s among American youth, who challenged rote learning, denied reality descriptions that were at odds with their own perceptions, and rejected the widespread effort to impose uniformity in the name of diversity.[2] Here the School shared a common problem with the State. Liberty has never been total, for individuals' pursuits of their diverse definitions of freedom create social conflicts. This has caused authoritative institutions to define freedom so as to avoid disorder and injustice. Each definition becomes a constraint for some and a shield for others. Against this narrowing experience, there are always people who will rebel, decrying the hypocrisy of an institution that says one thing but does another.

These paradoxes of democracy are of course related. The very breadth of democratic values provides convenient justification for any narrowing act by the State and School. For example, local control of the School has been a dominant value in our history, but so has the concept of equal educational opportunity. These have collided head on over the segregation issue since 1954, as the federal government's actions in the name of equality have restricted the school district's, which represent local control. In short, then, the potential for value conflict exists because of our pluralism, and the reality of these conflicts exists due to selective emphasis of values by those in authority.[3]

In a totalitarian State, such value disjunction rarely exists as all values and institutions are designed to achieve monolithic results.[4] In a democracy, however, values are diverse and value conflict is frequent, all to be worked out within the system by majority decision making. In both systems, however, the School is assigned prime responsibility for instructing the young in civic virtue. When such virtue is defined under totalitarianism as obedience to the State, all other civic values can be aligned to this central command. In democracies, however, in which individualism is stressed as a central virtue and where individuals differ about what civic virtue entails, the lack of consensus on values places an inordinate and perhaps impossible burden on the School.

We can illustrate these tensions by reference to the value of equality in American society.[5] One of the norms of citizenship in our society is egalitarianism, and national surveys of thirteen- and seventeen-year olds at our bicentennial celebration found the belief to be deeply rooted. Huge proportions of those surveyed opposed racial (96 percent), religious (97 percent), political (82 versus 92 percent of the two groups), and sexual (87 percent) discrimination in the job market.[6] Yet we live in a hierarchical system of unequal social statuses.

The paradox is that the School acts not only to socialize norms such as equality but also to select the persons who will get the most and least of society's rewards. In important ways, to be "educated" is to be sorted into groups that vary widely in skills, self-esteem, influence, and social status. Schools are selective in distributing rewards or allocating values, whether grading on the curve or applying differential admission requirements. School structures provide an important means of legitimating a whole system of inequalities for students as well as business and governmental leaders. By the end of high school, grades and other performance records largely determine whether a student goes on to a prestige college or begins low-skilled work. Meanwhile, the School has been propounding a vague "equality" as desirable behavior expected of apprentice citizens. Against this it also implicitly teaches the inequalities of society, even if only offered as something to be corrected. This conflict produces a parallel conflict in young people, a form of cognitive dissonance that has to be resolved, if at all, by possessing and acting on contradictory notions of equality.[7] The School, then, handles these conflicting ideas of reward differentiation, as well as of political socialization, by abstaining, leaving the young to sort out the contradictions.

Political Socialization and Systems Analysis

Systems analysis, particularly in its definition of the relationship between School and State, provides an additional theoretical perspective. Whether writers use systems terms or not, all agree that the primary relationship of the School and State is close in every nation. Further, while the School is everywhere subordinate to the State, it engages in a trade-off of needs and advantages. Thus, the School instills obedience to the law and the legitimacy of the State, while the State provides the School with funds, some protection from outsiders, and a near monopoly in educating the young.[8]

This broadly stated interrelationship is familiar in systems terms. The School is one of the agents that provides the State with *diffuse support*, defined by Easton as "broad political good will that a system generates through various means over the years . . . that helps members to accept or tolerate outputs to which they are opposed or the effect of which they see as damaging to their wants."[9] The securing of such support takes place as a result of *political socialization*, "those developmental processes through which persons acquire political orientations and patterns of behavior."[10] Political socialization orients the young to appropriate political values, attitudes, and behaviors.[11] To Easton, diffuse support is a theoretical explanation for the political system's ability to handle stress when its specific outputs fail to meet demands.

Political socialization not only affects what happens to the system's outputs, but it also has consequences for the input side. The young are taught what can be properly presented as demands and what roles can be properly performed by citizens in policy conversion. Such instruction helps limit demands to those the system can normally and usefully handle. For example, the fact that political authorities were never a source of assistance in bank crises before 1900 was clearly accepted then. However, by the 1930s, government intervention had become marginally proper, and in our own time unquestionably appropriate—indeed, expected. During the earlier era, lesser demands eased the task of political authorities, but in later periods an expanded view of their responsibilities overwhelmed them. Political socialization also defines proper role behavior for citizens. Inculcation of the view that voting is a proper means of effecting change whereas bomb throwing is not helps keep down the number of schoolhouses the political authorities must rebuild. Such role instruction also helps recruit and train political leaders attracted to political power and its uses.

In this fashion, the political system's persistence is enhanced by the School's political socialization. System-citizen interactions are regularized, citizen expectations about outputs made realistic for the system, their input demands shaped, and leaders attracted.[12] Although school operations in different States show considerable uniformity in such political socialization, its specific content—role expectations, for example—can vary with time and society. As Litt asked:

> Is this model student to be a member of a mass who does not question the rule of a superior and ordained elite, an industrial worker who needs the skill and understanding to know his role in modern society, or a child of the Enlightenment expected to participate in the voluntary mosaic of parties, interest groups, and informal circles of political opinion-formation?[13]

The variation and uniformity that exist in political socialization and the forces that account for them are basic research topics for which there are as yet few state and national cross-analyses.[14]

MODELS OF POLITICAL SOCIALIZATION

We wish now to bring together these philosophical, democratic, and systems analysis perspectives as they relate to political socialization. Two basic queries arise. What is attempted and what results in efforts to socialize American young people to the political system? Little empirical analysis bearing on these questions exists prior to the middle third of this century, but studies of earlier periods would probably not show patterns much different than today. When scholars did turn to the content of what was attempted in political socialization, they found highly similar values in the instruments of curriculum, textbook, and teacher.

There is no one necessary way these instruments must interact. Indeed, it is possible to argue, as Litt has, that two distinctive models of civic learning have operated at different stages in our history, that a third may be emerging now, and that these models reflect social changes and produce political learning changes.[15] A "rational citizen" model of political action dominated the nineteenth century, emphasizing a citizen's "mastery of the political environment [through] reasoned, voluntary effort" and the search for "harmony and political compromise." Instruction emphasized one's "rights, duties, and obligations"; that is, a citizen was to participate out of a sense of moral duty and be responsible for his use of power. Policy making was conceived of as a town meeting predicated on "rational deliberation . . . an open exchange of opinion in face-to-face meetings, and strong confidence in the ability of self-governing men to decide for the good of the community." The preparatory schools and strong liberal arts colleges generated this set of norms and infused it into public civic instruction through secondary textbooks and teacher training.

However, changes in society produced a new concept of civic education, the "allegiant American" model. The new urban immigrant masses threatened national consensus with their passionately different views about the nature of the State and its uses of power. Civic education took the form of "Americanization" textbooks and courses to integrate aliens into an allegiant consensus. The immigrant was to be swayed from "dirty" parties, patronage, and ethnic group conflict to accept nonpartisanship, the merit system, and "a harmony of community interests." All were taught a conventional wisdom about our history and institutions and given a common set of values about our politics and economics. These portrayed a nation working smoothly for the benefit of all, with room only for allegiance and no place for conflict.

A third alternative, not widespread in civic instruction, could be termed the "analytical." This seeks to develop skills of technical intellectual analysis that are highly abstract and impersonal—such as "models." The generating institution is the research group, which transmits its ideas to the large public universities. Indeed, an introductory college course in political science is invariably of this kind. These collegiate emphases are transmitted into public schools by teacher trainees taking such a course. The purpose is to analyze the empirical—as against the ideological—operations of political systems. Emphasis is upon how citizens, pressure groups, and political authorities actually conduct themselves, what values these behaviors reflect, and what comprehensive theory incorporates behavior and values.

THE INSTRUMENTS OF POLITICAL SOCIALIZATION

The instruments of political socialization can be woven into three instructional models. One emphasizes civic duties and obligations, rational deliberation, and compromise in policy making. A second emphasizes allegiance to a common culture, social harmony, and distaste for political agencies whose conflict threatens this harmony. The third emphasizes the technical ability to understand the nature of the political world in order that one can manage it. Which model best describes what is currently taught in American schools by the curriculum, textbooks, and teachers, as the School seeks to support the State?

Curriculum Content

What, for example, is known about the actual content of the curriculum? A major answer is—not much, because by 1980 only half of the fifty states even required such a course in their public schools. As for what can be said of the actual course offerings in curriculum design, the answer can be brief, as the findings generally agree. The curriculum is formalistically descriptive, weakly linked to reality, devoid of analytical concepts except legalistic ones, highly prescriptive in tone and—as a direct consequence of all this—noncontroversial. Few changes are found during a half century of social studies offerings: civics in the ninth grade, world history in the tenth, American history in the eleventh, and some government or social problems in the senior year.[16] This means that until recently, the curriculum contained little of the recent behavioral developments, comparative analysis, or international studies, and almost no sociology, anthropology, or psychology.[17]

From the elementary to the secondary schools, the instruction proceeds from an emphasis on indirect and symbolic patriotism to an explicit but selective use of facts about American history and government. Hess and Torney found widespread use of classroom symbols and rituals in the elementary schoolchild's world, for example, pledging allegiance, showing the flag or pictures of important events or people, singing patriotic songs. With the child's increasing interest in institutions rather than persons, more attention is given in successive years to specific political structures. This curriculum content has special empirical and normative perspectives. Empirically, it ignores events and conditions that contradict the ideal descriptions of the political system. The normative content emphasizes compliance with rules and authority while skimping citizens' rights to participate in their government (other than by voting). This in turn leads to a deemphasis on parties, interest groups, and partisan behavior.[18]

At the secondary level, more information is provided to the student, but it bears little relationship to the world portrayed by social scientists. One spokesman for a group that has closely studied this educational phase concluded that:

Today's high school student studies about government in much the same way that his parents studied government. Current high school civic and government courses continue to be based upon legalistic descriptions and ethical prescriptions. The social foundations of political behavior and the cultural forces that shape political roles and decisions are neglected. The relationships between certain kinds of political behavior and socioeconomic status, ethnic identity, or primary and secondary group memberships are ignored. Little or nothing is said about basic concepts of current political science such as political culture, political socialization, status, role, reference groups, and function. . . . The political world presented . . . bears little resemblance to the world of the politician.[19]

What dramatically distinguishes the perceptions of the politician from those of the teacher is the absence of controversy in the teacher's world. The clamor over issues that contemporary Americans are sharply divided over rarely enters the classroom; even the issues that once divided our ancestors may still be handled gingerly. American history courses characteristically leave little time for current politics; sometimes it is not even reached as the course fuzzes away somewhere after World War II.

This blandness is attributable to a lack of teacher competence at handling controversy and to pressures on teachers, textbook publishers, and school boards by special interest groups. We will note the pressure of "curriculum evangelism" used to assure a neutral if not favorable treatment for certain groups and values.[20]

Textbook Content

Textbooks are obviously another major instrument for political socialization. They played a powerful role in the decades after the Civil War training citizens in history and patriotism, when, in Wiggin's phrase, the textbook was "teacher to America." Indeed, the perspective of the southern white saturated the national perspective of Reconstruction due to the dominance of southern historians' ideas in secondary textbooks. More recently, the historical task of citizenship training still fills our textbooks.[21]

Again, the findings are much like those for the total curriculum—textbooks are as bland as the curriculum they serve. Noncontroversial, offering few conceptual and analytical tools for understanding political reality, jingoistic and narrowly moralistic (only the rare book mentions any mistake the United States has ever made in domestic policy and none in foreign affairs), naive in descriptions of the political process, overly optimistic about the system's ability to handle future problems—the criticisms of these books are repetitive and insistent. The instructional methods used are not much more attractive. At a chapter's end there are questions for review that stress formal facts. The question of what the individual student might do about all these facts is never raised. The naturalist fallacy—that by assembling enough empirical facts, one can make value judgments—pervades such instruction.

A vivid illustration of such blandness is in the treatment of minorities. Our society has always depended upon many minorities, what Walt Whitman called, "A Nation of nations." But until very recently whatever students could learn about this social fact from their books would be scant and stereotyped. Jews, Blacks, and other immigrants, as well as American Indians, were often not presented at all or only as picturesque human interest facets of history. They were never shown as having an impact on our history. The "melting pot" thesis of such books is the implicit reason for not presenting such historical evidence; somehow, the immigrant stepped off the boat and into a giant social fondue. Often explicit was a social harmony in which all groups were said to have lived, except for the regrettable aberration of the Civil War. Blacks disappeared from history textbooks after that war, except for an occasional patronizing reference to George Washington Carver—rarely to Frederick Douglass and never to William DuBois. Indians were presented as quaint natives who sometimes caused trouble that was quickly put down. America was "discovered" by an Italian or a Viking but never by Indians. It is hard to adequately parody such a narrow view of the pluralistic basis of American history; the actual presentations do so on their face.

Then, sometime in the 1960s, minorities began receiving more realistic treatment of their roles in history as a result of political and educational protest. A comparison of textbooks from 1949 to 1960 found some improvement for Jews but little for Blacks and immigrants of other races. By 1980, however, a fuller exposition of the Blacks' historical role—including changing terminology from Negro to Black— and removal of offensive characterizations were widely evident in textbooks. Pressure from the urban centers by the increasingly politicized Blacks was a major force in this change.[23] The rate of adopting these modified textbooks, however, was still influenced if not set by statewide decisions, as in California, where special interest groups could affect an entire state.

The Role of the Teacher

Intervening among curriculum, textbook, and student, the teacher has been regarded as a potentially powerful instrument for political socialization since the days of Athens. And, as Socrates learned when the Athenians executed him for his teachings, societies have always placed constraints upon such power. A review of teacher preparation provides important clues to the direction of such constraints. Despite some acceptance of social science courses, teacher training continues to emphasize preparation in history. Even the common social science major requires that one-third to one-half the coursework be in history, with the rest spread among numerous other fields, according to a 1959 study.[24]

The outlook, training, and methodology of the historian is not that of the social scientist, as historians have resisted the social scientists' behavioral revolution of the last quarter century. As a consequence, "the student comes to think of human activity in a descriptive, sequential, and narrative fashion rather than in an analytical and predictive way. History and historians do not address themselves to the problem of systematically developing theories of human conduct."[25] Moreover, such training inculcates a past rather than a present orientation in teachers that necessarily keeps them from directing students' attention to the social world around them. All this makes it easier for teachers to instill noncritical attitudes about the political and social world—and also makes it safer for them.

As social science courses are increasingly added to secondary school curriculum, the gap between the competence of the teacher and the potential quality of the offering may grow. Despite great student interest in government in the 1960s, for example, few teachers were qualified to offer the new thinking in political science as analytical tools. Many had only had an introductory course in college, which was often years behind them, and some had had none. In Kansas, "14.6 percent of the government teachers and 25.5 percent of the citizenship instructors had never had a college course in government." Better preparation should come with upgrading high school curricula by the professions and recent federal projects.[26]

Certain characteristics of civics teachers can be of considerable importance in their work of socialization. According to an Oregon study of the early 1960s, lack of controversy in textbooks was matched by teacher avoidance of controversy. The safer the topic, the less reluctance there was to express views. Those who were younger, more liberal, and more politically active, however, consistently expressed themselves more openly. The avoidance by most teachers sampled was partly a function of what one taught; those in social studies, English, and languages were more expressive and liberal than their colleagues in art and music. Issue avoidance in class did not carry outside the classroom, however, as most teachers agreed they would express themselves in their role as citizens. Yet "even for the expressive teachers the closing of the classroom door means goodbye to the world of politics."[27] We shall note some changes in this behavior, however.

Timidity—or lack of competence—in the face of controversy is not new. Thirty-five years ago Beale asked, "Are American teachers free?" and in his classic study found that they were not.[28] Countless other studies show that teachers are urged not to get involved in controversy, an insistence backed by sanctions of disapproval or dismissal.

Efforts to put constaints on teachers are not the monopoly of any particular group in this society but rather a recognition of their purported power as socializing agents. We have mentioned minority pressures that have recently moved textbook publishers to present a more complete and honest treatment. Teachers have also been charged with racism and bias by these same groups, while, from the other side, right-wing elements charge subversion if teachers do change. Unsafe because controversial, particular issues consistently appear in accounts of these conflicts. Favorable—or even any—reference to the United Nations, the right to dissent, civil rights, current politics, evolution, the role of Blacks in our history, the Soviet Union, sex education, family life, class and status conflict—again and again the same curriculum items appear at the hub of local community conflict with an embattled teacher.[29]

One curious feature of the teacher-as-socializing-agent is the wide evidence that teacher adherence to values normally defined as democratic is not very strong. Teachers' responses to attitude scales on civil rights raise questions about their knowledge of and attachment to civil rights values. If prevalent, this presents a picture of a socializing agent who is not particularly well trained for his or her task, noncombative, sensitive to community pressure, and uncertain about if not antipathetic to at least part of the democratic credo he or she is ostensibly to transmit.[30]

Upon review, these three instruments of political socialization—curriculum, textbooks, and teachers—share common features. They are uncritical of the political system, unconcerned with contemporary social conflict, and undemanding of the student. Formal exposure to politics—if any—is concentrated during the latter part of the curriculum, and much of that focuses in a selective way upon the past. The window opened to the student on her or his nation reveals a social monochrome, not a kaleidoscope, of people. They are characteristically seen interacting by accommodation not competition. The political system is presented as an arrangement of dust-dry institutions, and its presentation is formalistic; no live or lively people fill these positions of power. Our system's values are offered as an unchallengeable heritage of the past, to be accepted as fact and not opinion, whose content is given and whose clarity is obvious.

In short, if diffuse support for a political system is best created by exposing the young to a uniform set of stimuli in a structured way, then the instruments of American socialization surveyed are just such stimuli. The allegiant American model prevails, offering students "one nation, under God, indivisible, with liberty and justice for all." The instructional design, explicit or not, causes children to see their oneness and ignore their distinctness, with similar treatment for their allegiance and dissent, their cooperation and conflict. In our terms, then, all of this, if successful, looks like diffuse support.

Yet it remains to be seen what the effect is upon the young. When we ask how effective such socialization has been, we raise a more significant query than asking what the instruments are like. The answer here leads us into a more dynamic study of the citizen at the intersection of State and School.

THE EFFECTS OF POLITICAL SOCIALIZATION

The recent flood of research on this issue must necessarily be summarized here,[31] but several conclusions can be drawn. First, institutions other than the School are also socializing agents—family and peer groups, as well as reality signals (feedback) from distinctive events. Second, the School instruments previously described are found to have *little* effect for white middle-class Americans but substantially more for black Americans. Third, the psychology of the socialization process is very complex. And fourth, little enough is systematically known about these psychological aspects to allow valid generalizations about the socialization process. These comments should not be taken as overly critical, for only recently has anyone focused on this complex process. Just enough is known to conclude that current School theory of curriculum and instruction is misplaced and ineffective.

Causes and Effects of Socialization

The scholarly disregard—until quite recently—of the School as a political socializer is seen in the fact that Hyman's seminal volume in 1959 emphasized research on family influence but totally ignored that of the School.[32] The primacy of family influence on the political socialization of children has been challenged recently by Hess and Torney's study of over twelve thousand elementary children and confirmed in other details by a smaller national sample in the work of Jennings and Niemi. From these studies the family emerges as important in creating early gross attitudes of support for country and government and for shaping the child's party identification (in the last, the mother is more important than the father).[33] For other aspects of attitude, value, and cognition about the political world, however, other agents—such as the School, peers, and communications media—operate.

Clearly an elaborate theory is needed to explain why the child is not the mirror image of the parent. Such a theory may be something like Dennis's suggestion: "The views of the socialized are likely to follow the socializers who most often interact with him, present more explicit political content to him, and have higher salience, prestige, and capacity to influence him generally." And yet, as he concludes,

The comparative assessment of these forces and the extent to which they operate in concert or disharmony has only begun. There are still remarkably few published findings comparing different agency inputs with their ostensible socialization out-puts, or relating both to the properties of learner and teacher as intervening variables.[34]

In that case, what do we know about the effect of the School as a socializing agent? It must be kept in mind that the School's socializing stimuli are probably not the same everywhere in America. Hence, variation in curriculum, textbook, and teaching quality, as well as in the local community's demands upon such instruction, is probably associated with variations in what is transmitted. Thus, Litt showed that of three Boston suburbs with different statuses, each emphasized a different model of the three set out earlier. Even within the school site, Morgan recently showed that tracking produces greater differences within schools than between them in the lessons about democracy the students obtain.[35]

Yet repeated research finds that the impact of high school civics courses is minimal for white middle-class American youth, who after all constitute the large majority in schools. In a large national sample of high school students in civic courses, Langton and Jennings found little change in knowledge or attitudes over the couse of a class, which is ostensibly the behavioral objective of such courses. Blacks, on the other hand, particularly those of lower- and middle-class origins, did show significant increases in political knowledge, toleration, efficacy, and the desire to participate in politics. For them at least, the course content was new information; for whites it was redundant. The implication is that other agents, such as peer groups and family, can socialize whites before such courses enter their lives. But how and with what comparative effect we simply do not know at this time. Such insignificant findings lead one to question much of what is now offered as civic instruction in high schools. So much effort with so little evident result suggests either the need for change in the instruction at this level or a shift to instruction in earlier years where effects are more likely.[36] Many major questions on the means and results of political socialization remain,[37] though by the late 1970s scholarly interest in them had lagged.

In conclusion, then, the untangling of learning influences from home, school, and peers is extremely difficult; it is clear that research permits no answer as to *the* one socializing agent. What can be said is more complex but fairly consistent. As analysts of a large sample of high-schoolers concluded:

Although the impact of parents on their offspring varied enormously across the range of orientations, residues of that impact almost always remained when other relevant characteristics in the schools and larger environments were controlled statistically. . . .

When we turn our attention to the school, the picture is somewhat less uniform. In large part this is because it has been very difficult to pinpoint exactly which properties of the school are crucial in the socialization process. . . . Taking any single dimension of school life, its reverberations on adolescent political orientations are customarily modest. When these dimensions are combined, however, they suggest that the school has significant although not overwhelming importance.[38]

Our rough grasp of the exact nature of political socialization underlines the distance that research must go, but it also suggests some directions. For example, the once-common assumption by psychologists that little political learning occurs in childhood has been the basis for curriculum theory requiring civics only in secondary schools. But this assumption proved doubtful when scholars first searched for specifically political aspects of socialization during early life. It was found that as early as the second grade children conceived images of government and political leaders and held an extraordinarily and unsuspectedly benign attitude toward both political objects; the School seemed more influential than the family in many of these respects.

It was also once believed that attitudes toward authority within the family were transferred to political authorities, first via personalized attraction to idealized presidents and then to political institutions, eventually accounting for citizen acceptance of the political system's legitimacy. However, this purported tie evaporates as soon as children learn that families and government act differently, and that one's responsibilities within each are different. The psychological conceptualization of socialization has its critics, but at least the questions raised have relevance for other aspects of political studies.[39]

The "Hidden Curriculum" Possibility

Another strong perspective on civics learning emerged in the 1970s. Some interpreted the political socialization research just reviewed to mean that the School did not teach civic values—or anything civic—very well. Critics charged that instead schools transmitted other values, those flowing from the structure of education and the organizational imperatives of the profession. In short, there was a "hidden curriculum" being imposed on students, a case of "What we do is so loud you can't hear what we say."

This concept has several dimensions, summarized by Merelman as encompassing:

a set of common practices which, by teaching quite different behavior and power relationships, supposedly prevents the transmission of democratic values in the school. . . . It is alleged that the school teaches hierarchy, not democracy. Instead of student power in the school, we find teacher control over curriculum and adminis- trator control over the school building. Instead of genuine equality among students, we find invidious ability groupings. . . . Instead of liberty for students we encounter constant surveillance. Instead of the "personal interest in social relationships" envisaged by Dewey, we observe egotistic competition, for grades, for status, and ultimately, for admission to "appropriate" colleges and universities. Instead of the democratic citizen's enjoyment of choice and spontaneity, we discover the dead hand of delay and queing . . . of teacher dictates, of a fixed, externally prescribed, stultifying curriculum. Behind the pretence of "democratic" socialization lurks the reality of closely supervised, standardized training where students fight each other in order to please those in power. In sum, students cannot learn democracy in the school because the school is not a democratic place.[40]

The idea of a hidden curriculum fit well this decade's swelling disenchantment with American schooling, when the School was widely condemned for not teaching much of anything to anybody. But as Merelman charges of the "hidden curriculum" thesis, it claims more than it can substantiate. Conformist and alienated students are both offered as contrary evidence of the same thesis, clearly a non-disputable proposition if opposing evidence is acceptable.

The description of teachers, curriculum, and administrators as everywhere repressive is also inaccurate. After all, students do find areas of freedom for their own activities within the school, and teachers who emphasize student assertiveness in pursuit of academic goals cannot also be teaching submissiveness. Some authoritarian school practices have come under successful legal attack; in addition, little of this thesis takes into account the ties between students' backgrounds (which may also be highly authoritarian) and the values that the school teaches. Moreover, students find ways not to be dependent upon the system and not to surrender to the hidden curriculum that they experience—it is not all that "hidden," it seems. Nor is the evidence strong that students alienated from school are also alienated from the larger political system, as a study of over eighteen hundred high school leaders revealed.

An alternative explanation for the order, discipline, and hierarchy that underlie the hidden curriculum, Merelman urges, may stem not from a political explanation but rather from the nature of large organizations. Like other professionals, teachers are granted authority by the community to provide services deemed highly valuable to all, services requiring special training. Although that authority has been strongly challenged in the last decade in all professions, here and abroad,[41] normally the grant of authority has presumed that educators have special knowledge, both in substance and in methods of transmitting it. But teachers, facing large numbers of students, are called upon to provide not only learning but order as well. To achieve both, educators claim that ordered ways of learning are necessary because: knowledge is not gained randomly but sequentially (short division before long division); it must be standardized so teachers can teach the same knowledge at the same time; and students must be tested in standardized ways to determine what was learned and which students need more instruction. In short, at the heart of the hidden curriculum lie practices stemming from the need for professional control over the dissemination of knowledge and the maintenance of order within the organization, all justified by special professional rationales.

Note, however, the special problem that accompanies the teaching of political values. Given the pluralism of our political choices and values, the civics classroom is not a place where the teacher can impose a singular ideal with which all agree. Hence the student finds value relativism, not the usual conventional wisdom transmitted by professionals whose control of order rests on that wisdom base. If the teacher attempts to impose a single set of values in the traditional fashion of professionals, he or she will be faced with those in the community advocating other values—a most threatening situation.[42]

How, for example, can one deal with the key democratic values of popular sovereignty and political equality within the education structure when both challenge the very concept of that structure? Merelman suggests that for popular sovereignty, the School hires civics teachers who are not that much more knowledgeable than the students so that the latter will feel closer to their teachers and come to think that intellectual authority is not to be feared. As for political equality, grading practices and curriculum are adjusted in every course so that a large majority of students neither fail nor excel; the result is that the majority shares roughly the same knowledge as a community of equals. All this is facilitated if, as is very often the case, these values are taught as "facts." That way few students learn this crucial intellectual distinction. By treating values as accepted facts, the potential danger of someone inquiring into them can be avoided, and the necessary order of the school enhanced.

All of this suggests why few strong links have been found between schools and political socialization. Students cannot take seriously such "softness" in the school's text, teacher, content, and grading. These seek to teach overtly the opposite of the hidden curriculum that they know elsewhere and that imposes order and demands much. The ostensibly democratic values being taught, therefore, are kept poorly conceptualized and made difficult to apply to specifics, as almost all studies of students and adults demonstrate. Sadly enough, it may be the brightest students who see through the softness most easily and become disillusioned with schooling.

Like all large-scale critiques of social institutions, the notion of the hidden curriculum is challenged on grounds of its conceptualization, methodology, and interpretation of analytical results.[43] In the debate and analysis that will engage students of political socialization in the 1980s, how the school works its effect on political values will be a serious question. There should be little doubt, however, about the fact that schools do teach these values. Critical of the assumption that schools do not teach political values, Jennings assembled the results of twenty years of major studies in 1981, finding a strong relationship between the amount of education and the amount of political knowledge. The evidence was conclusive. In short, debate should no longer center on whether the School has effects on the values of the State. It is the how of it that is little understood and represents a major research topic for the years ahead.

POLITICAL THEORY AND POLITICAL LEARNING

What we do know about the political values the school teaches should be understood, for the teaching clearly shows the "political" quality of education. Research is in agreement about the content of this instruction, the map of politics that is taught the young. School socialization emphasizes: prescriptive learning but not analytical skills; the positive qualities of our history and social life but not the problem areas; and the harmony and unity of the political process but not its divisions. In short, we see here many of the features of the allegiant American model with its impersonal, abstract institutions of governance.

Most scholars summarized here are appalled at their findings, mainly because they judge from the analytical model. Their criticisms are that current civic instruction provides few political management skills, develops no techniques of analysis and inquiry to help citizens understand political reality, and presents little knowledge of our pluralistic, group-conflict political world—and of who wins and who loses that conflict. They complain of textbooks and teachers pressured by representatives of that society into concealing the complex reality of the very world they represent. By 1980 some even challenged the conventional wisdom that greater education brought greater support for racial tolerance.[44]

Just as people get the government they deserve, so their civic instruction reflects the dominant educational demands of the society. After all, the civic instruction portrayed here is useful for many people. The view of a harmonious world is easier for the teacher to transmit than facts that emphasize complex and subtle conflicts, even more so if the teacher is poorly trained. School boards can deflect local pressures more easily if civic content is at such a general, and hence acceptable, level that no particular group can take offense. Textbook publishers lose fewer sales if powerful group values are not questioned and the governing process is depicted as almost perfect. And, in terms of the larger political system, those socialized in this fashion are less likely to assert a right to participate more fully, to strive for more resources from government, and, if disappointed in that effort, to challenge the legitimacy of the political authorities, if not of the political regime itself.

Apathy by the many is highly useful to the few powerful whose political activities are made easier by the absence of the many. A curriculum that tells people that politics is not hard to understand thus encourages the many's belief that it is also not important and so should not claim their time and energy. A learning model that emphasizes inquiry or asks the student to look closely at the parade of reality is not useful to vocal minorities, who cooperate in limiting such inquiry. Socrates, it will be recalled, felt the consequences of his urgings that "the unexamined life is not worth living." There are few like Socrates in the world of American civics teaching.

A further conclusion is that the socialization content described here illuminates the theoretical perspectives of the opening section of this chapter. The tensions among plural, democratic values noted there are suppressed by the allegiant American model that stresses acceptance of a consensual society, just as they are aggravated by the analytical model that stresses a conflictual society. The School reduces challenge to a consensual ideal by the reality outside the class through several means. Most important is a curriculum that avoids contemporary politics and postpones consideration of that political scene to the last years of schooling.

Note the implications of this for systems analysis. The School's assertion that all is well and its avoidance of contradiction both contribute more emotional diffuse support of the State than do other means. Further support may stem from instruction that presents the political system as free from error in the past; as a set of impersonal institutions, not human beings about whom passions rage; and as vaguely embodying a creed that ties all Americans together. This homogenized view contains elements of support for the authorities, regime, and community of the political system.

But there may be a penalty the School pays for providing this kind of diffuse support; students move from a benign attitude toward government in their elementary years to one of cynicism in their high school years.[45] The School is certainly not teaching such cynicism directly; rather, additional learning is coming from elsewhere— parents, peers, the media, and reality. These inevitably set up a perspective that clashes with that offered by the School. The political events of the last two decades must thrust upon the students' attention a world of rancorous conflict, bumbling leaders, and group divisions almost without number. Against this, the School offers only the allegiant American world which does not conform to reality. Little research has dealt with what students learn about politics without civics,[46] when they are directly caught up in an aspect of reality such as the draft, desegregation, teacher strikes, and other characteristics of recent political school turbulence. We believe that the School's instruction—with its emphasis on the harmony, unity, and the perfection of American politics—must turn off many students, certainly the most aware. In sum, the short-term benefit of avoiding conflict via civics instruction may well be exceeded by the long-term costs of contributing more to the general disenchantment with American schooling. If so, this strategy of achieving diffuse support for the political system costs more than it is worth.

In the chapters that follow we deal directly with *specific* support for the political system resulting from satisfaction with system outputs. What we see when we turn to the political conversion of demands into outputs is not the simple "clean" process presented by the Schools but a divisive, difficult, and often messy struggle among conflicting groups.

NOTES

1. This section has been informed by reflections on this question by Heinz Eulau, "Political Science and Education: The Long View and the Short," *State, School, and Politics: Research Directions,* Michael W. Kirst, ed. (Lexington, Mass.: Heath, 1972).

2. Charles Silberman, *Crisis in the Classroom* (New York: Random House, 1970), documents much of this contradiction and dissent.

3. These reflections are elaborated upon in T. Bentley Edwards and Frederick M. Wirt, eds., *School Desegregation in the North,* chaps. 1, 13; Frederick M. Wirt and Willis D. Hawley, eds., *New Dimensions of Freedom in America* (San Francisco: Chandler, 1967, 1969).

4. For comparison with the USSR, see George Z. F. Bereday and Jaan Pennar, eds., *The Politics of Soviet Education* (New York: Praeger, 1960), esp. chaps. 3–4; George Z. F. Bereday and Bonnie B. Stretch, "Political Education in the U.S.A. and the U.S.S.R.," *Comparative Education Review* 7 (1963): 1–16; and Jeremy R. Azrael, "Patterns of Polity-Directed Educational Development: The Soviet Union," in *Education and Political Development,* James S. Coleman, ed. (Princeton: Princeton University Press, 1965), pp. 233–71.

5. The following was suggested by Kenneth Prewitt, "Social Selection and Social Citizenship," in *State, School and Politics,* Kirst, ed. Prewitt leans on two earlier essays: Talcott Parsons, "The School Class as a Social System: Some of Its Function in American Society," *Social Structure and Personality* (New York: Free Press, 1964), pp. 129–54; and T. H. Marshall, "Citizenship and Social Class," *Class, Citizenship and Social Development* (New York: Doubleday, Anchor, 1964).

6. National Assessment of Educational Progress, *Education for Citizenship: A Bicentennial Survey* (Denver: National Assessment of Educational Progress, 1976), chap. 3.

7. For a classic statement of these notions and their origins in the clash between class realities and the American creed, see H. Lloyd Warner, *Democracy in Jonesville* (New York: Harper & Row, 1949); and A. B. Hollingshead, *Elmtown's Youth: The Impact of Social Classes on Adolescents* (New York: Wiley, 1949).

8. On these interrelationships, see David Easton, "The Function of Formal Education," *School Review* 65 (1957): 304–16; Byron G. Massialas, *Education and the Political System* (Reading, Mass.: Addison-Wesley, 1969), chap. 1; and Dean Jaros and Bradley C. Canon, "Transmitting Basic Political Values: The Role of the Educational System," *School Review* 77 (1969): 94–107.

9. David Easton, *A Systems Analysis of Political Life* (New York: Wiley, 1965), p. 273.

10. David Easton and Jack Dennis, *Children in the Political System* (New York: McGraw-Hill, 1969), p. 7. The definition is not so simple as it looks; see Fred I. Greenstein, "A Note on the Ambiguity of 'Political Socialization': Definitions, Criticism and Strategies of Inquiry," *Journal of Politics* 32 (1970): 969–78.

11. The contents of these orientations are usually conceptualized broadly as values, affect, and cognition, but role behaviors may be taught without such prior understanding. For a summary of scholars' agreement on this orientation content, see Jack Dennis, "Major Problems of Political Socialization Research," *Midwest Journal of Political Science* 12 (1968): 91–98; Richard Dawson, Kenneth Prewitt, and Karen S. Dawson, *Political Socialization,* 2d ed. (Boston: Little, Brown & Co., 1977).

12. A fuller explanation of the theoretical and conceptual elements here is developed in Easton and Dennis, *Children in the Political System,* pt. 1, esp. chap. 3. Easton reminds us in private correspondence, however, that schools are not always successful in bolstering a system. In Quebec, he notes, many teachers are accused of fostering "separatist" sentiment among their students.

13. Edgar Litt, "Education and Political Enlightenment in America, *Annals of the American Academy of Political and Social Sciences* 361 (1965): 35.

14. The first systematic examination of civic education was an eight-country study directed in the late 1920s by Charles E. Merriam; see his *The Making of Citizens: A Comparative Study of Methods of Civic Training* (Chicago: University of Chicago Press, 1931). Political science concern on the subject was dropped for another quarter century until Easton's writing in the 1950s and Herbert H. Hyman's *Political Socialization* (New York: Free Press, 1959); although this study ignored schools as a socializing agent in its focus upon the family. The first fully cross-national studies in the mode indicated in the text were Gabriel A. Almond and Sidney Verba, *The Civic Culture: Political Attitudes and Democracy in Five Nations* (Princeton: Princeton University Press, 1963; Almond and Verba, *The Civic Culture Revisited* (Boston: Little, Brown & Co., 1980).

15. The following quotations are drawn from Litt, "Education and Political Enlightenment." The model labels are by the present authors.

16. Frederick R. Smith, "The Curriculum," in *New Challenges in the Social Studies*, Byron G. Massialas and Frederick R. Smith, eds. (Belmont, Calif.: Wadsworth, 1965).

17. M. Kent Jennings, "Correlates of the Social Studies Curriculum," in *Social Studies in the United States,* C. Benjamin Cox and Byron G. Massialas, eds., (New York: Harcourt Brace Jovanovich, 1967), pp. 289–309.

18. Robert D. Hess and Judith V. Torney, *The Development of Political Attitudes in Children* (Chicago: Aldine, 1967), pp. 105–15. For an extended analysis, see Hess and Torney, *The Development of Basic Attitudes and Values Toward Government and Citizenship During the Elementary School Years, Part I* (Chicago: University of Chicago, Cooperative Research Project no. 1078, 1965).

19. John J. Patrick, "The Implications of Political Socialization Research for Curriculum Development and Instruction in the Social Studies" (Paper read at the 1968 American Political Science Association convention; the author is an associate of the High School Curriculum Center in Government, Indiana University, whose occasional papers illuminate this field and whose efforts are directed toward reforming this curriculum.)

For specific content analysis, see Franklin Patterson, "Citizenship and the High School: Representative Current Practices," in *The Adolescent Citizen*, Franklin Patterson et al. (New York: Free Press, 1960), pp. 100–75; Frederick R. Smith and John J. Patrick, "Civics: Relating Social Study to Social Reality," in *Social Studies,* Cox and

Massialas, eds., pp. 105–27; Byron G. Massialas, "American Government," in ibid., pp. 167–95.

For some curriculum reform suggestions, see Donald W. Oliver and James P. Shaver, *Teaching Public Issues in the High School* (Boston: Houghton Mifflin, 1966); Byron G. Massialas and C. Benjamin Cox, *Inquiry in Social Studies* (New York: McGraw-Hill, 1966), esp. chap. 2.

20. John P. Lunstrum, "The Treatment of Controversial Issues in Social Studies Instruction," *High School Journal* 49 (1965): 13–21; for a fuller picture, see Massialas and Cox, *Inquiry in Social Studies*, esp. pp. 158–60. A detailed study of right-wing pressures upon textbooks and curriculum is Jack Nelson and Gene Roberts, Jr., *The Censors and the Schools* (Boston: Little, Brown & Co., 1963).

21. For a thorough historical study of these instruments in inculcating nationalism, see Gladys A. Wiggin, *Education and Nationalism* (New York: McGraw-Hill, 1962); the role of the textbook is examined in chap. 9. On the Southern perspective, see Bernard A. Weisberger, "Dark and Bloody Ground of Reconstruction Historiography," *Journal of Southern History* 25 (1959): 427–47.

22. The earliest such analysis may have been Bessie L. Pierce, *Civic Attitudes in American Schools* (Chicago: University of Chicago Press, 1930). The study covering the most texts (93) is James P. Shaver, "Reflective Thinking Values and Social Studies Textbooks," *School Review* 73 (1960): 226–57. See also Mark M. Krug, " 'Safe' Textbooks and Citizenship Education," ibid. 68 (1960): 463–80; Edgar Litt, "Civic Education, Community Norms, and Political Indoctrination," *American Sociological Review* 28 (1963): 71–72; Byron G. Massialas, "American Government: 'We Are the Greatest,' " in *Social Studies*, Cox and Massialas, eds., pp. 167–95; Smith and Patrick, "Civics"; Stanley E. Ballinger, "The Social Studies and Social Controversy," *School Review* 71 (1963): 97–111. For studies of alternatives, see Massialas and Cox, *Inquiry in Social Studies,* chap. 9.

23. Content analyses of the earlier omissions are found in sources cited in n. 22. For specialized studies, see United States Congress, House Committee on Education and Labor, Ad Hoc Subcommittee on De Facto School Segregation, *Books for Schools and the Treatment of Minorities* (1966); the foregoing is popularized in John Brademas, "Don't Censor Textbooks—But Let's Keep Out Biased or Inaccurate Information," *Nation's Schools* 79 (1967): 38–52; for a study of a special distortion, see Virgil J. Vogel, "The Indian in American History," *Integrated Education* 6 (1968): 16–32; For studies of changing content, see Lloyd Marcus, *The Treatment of Minorities in Secondary School Textbooks* (New York: Anti-Defamation League of B'nai B'rith, 1961); and Sol M. Elkin, "Minorities in Textbooks: The Latest Chapter," *Teachers College Record* 66 (1965): 502–08.

24. National Education Association, *The Education of Teachers: Curriculum Programs* (Washington, D.C.: NEA, 1959), pp. 173–92, as cited in Massialas and Cox, *Inquiry in Social Studies,* chap 12.

25. Ibid., p. 285; for elaboration see John R. Palmer, "The Problem of Historical Explanation," *Social Education* 27 (1963).

26. The Kansas figure is cited in Harlan Hahn, "Teacher Preparation in Political Science," *Social Education* 29 (1965): 86–89. Symptomatic of professional social scientist interest is the development in the American Political Science Association in 1970 of a Pre-Collegiate Education Committee and earlier the work of the center

mentioned in n. 19, to develop a model curriculum. Indicative of new thinking on such preparation is Massialas and Cox, *Inquiry in Social Studies*, chap. 12. It is striking how often this course is taught by an athletic coach.

27. Harmon Zeigler, *The Political Life of American Teachers* (Englewood Cliffs, N.J.: Prentice-Hall, 1967), chap. 4, quotation at 113.

28. Howard K. Beale, *Are American Teachers Free?* (New York: Scribner's, 1936).

29. For case studies, see Joseph F. Maloney, *"The Lonesome Train" in Levittown* (University, Ala.: Inter-University Case Program, No. 39, 1958); Donald W. Robinson, "The Teachers Take a Birching," *Phi Delta Kappan* (1962): 182–88. For more systematic analysis of teacher constraints and sanctions, see Zeigler, chap. 5; and Howard S. Becker, "The Teacher in the Authority System of the Public School," *Journal of Educational Sociology* 27 (1953).

30. For a review of research on this attitudinal dimension, see Merlyn M. Gubser, "Anti-Democratic Attitudes of American Educators," *School and Community* 54 (1967): 14–16; see also John C. Weiser and James E. Hayes, "Democratic Attitudes of Teachers and Prospective Teachers," *Phi Delta Kappan* 47 (1966): 476–81.

31. A full review is found in Dawson et al., *Political Socialization*, and M. Kent Jennings and Richard G. Niemi, *The Political Character of Adolescence: The Influence of Families and Schools* (Princeton, N.J.: Princeton University Press, 1974), pp. 327–28; see also William R. Schonfeld, "The Focus of Political Socialization Research: An Evaluation," *World Politics* 23 (April, 1971): 544–78.

32. Hyman, *Political Socialization.*

33. Hess and Torney, *The Development of Political Attitudes in Children*, chap. 5; M. Kent Jennings and Richard G. Niemi, "The Transmission of Political Values from Parent to Child," *American Political Science Review* 62 (1968): 169–84, involving a national sample of 1,669 seniors. Another study of these data shows that it is the mother rather than the father who is more influential in shaping partisan affiliation and attitudes on some public issues; see M. Kent Jennings and Kenneth P. Langton, "Mothers vs. Fathers: The Formation of Political Orientations Among Young Americans," *Journal of Politics* 31 (1969): 329–58.

34. Dennis, "Major Problems," p. 109. For a similar judgment drawn from a review of the literature, see Vernon M. Goetcheus and Harvey C. Mansfield, "Innovations and Trends in the Study of American Politics," *Annals of the American Academy of Political and Social Science* 391 (1970): 178–81; and Dawson et al., *Political Socialization*, pp. 215–18.

35. See Litt, "Education and Political Enlightenment," n. 22; Edward P. Morgan, *Inequality in Classroom Learning: Schooling and Democratic Citizenship* (New York: Praeger, 1977) shows in three high schools the great variety of factors working in the teaching of civics.

36. Earlier research with null findings includes Roy A. Price, "Citizenship Studies in Syracuse," *Phi Delta Kappan* 33 (1951); 179–81; Earl E. Edgar, "Kansas Study of Education for Citizenship," ibid.: 175–78; Roy E. Horton, Jr., "American Freedom and the Values of Youth," in *Anti-Democratic Attitudes in American Schools*, H. M. Remmers, ed., (Evanston: Northwestern University Press, 1963), pp. 18–60; Litt, "Education and Political Enlightenment"; Patterson, "Citizenship and the High School," pp. 71–73.

For similar results in college, see Albert Somit et al., "The Effect of the Intro-

ductory Political Science Course on Student Attitudes Toward Political Participation,"
American Political Science Review 52 (1958): 1129–32; James A. Robinson et al.,
"Teaching with Inter-Nation Simulation and Case Studies," ibid. 60 (1966): 53–65.

The Langton-Jennings study is "Political Socialization and the High School Civics
Curriculum in the United States," ibid. 62 (1968): 852–67, with exchange following at
ibid. 63 (1969): 172–73. Curriculum revisions flowing from such findings have been
suggested by idem and by Patrick.

37. Dennis, "Major Problems"; see also Dawson et al., *Political Socialization.*

38. Jennings and Niemi, *The Political Character of Adolescence,* pp. 327–28.

39. The findings grossly simplified here are drawn from Hess and Torney,
Development of Political Attitudes; Easton and Dennis, *Children in the Political System*; Fred I.
Greenstein, *Children and Politics* (New Haven: Yale University Press, 1965). For some
criticisms, see Goetcheus and Mansfield, "Innovations and Trends"; Sheilah R.
Koppen, "Children and Compliance: A Comparative Analysis of Socialization
Studies," *Law and Society Review* 4 (1970): 545–64; Dean Jaros et al., "The Malevolent
Leader: Political Socialization in an American Sub-Culture," *American Political Science
Review* 62 (1968): 564–75; Schonfeld, "The Focus of Political Socialization Research";
R. W. Connell, *The Child's Construction of Politics* (Carleton, Victoria: Melbourne
University Press, 1971).

40. Richard M. Merelman, "Democratic Politics and the Culture of American
Education," *American Political Science Review* 74 (1980): 320; the following paragraphs,
unless noted otherwise, are drawn from this source, 319–32. See the extensive
bibliography on the hidden curriculum concept at this source for support of
propositions in the following paragraphs.

41. Frederick M. Wirt, "Professionalism and Political Conflict," *Journal of Public
Policy* 1 (1981): 61–93.

42. This threat from community pressure appears in all studies of the civics
teacher; see Zeigler, *Political Life of American Teachers,* passim, and Massialas, *Education
and the Political System,* chap. 6.

43. The following is drawn from: Kent Jennings, "Comment," *American Political
Science Review* 74 (1980): 333–37; Merelman, "A Reply to Richard M. Jennings," ibid.:
338–41; and Jennings, "Communication," ibid. 75 (1981) in press.

44. Mary Jackman, "General and Applied Tolerance: Does Education Increase
Commitment to Racial Integration," *American Journal of Political Science* 23 (1978): 303–
25; challenged by Michael Corbett, "Education and Political Tolerance: Group-
Relatedness and Consistency Reconsidered," *American Politics Quarterly* 8 (1980): 345–
60.

45. Greenstein, "Note on the Ambiguity." Although this work draws data from
before the turbulent national events of the last two decades, this finding has been
confirmed by all later longitudinal studies; see Dawson et al., *Political Socialization,*
passim.

46. Frederick M. Wirt, "Politics without Civics," *Society* 14 (1977): 46–48.

4

The Origins and Agents of Demand Inputs

The political system is not subject to the input of support alone, for demands provide the more continuous, contentious stuff of governance. We turn in this section to the exchange, across boundaries, of wants that arise from unsatisfied values. These values generate stress in the social environment—some of which produce demands upon the political system. Essentially, then, such demands originate in the conflict among basic social values and are transmitted into the political system. The next chapter carries us one step farther to examine the channels of access to the system's conversion process. Our present inquiry, however, investigates how stress arises through value conflicts and what agents transfer the resultant demands across the system's boundary.

VALUES AND THE ORIGIN OF CONFLICT

Individualism and Majoritarianism

The first and perhaps still best commentator on American political life noted a curious contradiction in its fundamental values. Alexis de Tocqueville pointed to the individualistic and the collectivist impulses whose clash provided a vital dynamism to the America he knew in the 1830s. Being a good aristocrat, he feared that the collectivist impulse would triumph, with its adoration of the majoritarian principle. We believe that stress swirling in our society today still stems from the confrontation between individual and group pressures to define "politics" or government.

The fundamental value may well be individualism, with its roots in Greek and Christian beliefs. It is reflected in our economic processes, our record of violence, and the restlessness of spirit characterizing the westward migration in the 1800s and the city migration of the 1900s. The political reflections of this value can be seen in the bills of rights in national and state constitutions. These draw those lines around the individual that constitute tyranny for government to cross. Such declarations are also designed to guard any minority against an equally possible tyranny by popular majorities. Yet the problem is that majorities have special authority in a democracy, so the conflict of minority right and majority rule has been endemic.

The interaction of the two principles is influenced by the mediation of the political system. If all persons are regarded as important, their wishes must be responded to by that system. But people's wishes are many and often conflicting, so if it is to persist, government must regulate these conflicts so they remain within tolerable levels. The operating principle of such regulation is that a given policy will take the direction preferred by the majority. Of course, this is a simplification of a very complex body of theory, as "majority rule" is a concept whose ambiguity is exceeded only by its sister concept of "majority will."[1]

If our history has evinced conflict between individualism and majority rule, our political practices and institutions have also reflected this conflict. Thus minority rights are protected by numerous devices, including the two-thirds requirement to pass school tax levies. Majority rule can be seen in the American concern to *elect* everyone in sight, including members of the sixteen thousand school boards—the only nation to do so. Many of the constitutional principles are barriers against temporary majorities, for example, separation of power, checks and balances, federalism, and civil rights. For instance, school boards may issue policies, but they are subject to taxpayer suit, popular referendum, and even recall of officials. The national will may call for outlawing school segregation, but the power of southern congressmen can long thwart that will. Or, when passed, a law may be opposed by local minorities prepared to hold the line for another generation, if possible.

Such individualism operating in political channels might tear the society apart if not checked. To a degree that is not fully clear, diffuse support for the political organization—the accepted basic rules of governance—has contributed to the creation of a political community, the sense that Americans want to exist together. However, diffuse support is not absolute or very thorough among Americans because of the splintering effect of individualism.

Possibly this centrifugal pull of individualism has been checked by our tendency to live and socialize mostly with those who agree with us.[2] In much of our past, American society consisted of islands of conformity, each oriented to different values and indifferent to or unaware of the others. The Bible Belt schools ignored evolution while urban northern schools treated it fully; rural Protestant schools might require prayers while urban liberal enclaves ignored them. Such cultural isolationism broke down, however, when outside forces disrupted the civil serenity—the issues of slavery and union a century ago, the movement from farm to the city seventy-five years ago, and the impact of communications media in the last fifty years. These changes evoked new needs of and stresses and demands on the political system; one of those demand sets arose over conflicting claims on the nature of schools.[3]

The variety of group and region, policy set and community life reflects that basic individualism in American life.[4] Not for us the French school system in which at a given hour every child of a given age in every school is learning the same thing. The very thought is unthinkable for us, and so our philosophic individualism reinforces social differentiation, and both are reflected in the kind of political system we have.[5] The rate of exchanges between the environment and the political system is enormously affected by a value system which emphasizes that one *should* translate private preference and need into public policy. Such exchanges are also augmented by an environment of great social diversity that necessarily generates more wants and demands than a homogeneous environment does.

Pragmatism and School Policy

Another basic American value influences this series of boundaries exchanges—pragmatism.[6] While the political system began with all its subsystems relatively uninvolved in the lives of its citizens, that condition continued only so long as private action was competent to meet wants. When that failed, Americans showed no reluctance in turning to the political system and public policy. Such a resort was first restricted to local political authorities, but if this proved inadequate, then state authorities and, in time, federal authorities were resorted to. There are special aspects of this political pragmatism: collective action in the name of individualism and a blitheness about ignoring "states rights" doctrine if necessary.[7]

In seeking authoritative allocation of resources, individuals let no doctrine stand in their way.[8] One general cultural value—individualism—generated inputs into the political system that another value—majority rule—authorized as legitimate behavior. But in addition, pragmatism—undeterred by bonds of the past, stimulated by the challenge of a new society, and mobilizing collective, mutual interests—provided a crystallizing value. Combined with the other two, it made innumerable exchanges across that intangible boundary between the private and public systems possible.

We can illustrate this value complex in school policies. The desire for education has *not been* a major value from the founding of this republic in the sense that everyone wanted it. Indeed, many reasons existed for opposing the establishment of early public schools, echoes of which are still heard today.[9] Yet along the way signs appear that many Americans *did* accept this value: the *national* commitment to use land sales to finance schools and colleges, for example, the Northwest Ordinance of 1787 and the Morrill Land Acts of 1862 and 1890; the *states'* commitment to provide a free public education at least to the grammar school level, then to high school, and now to some college; local *communities'* efforts at private support to reinforce state efforts in the private academies and colleges of the nineteenth century; and the constant shaping of the curriculum to meet the special concerns of Americans, for example, in farm, industrial, and military training classes.[10]

All this was not by any means a function of governmental action alone; the nationalizing force of professionalism has been of much greater consequence over a much longer period. The growth of professional standards for administration, teaching, curriculum, testing, and other elements of education were all a phenomenon of the last and not this century. Before this force emerged, the fabric of American schools was plaid and a rather ragged plaid at that. Experience drawn from testing a jumble of ideas transmitted through new journals and new training for the emergent profession did far more than the political system to impose a striking uniformity on American instructional practices. Pragmatism shows everywhere in the early history of this profession, for what worked well in one site was soon transmitted elsewhere.

In the face of this powerful nationalizing force, the belief in local control of schools never wavered, nor does it today even when the existence of local control seems much in doubt. Yet those favoring local control in earlier times were also busy adopting the innovations that professional administrators and teachers proclaimed as the best methods. In this fashion, American schools everywhere accepted a standard set of graduation requirements (thus the Carnegie unit concept), learning theories and their instructional practices, teacher- and administrator-training standards, and so on.[11] So it was that local control was eroded by the local adoption of nationwide professional standards.

If the political system's relationship to education has varied over time, so has the citizen's.[12] The belief that "education is a good thing" has had different meanings in the pluralist perspectives of our society. Early on, education was considered important for religious training. In colonial Massachusetts, in what Meyer has called "The Bible Commonwealth," the first schooling law was known as the "Old Deluder Satan Act"; a favorite early textbook was John Cotton's *Spiritual Mild for Babes Drawn Out of the Breasts of Both Testaments*; and the enormously popular *New England Primer* featured a biblical alphabet, *A* being "In Adam's fall/We sinned all."[13]

Schooling subsequently was endorsed for various pragmatic goals: transmission of basic literacy, i.e., the three Rs; provision of trained labor, i.e., vocational training for farmers and industrial workers; molding into one culture the diverse cultures of our immigrants, i.e., "Americanization"; and the absorption of "culture" in the popular sense, i.e., humanist and liberal education. Then, too, across time education has been supported by many—but not all—for the boost it provides children in the economic and status struggle or for its usefulness as a custody agent when parents are at work.

EQUALITY, EFFICIENCY, AND FREEDOM TO CHOOSE: AN INHERENT CONFLICT

Equality has become an increasingly important value in debates about school policy.[14] Equality includes several different concepts, for example, ensuring equal educational outcomes, equal access to education, or equal treatment of students. Many policy debates involve all of these under the general rubric of "equal education opportunity."

Equal access was the first of these concepts to become widespread as a minimally acceptable level of local school services. Most states guaranteed a minimum expenditure per pupil in each locality by means of a minimum-foundation school finance program. The federal antidiscrimination and desegregation laws are another prominent example of equal access. Equal treatment came later as school policy makers realized that learners have widely varying characteristics and abilities that require different resources for specific circumstances. It was seen that access is not enough and must be supplemented through special programs. For example, less fortunate children needed compensatory or special education to reach the same "starting line" as others in the competition for adult success.

By 1970, still another concept of equality had entered the political system—that is, equality should be conceived of as similar pupil outcomes. Such outcomes could be pupil achievement-test scores or universal attainment of minimum basic skills.[15] Proponents of this view contend that schools rather than pupils should be held responsible for substandard pupil attainment. They felt that as academic achievement is crucial for adult success, equal achievement outcomes are necessary for equal chances to enter adult occupations or earn income. A standard of equal outcomes would break the link between low school achievement and low socioeconomic status.

American culture exhibits a deep attachment to efficiency with values such as the Protestant ethic and the profit motive. Repeated schemes to produce school efficiency have been introduced throughout our history. Around 1900, for example, schools were under pressure to adopt scientific management techniques including time and motion studies.[16] In chapter 10, we trace the more recent movement toward education accountability including management by objectives and teacher evaluation. Those who value efficiency advocate greater productivity and cost savings; however, many policies designed to enhance equality conflict with school efficiency. Court-mandated integration increases transport costs per pupil. Special compensatory programs may also add costs without increasing pupil achievement. Federal regulations requiring the placement of handi-capped children in regular classrooms may prohibit lower-cost in-structional methods. Efficiency advocates stress that between 1940 and 1970 per pupil expenditures for American public schools increased 500 percent, even discounting for inflation. Yet measures of academic achievement were mixed and may have even gone down for some students.[17] The recent addition of school personnel such as reading specialists and teacher aides to achieve equality adds costs but not necessarily outputs from the perspective of these critics.

American individualism discussed earlier underlies another strongly held value surrounding school policy—the freedom to choose or select from different courses of action. One manifestation of this is our market economy; another is local control of education by sixteen thousand separate school boards. Some school policy makers resist central control by state and federal governments; others would like public schools to compete with private schools through competitive funding techniques such as vouchers or tuition tax credits.[18]

But free choice conflicts with equality and efficiency. Local school boards could choose segregated schools or inadequate funding for the handicapped. Others might choose high-cost instructional techniques or inefficient managerial policies. One way to change local politics is through mandates from centralized nonlocal authorities, and the federal and state governments have been mandating equality-oriented policies for the last fifteen years. Yet these centralized policies of equality or efficiency restrict local choice. In short, these three values cannot all be simultaneously maximized. Using all three entails political trade-offs within the conversion process of the political system. Local school boards contend that they must cut back on programs preferred by local residents such as music and arts in order to cover the cost of federal or state mandates for handicapped and bilingual children. Local boards are required to hire teachers with special bilingual credentials, but they assert that the types of training required are inefficient.

Conflicts around these three competing values are likely to become more intense in the 1980s. The federal government currently appears willing to ease up on its priority for equality and permit wider local and state choice, and the Reagan administration proposal to remove the strings from federal categorical programs for the handicapped and disadvantaged is a definite tilt toward free (local) choice. In addition, the fiscal stress in several states such as Michigan will cause an increased search for efficient policies such as closing low-enrollment schools. In California, Proposition 13 caused school districts to charge fees for school athletics, thereby restricting equality of access for poor families to participate in sports programs.

Filtered through the pluralist prism of our society, general values take on different definitions. The private pursuit of individualistic interests sometimes produces cooperation and accommodation among groups. Yet other groups come into conflict and find that private subsystems provide insufficient resources for satisfying their values.[19] As a result, some groups are rewarded and others are not. The consequent stress can generate a drive to mobilize additional resources by those unrewarded. Such a drive can take the form of transferring the struggle from the private into the political system. That system, in turn, seeks to maintain support for its political objectives by finding different ways of adjusting to such demands.

Each school system reflects the prevailing values in that district to some degree. The guardians of community values—religious, economic, patriotic—for whom schools are important instruments for keeping the faith operate at this level. We have seen how the indoctrination function dominates schools when they teach about our government. Given insulation from outside forces, such local guardians of orthodoxy can exist without challenge. But in this century challenges abound—the growth of national communication media, greater geographical mobility stemming from the economy or wars, professionalism, and so on. Control over schoolpeople locally has been weakened by professionalism, as noted above, or by the militancy of teachers increasingly unwilling to accept the dominance of parochialism.

However, we are nevertheless far from the bland homogeneity of the French school system. Some schools still hold the theory of evolution suspect, and others offer calculus or Asian history. The decentralizing impulse of pluralism clashes with the centralizing pull of nationalizing forces, such as professionalism and now federal laws. In this, education is not unique; it merely reflects the tensions of a federal system that emerge in many other policy areas as well. But whatever the balance between these conflicting values in earlier eras, it has been altered drastically by new nationalizing forces.

We need to know more about the specifics of this exchange and conversion process. Thus, who are the agents that transfer demand inputs into the political system from their position on its boundaries? "Transfer agents" is an abstraction for which we need some flesh-and-blood referents. For our purposes, we focus upon the roles of interest groups, electoral mechanisms, and local power structures. Each performs latent and manifest functions. Latently, each is involved in boundary transfer activities that have consequences for the ability of the political system—in this case the school—to persist as it seeks to cope with stress-generated demands. Manifestly, each speaks for or transmits the variety of American individualism involved in the swirl and clamor of local school politics. Both functions tell us much about how Americans give their educational values a political form when they seek to transfer private preference into public policy.

INTEREST GROUPS AS TRANSFER AGENTS

Interest groups, intermediate between citizens and educational political authorities, are involved in the full spectrum of private demands upon the school as a political system. That is, they make claims for justice, help, reward, or recognition. They do more, however, than just transmit political desires from citizens to officials. As transfer agents for the political system, interest groups can often reformulate demands so that they differ somewhat from citizens' desires. Moreover, interest groups do not confine their activities to just the input and conversion phases of the political system; they also provide feedback on the implementation of school policy. They are often mobilized by competing claims for the scarce budget resources of educational agencies. Despite such political activities, the tradition that overt politics and schools should be separate has shaped the nature of school interest groups.

There are many reasons why individuals join interest groups and why collective action comes about, and there has been an impressive growth in the numbers and types of educational interest groups over the past decades. This complex array of groups is part of the greater political turbulence with which educational policy makers must contend. The broad spectrum of interest groups reflects a weakening national consensus about educational goals over the last two decades and the diminishing influence of broad-based groups such as school boards and PTAs. Moreover, reforms such as compensatory, bilingual, and special education have created their own separate constituencies to preserve these new school functions. In addition, compensatory, bilingual, and special education programs spawn cohorts whose prime allegiance is to the program rather than the broad-based concept of a common school. Categorical initiatives from Washington and the state house have generated a jumble of interest groups that includes local project directors, parent groups, and federal and state categorical administrators.

Educational interest groups are also created as spin-offs of broader social movements, including women's liberation in the 1960s and the Moral Majority in the 1980s. These movements form political action groups with sections devoted to educational policies. For example, the National Organization of Women (NOW) may urge a state board of education to include a broader variety of female occupations in textbooks, or the Moral Majority will appear before local boards advocating that the story of creation be taught alongside evolution in science classes.

Another type of interest group includes networks of interstate experts and advocates who focus on particular policies such as school finance reform or competency education. These "policy issue networks" are not so broad based as social movements, and they emphasize technical expertise and assistance in their lobbying strategy. All of these newer interest groups are in addition to the collective action groups that have been around for years, including the Council for Basic Education and the School Administration Association. We will turn to these shortly.

This complex and shifting kaleidoscope of interest groups naturally confronts educational administration with a much broader range of demands than they faced even a few years ago. Any contest changes its nature when the number of participants changes. Two tenth graders engaged in a schoolyard fight, one black and one white, are most likely working out their masculinity in a fashion characteristic of that age. But if a hundred students of each color are involved, it is not merely a melee; there are likely to be racial overtones to the fighting. So increasing the number of participants facing the administrator means that he or she is in a different kind of contest than before, a contest in which one's role definition will change. Cuban has noted how role definitions have altered through this century as a result of new social environments affecting big city superintendents.[20] In one sense, the current period is the most exciting since reformers started pulling schools out from under political bosses and machines a century ago, but in another, it is also unpleasant for those involved.

One of the major changes is that the administrator is now working with these new interest groups. A major key to achieving education policy outcomes is to build a majority coalition from shifting alliances. Sometimes NOW will join forces with a local PTA, but at other times it opposes local preferences and aligns with a state organization made up of compensatory education parents. Because education has lost its diffuse support, appeals for loyalty to general public education are insufficient to mobilize interest group support for many things, including increases in local taxes. Splintered interest groups want a specific "payoff," such as access ramps for handicapped children. As Cuban notes, the role of the local school superintendent as an administrative chief has long since changed to that of a chief political negotiator and coalition builder. The objective of the next section is to categorize the interest groups, explain their formation and growth, and underline the necessity of coalition formulation.

The Role of Interest Group Entrepreneurs

If the social and structural forces at work in our society create interest groups, why do so many individuals join and contribute to them? The initial simple answer was that people join a group because they agree with the group's goals. Mancur Olson, in his *The Logic of Collective Action*, changed this straightforward emphasis on motivations.[21] As an economist, he stressed that individuals will *not* contribute to interest groups if they receive the same benefits through nonparticipation—as a "free rider." Why join the local teachers' organization if everyone receives wage increases through the efforts of those who give time and money? Olson answered this puzzle by focusing on the private benefits an organization can extend to or withhold from individuals. Anything of tangible value—group insurance programs, newsletters, tire discounts—can be contingent upon individual contributions. Interest groups therefore attract members and resources by supplying benefits only tangentially related to politics or specific public policies. Yet interest group political activities are possible because the people who join want private benefits, not because they share common values or goals.

Olson's thesis has gone through several adaptations, and these help explain the broad array of motives for individual contributions to groups. Salisbury has demonstrated that ideology, moral principles, and social pressures can generate collective action.[22] In an analogy to the marketplace, lobbyists form groups because, like entrepreneurs, the benefits they can obtain exceed the costs they must invest in mobilizing others. Members of a group also join because the cost-benefit ratio is favorable. Benefits are not merely material, such as good teacher contracts. They can also be "solidary," the intangible psychological reward that comes from belonging—the pleasure of sharing the company of like-minded others—as in a group of mothers protecting the neighborhood school against dangerous drugs or suspect curricula. Benefits can also be "expressive," so that one's personal goals are incorporated into and expressed by group action. An example would be a belief in the value of education manifested by work in the PTA. Common Cause is a classic example of all these. Other analysts have emphasized the motive of "imperfect information" whereby individuals underestimate their ability to become a free rider or overestimate the importance of proposed education legislation for their job performance. Moe broadens individual motives for collective action by positing that people join interest groups because they like to go to meetings or have feelings of responsibility.[23]

Because of this variety of possible motivations, we cannot predict what types or amounts of inducements will make people join a group. Politics need not be a by-product of membership gained through discounts for auto rentals or tax shelter annuities. Interest group entrepreneurs can attract members through ideological appeal, emphasis on fairness, social pressure, and the structuring of meetings. We lack empirical studies on the perceptual and value characteristics that motivate membership in education lobby groups. We do know, however, that there are numerous motivations and that the interest group leader is well advised to develop diverse appeals. However, at the core of this exchange, one trades group dues for individual benefits.

A recent key change in education politics has been the decline of loyalty as a motivation for supporting education interest groups. The PTA, AAUW, and National Committee for the Support of Public Schools have all lost ground in membership to state Title I ESEA coordinators, the Ford Foundation, and parents of limited-English-speaking children. Selective benefits are increasingly organized around categorical programs or professional specialties. Moreover, loyalty to the harmony of the education profession no longer inspires the membership it did when National Education Association (NEA) headquarters included administrators, professors, and schoolteachers under one roof.

A reflection of all this activity is the fact that expenditures for group action have grown dramatically since 1960. There has been an "arms race" that results in Washington or state capitol lobby offices for cities, categorical groups, low wealth school districts, and woman's organizations. Two examples illustrate this point. Table 4.1 is a listing of groups on one side of a current school issue; they are opposed to federal tax credits in Washington. This staggering variety illustrates two qualities of current school politics. Education policy touches on a mosaic of American values—religious, ethnic, professional, social, economic—which often clash in politics. Table 4.1 also illustrates the shifting quality of coalitional policy making, for this amalgam alters for other school issues. For example, some groups will drop out if the issue does not involve federal aid to private schools.

Another perspective on the recent proliferation of interest groups is seen in table 4.2, which is a statewide collective that supports increased state aid in California. Note how many separate school employee and support groups are represented in Sacramento. Although rarely studied, much the same situation probably exists in most if not all the states.[24]

A CLASSIFICATION OF SCHOOL INTEREST GROUPS

Differences exist among these groups—for example, in temporary versus permanent organization, special versus broad interests, and larger versus limited resources—categories quite like those found in interest groups of other areas. The National Education Association (NEA) illustrates the qualities of permanent organization, broad interests, and large resources while taxpayer-revolt groups exemplify the temporary, narrow, and limited-resource type of group. A major distinction we will employ for a closer examination of all such groups centers on the thoroughness of their interest in the many facets of education. Thus, we divide such groups into those for whom education is an end and those for whom it is a means to other ends. The first is filled with professional educators or those professionally oriented, the second with those wishing to use the school to serve other values, such as reducing taxes, protecting moral or patriotic values, and so on.

Table 4.1
Groups Officially Opposing Tuition Tax Credits—1980

American Association of Colleges for Teacher Education
American Association for Health, Physical Education, and Recreation
American Association of School Administrators
American Civil Liberties Union
American Ethical Union
American Federation of State, County and Municipal Employees
American Federation of Teachers, AFL-CIO
American Humanist Association
American Jewish Congress
Americans for Democratic Action
Americans United for Separation of Church and State
A. Philip Randolph Institute
Association for International Childhood Education
Baptist Joint Committee on Public Affairs
Coalition of Labor Union Women
Council for Educational Development and Research
Council for Exceptional Children
Council of Chief State School Officers
Council of Great City Schools
Division of Homeland Ministries, Christian Church (Disciples of Christ)
Federal Education Project of the Lawyers Committee for Civil Rights under the Law
Horace Mann League
Labor Council for Latin American Advancement
League of Women Voters
National Association for the Advancement of Colored People
National Association of Elementary School Principals
National Association for Hearing and Speech Action
National Association of Secondary School Principals
National Association of State Boards of Education
National Coalition for Public Education and Religious Liberty
National Committee for Citizens in Education
National Congress of Parents and Teachers
National Council of Churches
National Council of Jewish Women
National Council of Senior Citizens
National Education Association
National School Boards Association
National Student Association
National Student Lobby
National Urban Coalition
National Urban League
Student National Education Association
Union of American Hebrew Congregations
Unitarian Universalist Association
United Auto Workers
United Methodist Church
United States Student Association

Table 4.2
A California Collective Education Interest Group—1981

Education Congress of California

American Association of University Women—California Division
Association of California School Administrators
Association of California School Districts
Association of Low Wealth Schools
Association of Mexican-American Educators, Inc.
California Association of School Business Officials
California Congress of Parents and Teachers, Inc.
California Federation of Teachers, AFL-CIO
California Personnel and Guidance Association
California School Boards Association
California School Employees Association
California School Nurses Organization
California Teachers Association—NEA
The Delta Kappa Gamma Society—Chi State—California
League of Women Voters of California
Los Angeles Unified School District
Schools for Sound Finance
United Teachers of Los Angeles

Professional Interest Groups

For many years the most numerous interest group—teachers—exerted only minimal political influence. Schoolteachers had traditionally been reluctant to use collective action for transmitting demands to political authorities either within or outside school systems. The doctrine of the school administrator also played down the usefulness of teachers' collective organizations, stressing instead negotiations by individual professionals. This traditional doctrine also emphasized the authority of the superintendent and played down democracy and participation as used in the current popular sense. Later, an altered conception of administration favored teacher participation only for its effects on morale building and consequent improved performance. Not surprisingly, until recently the views of teacher representatives differed only slightly from the administrators' tenets.

A review of the history of the NEA will help to illuminate the norms of the professional educator. This group wanted a unified profession that should not split into opposing interest groups competing for scarce educational resources or should not engage in public conflict

over competing educational values. As the leading national organization, the NEA concentrated its efforts at the national and state levels.
It gave scant attention either to local interest groups of teachers or
collective pressure to change local school policy. Educators were
inculcated with the "professional" need for a harmony of interests and
a resulting agreement on educational goals for young children. Group
activity, when reinforced by formal arrangements such as interest
groups, would only lead to unnecessary and harmful conflict. With
that perspective, until 1960 the NEA as a national organization
focused its concern on standards and ethics and lobbied for general
federal aid for buildings and salaries, conduct and dissemination of
research, and technical assistance for state affiliates.[26]

This group's resources are not minor. In 1981, it has 1,650,000
members, representing about 60 percent of our public schoolteachers.
It has an extensive bureaucracy and hierarchy, although policy is
usually made by the executive staff with the concurrence of a board of
ninety-two directors and an executive committee of eleven.[27] Its national budget is currently $74.5 million. Every state has its own
teacher's association, which is frequently a powerful interest group at
the state level. There are over eighty-five hundred dues-paying local
school affiliates that filter their money through the state affiliates.[28]

At the national level, the NEA functions as an umbrella for major
segments of the profession. Within the national organization there are
over seventy-five departments, divisions, commissions, and committees. Separate professional organizations within NEA exist even for
audio-visual specialists, as well as for home economics and speech
teachers. The Political Action Council (PAC) of NEA plans to spend
$1.6 million in 1981–82 supporting political candidates at the state and
national levels. In one building the NEA houses groups with specialized
orientations and values that increasingly compete with each other in
the political system. Principals and counselors feel they are not well
represented by either teachers or administrators, that they are in an
intermediary position. These divisions over priorities for money and
values within the profession have spawned professional competitors
who argue their cases before school boards and legislatures.

The most noticeable NEA competition exists within the teaching
profession itself. The American Federation of Teachers (AFT) restricts
its membership to teachers and administrators who have no direct
authority over teachers. The AFT has affiliates in one-half of the states,
a 580,000 membership concentrated in large cities or nearby, and a

budget of $22 million, much smaller than the NEA. While the two teachers' groups can take common positions on some policy issues, for example, increased state aid for teacher salaries, their differences on others are not concealed.

AFT executives contend that professional unity is a myth because value conflicts are inevitable between teachers and their managers who administer the school.[29] AFT rhetoric is replete with *we* and *they*, terms reflective of a split between an aggressive labor union and its employer. The AFT's willingness to resort to a strike has been attractive to urban teachers but has shattered the professional ethic of low-profile interest group activity. The organizing success of the AFT in the 1960s led to the NEA taking a more militant stance in stressing collective bargaining.

The differences between the two are not merely over goals but over the organization of political efforts. If the AFT has succeeded more in big cities, the NEA has been more effective at the state level, where its affiliates—one of the largest organized interest groups in the states— spend much time dealing with state politicians.[30] The AFT, on the other hand, has few effective state federations, concentrating its efforts at the local level. Both groups have Washington offices, but until 1968 neither had been very successful in getting political demands approved by the president and Congress.[31] This changed dramatically during the 1970s when the NEA endorsed Jimmy Carter and became a major factor in his campaign structure.

The major administrative groups of superintendents and principals now frequently make their own different demands on the political system and maintain their own offices at the state and federal levels. The National Association of School Boards has traditionally joined forces with the administrator-teacher groups at the state and federal levels— but not when these groups cannot agree.

These divisions among professional educators should not be overestimated, for other forces work toward their unity. The tradition of a unified profession and the common training and experience of professional educators have led to an agreement on many fundamental values, a factor tending to restrict the range of interest group activity. For example, most administrators have come up through the teaching ranks, and accrediting associations are usually staffed by professional educators. Indeed, the faith that the public has in accreditation makes regional accrediting agencies a professional interest group of considerable importance, often bringing irresistible pressure to achieve their standards of faculty, budget, facilities, and curriculum.

Professionally Oriented Interest Groups

Other groups, although not composed of professionals, are also interested in educational policy as an end in itself. Like educators, they provide schools with diffuse support, but also like educators, they differ on some aspects of school governance and hence provide demand inputs. These demands may represent their whole purpose or only a secondary interest.

The National Congress of Parents and Teachers is not only the largest group in this category, it is the largest volunteer organization in the nation. The PTA is a loose confederation of about forty thousand local units and eight million members concerned primarily with specific problems facing *specific* schools. It is most influential and active at the local or district level, where its heterogeneous membership precludes agreement on controversial issues.[32] Although the membership is now one-third male, the organization is still dominated by women.[33]

Analysts of PTA accomplishments stress the generally dependent and close relationship it has to school administrators. Koerner expressed it this way:

the American PTA is rarely anything more than a coffee and cookies organization based on vague good will and gullibility. It is chiefly useful to the administration for raising money for special projects and persuading parents who are interested enough to attend meetings that the local schools are in the front ranks of American education.[34]

But as we shall see in the next chapter, such participation can have important positive social and psychological benefits for individuals.

The PTA's role locally is amplified at the national and state levels. However, it does not provide an independent source of demand inputs into school policy but rather proceeds as an instrument of educators who use it to reinforce or implement *their* policy inputs. Indeed, the national PTA is a resolute member of the Big Six—a coalition of three professional groups and three lay groups in education: American Association of School Administrators, NEA, Council of Chief State School Officers, National School Boards Association, National Association of State School Boards, and National Congress of Parents and Teachers. At another level, a study of three states in the

Midwest concluded that the PTA is viewed by legislators as a useful friend but not a very bothersome enemy. In effect, the values of the PTA leadership and the school professionals are similar, and as a consequence the PTA does not sponsor many conflict-oriented demands.

The PTA is not, however, the only professionally oriented lay interest group. The Council for Basic Education is an organization that has emphasized values different from those of the PTA and has become known as a "critic of public education." The CBE believes that the schools have neglected the fundamental intellectual disciplines in their purported overemphasis upon social adjustment. Its intentions are to see

that school administrators are encouraged and supported in resisting pressures to divert school time to activities of minor educational significance, to curricula over- emphasizing social adjustment at the expense of intellectual discipline, and to programs that call upon the school to assume responsibilities properly belonging to the home, to religious bodies, and to other agencies.[35]

The CBE attempts to influence school authorities primarily through publications, conferences, and other uses of the media. It does not have local chapters but has provided material to local groups who are interested.

Professionally oriented interest groups can also be found among numerous organizations that embrace education as a secondary concern, for example, the League of Women Voters and the American Association of University Women. These groups exist to promote general social improvements, a part of which touch on school programs and processes. Most of these groups only attempt to influence the political conversion process for education when the members are deeply and widely concerned about a particular aspect of school policy. This occurs intermittently, however, such as when the state constitution for education is revised. Like the PTA, these are non-issue-specific groups that provide support for the ongoing system and inject little conflict into it. They also constitute a resource for decision makers in times of crisis.

Transcendental Groups

Several kinds of interest groups view the schools as a means to accomplish ends that transcend the schools, for example, reducing the tax burden, eradicating communism, and so on. Around the turn of the century taxpayer organizations began to mobilize support for the elimination of "wasteful" public spending. Of particular interest, however, is the finding that taxpayer organizations have been *supporters* as well as opponents of increased tax support—depending on the tax source. They are strongly opposed to local property taxes but on occasion will support increases in state sales or income taxes.

Distinct from those whose main interest is material are those whose concern is with the moral instruction in the schools; the overlap of the two, however, needs study. The educational function of moral indoctrination dating from our schools' colonial origins never really disappeared with the *New England Primer*. The concern for the religious instruction function has not disappeared either, as seen in the continuing outcry against and disobedience of Supreme Court decisions banning Bible reading and school prayers.

The main function of these groups is to guard orthodox values. Their support of the schools is secondary to their concern for maintenance of chosen community norms. The school is viewed as only one of many institutions whose moral sanctity must be protected against subversion or direct challenge. Constituting what LaPiere has called "societies for the prevention of change," they maintain a protective surveillance over teachers' drinking and dating in small rural towns, students' music, dancing, and clothing in suburbia, and teachers' and administrators' "Americanism" everywhere. Few such groups have more than a local organizational basis, although their frequent church associations might imply otherwise. Their tactics lean heavily on direct contact with suspected deviants who are challenged to prove their moral worth. These tactics can escalate into board confrontations or, in small towns, into whispering campaigns. In smaller communities, more homogeneous and hence with fewer independent bases for defense of those challenged, educators have little recourse. They walk a very narrow line, not only in their individual morality but also in what they transmit to students.[36]

Crisis Interest Groups

Despite the broad variety of interest groups in public education, not all interests or values are reflected in organized groups. Furthermore, existing groups may choose not to carry certain demands to school officials. Subsystem stress over value concerns can, however, activate people who share attitudes and values but as yet have no interest group to reflect their values. Feeling the strong need to impress their values on school policies, they create new organizations whose life is temporary.

A typical illustration of this was in a northeastern suburb, where two newly organized interest groups were created in one year and then dissolved after the school board elections.[37] One was a "taxpayers association," formed to defeat three board members and cut back school expenditures. The superintendent countered with an interest group called Save Our Schools in order to reelect the incumbent board members and pass the budget. Both groups played important roles in conveying their special values and demands in a political system where local groups had not traditionally been important.

Integration crises across the country frequently spawn "Parents to Preserve Neighborhood Schools" as a counterweight to civil rights groups advocating integration. Such groups disband after the integration crisis passes. Aside from such case studies, there has been no systematic examination of crisis interest groups.

Testing Agencies and Foundations

Several groups that do not fit the usual conception of an interest group influence the political system of American schools. Although this country does not have a system of national exams, we do have several national testing agencies. The most important is the Educational Testing Service in Princeton, New Jersey. Most American schools do not have a choice in whether to provide their best students with courses in most of the subjects covered by College Board Achievement Exams. Because high school administrators want their students to score well on these exams, they do not have absolute flexibility to teach what they want. These external constraints reflect value judgments on what should and should not be taught, albeit urged in the interest of professionalism. This is one of those forces of professionalism that we earlier argued may be a more powerful external constraint on local school policy than local demands or federal laws.

Further, while private philanthropic foundations are not thought of as interest groups, they have exercised a major influence on school issues such as curriculum reform, teacher training, testing, finance, facility design, educational television, and so on. The foundations have used their grants to generate stress over value concerns. When the Ford Foundation finances the development of many instruments to assess national achievement in education, it is helping to create a political issue that pits those who oppose national testing against supporters of increased accountability by professional educators. A decision on whether to permit national assessment had to be made by conversion systems at all levels, for example, local school boards, state departments of education, and the United States Congress. Consequently, the questions and approach in the approved assessment represented many compromises.[38]

A foundation does not behave as a conventional interest group does by seeking access to public policy makers and then advocating its case for public money or support. However, by using grants to start experiments and demonstration projects (often reflecting special value orientations), foundations may make value conflicts more visible. This in turn can create a new demand that provides an existing or new interest group with an issue. These interest groups may substantially modify the content of the demand as it is transmitted to the school board or state legislator, but the foundations need an interest group in order to reach the political authorities through collective pressure. Foundations give twice as much money to education as any other category of interest group.[39]

We now move closer to the political system and its reaction to stress by studying elections and local community power structures. These are the input targets of interest groups articulating social values, and hence they partake of a partial or preliminary allocative function. The process of electing members to local school boards is a formal, visible, and legitimized point of access for expressing stress-generated wants. The operations of a community power structure in treating school policy is informal, often covert, and not legitimized. But both process demands and set the conditions by which authoritative allocations are made in the conversion aspects of the school's political system.

CONCLUSION

This chapter has introduced major components of the conversion process by examining only the input side. We have suggested some of the basic values in the social environment that influence the conversion process and have indicated how interest groups act as transfer agents for these values. The energizing force that impels the input phenomenon is environmental stress arising out of unsatisfied values.[40] This phenomenon generates felt needs, and satisfaction is sought by turning to the political system. When such a force is set into motion, it crosses the boundary between private and public systems in distinctive ways. The presentation of demands by interest groups is not restricted to an education-policy process, as interest articulation is widespread for most policies.

NOTES

1. For analysis, see Willmoore Kendall, *John Locke and the Doctrine of Majority-Rule* (Urbana: University of Illinois Press, 1941); Henry Steele Commager, *Majority Rule and Minority Rights* (New York: Oxford University Press, 1943); Herbert McClosky, "The Fallacy of Absolute Majority Rule," *Journal of Politics* 11 (1949): 637–54; J. Roland Pennock, "Responsiveness, Responsibility, and Majority Rule," *American Political Science Review* 46 (1952): 791–96.

2. Evidence is found in Samuel A. Stouffer, *Communism, Conformity, and Civil Liberties* (New York: Doubleday, 1955); James W. Prothro and Charles M. Grigg, "Fundamental Principles of Democracy: Bases of Agreement and Disagreement," *Journal of Politics* 22 (1960): 276–94; Herbert McClosky, "Consensus and Ideology in American Politics," *American Political Science Review* 58 (1964): 361–82. For similar evidence about teachers, see chap. 2, n. 30, above.

3. Hugh D. Graham and Robert Gurr, *The History of Violence in America* (New York: Bantam Books, 1969).

4. On the impact of regionalism, compare Norval D. Glenn and J. L. Simmons, "Are Regional Cultural Differences Diminishing?" *Public Opinion Quarterly* 31 (1967): 176–93; Samuel C. Patterson, "The Political Cultures of the American States," *Journal of Politics* 30 (1968): 187–209; Daniel J. Elazar, *American Federalism: A View from the States* (New York: Crowell, 1966); and Ira Sharkansky, *Regionalism in American Politics* (Indianapolis: Bobbs-Merrill, 1969). On sex and income differentiation, see Lester W. Milbrath, *Political Participation* (Chicago: Rand McNally, 1965), chap. 5; V. O. Key, Jr., *Public Opinion and American Democracy* (New York: Knopf, 1961), chap. 6.

5. These combinations are explored in Oliver P. Williams et al., *Suburban Differences and Metropolitan Policies: A Philadelphia Story* (Philadelphia: University of Pennsylvania Press, 1965).

6. The following relies upon Currin Shields, "The American Tradition of Empirical Collectivism," *American Political Science Review* 46 (1952): 104–20.

7. Louis Hartz, *The Liberal Tradition in America* (Chicago: University of Chicago Press, 1955).

8. Elazar, *American Federalism.*

9. H. G. Good, *A History of American Education* (New York: Macmillan, 1956), chap. 4.

10. Ibid., chap. 5.

11. Although the themes of these two paragraphs are not usually put this bluntly,

most history of education studies support them, for example, in Good, *History of American Education.* For a detailed study of this process, see Lawrence A. Cremin, *The Transformation of the School: Progressivism in American Education, 1876–1957* (New York: Vintage Books, 1964).

12. A historical catalog of this expansion includes Ordinance of 1785; Ordinance of 1787; 1862, First Morrill Act; 1887, Hatch Act; 1890, Second Morrill Act; 1914, Smith-Lever Agricultural Extension Act; 1917, Smith-Hughes Vocational Act; 1918, Vocational Rehabilitation Act; 1933, School Lunch Program; 1935, Bankhead Jones Act (amended Smith-Lever); 1936, George Dean Act (amended Smith-Hughes); 1937, First Public Health Fellowships granted; 1940, Vocational Education for National Defense Act; 1944, GI Bill of Rights; 1950, National Science Foundation Act; 1954, Cooperative Research Program; 1958, National Defense Education Act; 1963, Higher Educational Facilities Act; 1963, Manpower Defense Training Act; 1964, Economic Opportunities Act; 1965, Elementary and Secondary Education Act. For a review, see *Congressional Quarterly, Federal Role in Education,* 2d ed. (Washington: Congressional Quarterly Service, 1967).

13. Adolphe E. Meyer, *An Educational History of the American People*, 2d ed. (New York: McGraw-Hill, 1967), chap. 2.

14. Walter J. Garms et al., *School Finance* (Englewood Cliffs, N.J.: Prentice-Hall, 1978), chap. 2.

15. Charles Benson, *The Cheerful Prospect* (Boston: Houghton Mifflin, 1965).

16. Raymond Callahan, *The Cult of Efficiency* (Chicago: University of Chicago Press, 1962).

17. Frank E. Armbruster, *Our Children's Crippled Future* (New York: Quadrangle, 1977).

18. John E. Coons and Stephen Sugarman, *Education by Choice* (Berkeley: University of California Press, 1978).

19. James Sundquist, *Politics and Policy* (Washington, D.C.: Brookings Institution, 1968).

20. Larry Cuban, *Urban School Chiefs Under Fire* (Chicago: University of Chicago Press, 1976).

21. Mancur Olson, *The Logic of Collective Action* (New York: Schocken, 1965).

22. Robert Salisbury, "An Exchange Theory of Interest Groups," *Midwest Journal of Political Science* 13 (1969): 1–32.

23. Terry Moe, *The Organization of Interests* (Chicago: University of Chicago Press, 1980). For a market theory analysis, see Michael Hayes, *Lobbyists and Legislators* (New Brunswick, N.J.: Rutgers, 1981).

24. See Roald Campbell and Tim Mazzoni, *State Policy Making for the Public Schools* (Berkeley: McCutchan, 1976).

25. Alan Rosenthal, *Pedagogues and Power* (Syracuse, N.Y.: Syracuse University Press, 1969), pp. 6–10. For a full current history, see G. Howard Goold and Arvid J. Burke, "The Organized Teaching Profession," in *Education in the States: Nationwide Development Since 1900,* Edgar Fuller and Jim B. Pearson, eds., (Washington, D.C.: National Education Association, 1969), chap. 14.

26. James Koerner, *Who Controls American Education?* (Boston: Beacon Press, 1968), p. 26.

27. Ibid., p. 27.

28. Anthony Cresswell and Michael Murphy, *Teachers, Unions, and Collective Bargaining* (Berkeley: McCutchan, 1980).

29. For a general background on the American Federation of Teachers, see Patrick W. Carlton and Harold I. Goodwin, *The Collective Dilemma: Negotiations in Education* (Columbus, Ohio: Jones, 1969). AFT publishes a monthly newspaper. *American Teacher*, which provides current information on AFT policy directions.

30. Thomas H. Eliot, Nicholas A. Masters, and Robert Salisbury, *State Politics and Public Schools* (New York: Knopf, 1964).

31. James Sundquist, *Politics and Policy* (Washington, D.C.: Brookings Institution, 1968), pp. 155–200. In 1969, the National Education Association was a crucial part of the Emergency Committee for Full Funding. This committee was able to persuade Congress to increase the president's education budget by over $500 million.

32. For an elaboration on this view, see Koerner, *Who Controls American Education?* pp. 32–33.

33. Roald I. Campbell et al., *The Organization and Control of American Schools* (Columbus, Ohio: Charles E. Merrill, 1978), pp. 327–66; William T. Kvareceus, "PTA: The Irrelevant Giant," *The Nation* 5 October 1963, pp. 200–1.

34. Koerner, *Who Controls American Education?* pp. 147–148.

35. Descriptive leaflet, Council for Basic Education (Washington, D.C., n.d.), pp. 3–4.

36. See Richard LaPiere, *Social Change* (New York: McGraw-Hill, 1965), p. 197; Mary A. Raywid, *The Axe-Grinders* (New York: Macmillan, 1962); Jack Nelson and Gene Roberts, Jr., *The Censors and the Schools* (Boston: Little, Brown & Co., 1963). The distinction offered here borders on that of the "sacred and secular communities" analyzed in Laurence Iannaccone and Frank W. Lutz, *Politics, Powers and Policy: The Governing of Local School Districts* (Columbus, Ohio: Charles E. Merrill, 1970).

37. Lesley H. Browder, "A Suburban School Superintendent Plays Politics," in *The Politics of Education at the Local, State, and Federal Level*, Michael W. Kirst, ed. (Berkeley: McCutchan, 1970).

38. Ralph Tyler, "National Assessment: A History and Sociology," in *New Models for American Education*, James Guthrie and Edward Wynne, eds. (Englewood Cliffs, N.J.: Prentice-Hall, 1971), chap. 2.

39. For a good overview, see Robert J. Havighurst, "Philanthropic Foundations as Interest Groups," in *Education and Urban Society* vol. 13, no. 2, 1981, pp. 193–218.

40. For an analysis of the curriculum area, see Jon Schaffarzick and Gary Sykes, *Value Conflicts and Curriculum Issues* (Berkeley: McCutchan, 1979), pp. 191–214.

5

Access Channels
To School Policy Making

MODES OF CITIZEN POLITICAL CONTROL

Although demands originate outside the political system, some become political when they "are voiced as proposals for decision and action on the part of the authorities."[1] Some demands enter the political system, others do not. This screening occurs for at least two reasons. It may be that the kind of valued interest seeking legitimation is not broadly accepted (for example, a Mafia interest) or that the resources each interest possesses are inadequate (thus the exclusion of the very poor).

Public preferences have concerned school professionals long before the recent turbulent politics of education. Given the condition, rare among nations, that our citizens vote upon school governors and some programs, it is not surprising that these school officials have long sought to detect and defend themselves against such control. Reformers tried to depoliticize education by substituting nonpartisan for partisan elections and election at large for election by ward, but citizens still possessed the means to control those given authority over school matters.

In the past, educators have concealed their concern for this participation by not calling it "politics" but "community relations." Educational journals were once preoccupied with ways of selling professional views to the public. Little of this persuasion rested upon empirically researched propositions, however; more often it was a nice story about how a bond issue was maneuvered to success in Hoggsville, Arkansas. In the decade following World War II, validation of some propositions on mobilizing citizen support began to appear.[2]

Popular participation in school policy making has traditionally taken two forms—election of officials and referendums on issues. We treat the referendum process in a later chapter because it partakes more directly of demand conversion than the election of officials does. *Local* school elections operate independently of political parties. Contrary to popular impression, political parties at the *national* level have sought unsuccessfully to serve as a link between citizens and school policy. For almost a century of national party platforms, education has been among "the predominant forces in operation during election years."[3] Yet schools have not escaped citizen control by avoiding the clutches of national parties, for there is still direct and indirect popular control. Directly, there is the widespread practice of electing school boards at the local level and boards and superintendents at the state level.[4] Indirectly, control exists in the election of state legislators, executives, and judges, whose broad responsibilities include authority over many aspects of public education.

THE ARROYOS OF SCHOOL BOARD ELECTIONS

Although 85 percent of local school boards in this country are elective, the politics of these elections was a great unknown until recently.[5] We are aware that these officials, five to seven on a board, almost always seek their three-year or four-year terms on a non-partisan ballot. We also know that the board appoints a superintendent, usually professionally trained, who operates under its general policy guides and who may be removed by it. The exception to this pattern is the appointment method found most often in our biggest cities. In the usual community, the theory of democratic control makes the board member a pivot between community demands and school operations. We examine how that role is performed in the next chapter, but first we must see whether the election of board members is a major channel for popular inputs to the school political system. There were some widespread general impressions about this citizen-elected official interaction when the first edition of this book was written a decade ago. But more recent studies have provided a much more complex picture of school board representation.

The "Dark Continent" of Board Elections

What was known raised more questions than it settled. One clear point is that there is little voter turnout for board elections, even more indifference than that for other government offices. Yet the reasons for such low turnout are not clear. Is it because of the nonpartisan myth of school politics or because elections are held in off years and at primary dates when turnout is low for all contests? If there is variation in the degree of citizen participation in different states or cities, what accounts for it? Does the mere requirement of nonpartisanship preclude political parties from playing a direct role as they do in Detroit or do voters' party identifications influence their choices, as they do in some city council races? Does low turnout benefit some groups but not others? That is, might board elections more often represent the weight of Republicans—who go to the polls more than Democrats—and consequently more often represent the viewpoint of groups attracted to the GOP?[6]

Another clear finding is that campaigning in school contests is very limited, candidate visibility very low, and the contest rarely based on specific policies. Is this again attributable to the nonpartisan myth, which requires participants to act as if they were not engaging in political acts? Or is it due to the lack of highly visible issues that might stimulate popular interest? What are the conditions under which election contests become visible and the public highly participant? Further, although most boards are elected, a minority in significant American cities are appointed. What difference does this make in representative roles? Is there any difference in policy orientation under the two methods, and, if so, can such differences by traced directly to the methods? Crain had shown that boards immune from elections were somewhat more able to move toward school desegregation than elected boards.[7]

Recruitment: Few Are Called, Even Fewer Chosen

Among the new knowledge of school politics available in the 1970s was a better conceptual picture of how board members are recruited to that office. In any political system, leaders must be recruited to fill the constitutional positions, but this process is not random. Rather the qualities of this process are in harmony with the dominant values of the larger system, just as the selection of kings and presidents tells us much about the value of their respective societies.[8] Moreover, the process in which a mass of citizens provide a very few decision makers is a winnowing of those failing to meet the dominant values. Successful recruitment must be followed by effective role learning in the new position of authority, and that in turn by successful role performance before a political system produces its leadership.

The relevance of this conceptual understanding to actual local politics was promoted in the work of Cistone during the 1970s.[9] Recruitment to broad membership in North American school elections is a process of many being excluded, a few being called to office, and even fewer becoming leaders. Being recruited is the outcome of possessing political opportunities, some formal, some practical. The unequal distribution of these opportunities is what provides a first screening of the total population. Formally, the legal code may set down minimum requirements—being a qualified voter, a district representative—but clearly these only screen out from the enormous numbers those who do not qualify to vote. Practically, eligibility is screened by social status, political resources, age (the more eligible have more of these), and sex (men get elected disproportionately in government). The fact that such opportunities are structured in society, some having many and many having little, means that most citizens are filtered out of the recruitment process.

Note the results of this process in the social composition of school boards. When the Progressive reforms of nonpartisanship in school matters finally settled into place across the nation, the large working-class membership had almost disappeared from school boards, and white middle-class dominated everywhere. Moreover, most members were male, married with children in the public schools, and active in the community. From the landmark study by Counts in 1924 to a replication by the National School Boards Association almost fifty years later, all the research substantiates this finding.[10] High social status alone does not give entry to the school board, but community activity—whether civic, business, political, or educational—joined with high social status provides training for office that few of the well-off actually use. We will consider whether or not this condition affects representativeness in policy decisions in the next chapter. However, in the recruitment stages, the eligibility processes of our democratic system leave behind a vast majority of Americans who cannot or will not seek entry or who simply don't care for the game.

Selection: Democratic Reality and Theory

Given even the small number who are eligible, the selection process pares the list even more. The major in-depth study done on a national sample of board members by Zeigler and Jennings labels as "precipitating conditions" the factors that moved some of those eligible to run for office.[11] Although most credited encouragement from others, 23 percent were self-starters whom no one had encouraged. This lot stands as a corrective to a view of school boards as "closed systems" which outsiders cannot penetrate. Most members, however, did point to a supportive network of significant others who induced— or pushed—them to run, such as other board members (29 percent), citizen groups (21 percent), friends and neighbors (21 percent), and the remainder who were split between school professionals and political figures. The number of these sources of support may be misleading, for in most districts sampled, members either were sponsored by previous board members, were initially appointed to fill an unexpired term, or both. Tendencies toward a closed decisional system were reinforced by the absence of competition for these seats in about one-quarter of this district sample. Significantly enough, a high degree of sponsorship was closely associated with lack of competition ($r = -.40$).

Using elections to select school boards always generates questions about the validity of elections in a democracy. Thus, the continuing criticism of the unrepresentational nature of board membership just noted has implied that without such "virtual representation," the people cannot be well served. This further implies a theory of democracy in which only those with like characteristics can speak for like-minded constituents. On historical grounds alone this is rather simplistic, for leaders in expanding civil liberties or social policy for the less-favored have been drawn largely from higher social status groups. Franklin D. Roosevelt and John F. Kennedy were far removed in status from the millions of poor and ill-favored who saw them as their leaders.

Board members in the 1970s, individually or collectively, have been studied within the context of more complex theories of democracy and representation than this. Theories of popular democracy were applied to studies of school referenda.[12] Theories of federalism were cited to illuminate the emerging school policy program from among "the family of governments." [13] In all this the natural sequence of how knowledge is built becomes visible. It moves from the particular case study—heavily descriptive, bound to time and place— to preliminary theories, which seek to generalize across such particulars and generate testable propositions about social behavior. These, in turn, could build an established theory. Several of these efforts are applicable in the study of elections to school boards. Each springs from a model of democracy that links citizens to policy makers through the electoral process.

The Zeigler-Jennings Study.   Probably the largest scale effort was drawn from the eighty-eight-district national sample analyzed by Zeigler and Jennings. While others have criticized this work for its design and its conclusions on the superintendent's responsiveness to the board,[14] almost no one challenges its findings on the model of citizen-board linkage through elections.

The authors deduced the major aspects of a popularly held democratic model, including beliefs

> . . . that the opportunity to seek office should not be restricted unduly, that a choice of candidates is ordinarily preferable to only one, that public attention should be engaged, that elections should be fair, and that the losers should step out in favor of the winners. Such elements lie at the heart of democratic selection procedures.

Subsequent analysis of board elections demonstrated, in the authors' words, that reality "scarcely meets the stiff requirements of the democratic ideal." [15]

Their quantitative analysis can be summarized broadly.[16] Just over half the board members faced any competition in their election bid. Moreover, another requirement of democratic competition is missing. That is, democratic theory assumes that officeholders have *ambition* to remain or to move to higher positions; ambition is what makes officials responsive to voter demands. But this research finds that board members have little ambition. Also, board members rarely move on to high state or national office; President Jimmy Carter was an exception. Only about one-third of the board members interviewed aspired to higher office, figures much lower than for state and national legislators. Indeed, four of five explicitly ruled out any interest in higher office, a finding parallel to those found among city council-members in a large California study.[17] In this tepid electoral climate, there are few signs that board members are bound to heed public demands because of their ambition.

Are these elections contentious, with candidates taking opposing stands on school issues? The democratic model assumes the presence of such candidate-related choice for the voters. Yet in only 58 percent of the contests did members report that their ideas about schools differed much from other candidates'. When the opposition included incumbents, however, many more differences with them were reported than when there were no incumbents; in short, incumbency offers a visible target for challenging policy ideas. The data of the Zeigler-Jennings study support the democratic proposition that opposition is useful if voters are to choose among policy ideas, but this opposition does not occur often.

Moreover, few of the differences were over educational programs and personnel, which one would expect to be central to electoral school conflict. The issue content of voters' choices more often dealt with the board—its role and operations, composition, or community relationship. Physical and fiscal problems or civil rights issues were somewhat less evident in election competition. These concerns are much more visible to the community than educational issues are, particularly when the latter are obscured by professionals' claims. Thus when incumbents are among a candidate's opposition, that board's role will more likely be an issue than when no incumbent is in the lists.

Public involvement in board elections is low, as any voting study will show. Another form of involvement, the formation of citizen support for particular candidates, does occur, but again only among the minority that votes at all. About half the candidates in the Zeigler-Jennings study reported no public group support. The presence of incumbents again changes the electoral context; there was more public support than when no incumbents faced the voter. So the incumbent's record seems to encourage group mobilization, providing a personal focus to school issues of considerable complexity.

Time and again what emerges from studies of board elections is that they are channels to the political system that are little used. Like those arroyos of the Southwest, only rarely is there intense turmoil surging through these channels. However, there are occasions that can have the effect of the flash floods through these desert courses, that is, enormous conflict followed by altered features in the immediate environment. Much more often, however, these election campaigns offer only slight differences in ideology or policy orientations. This is a condition that makes the democratic model of informed choice between significant policy options by a sizable electorate more a fiction than fact.

Competition and Responsiveness

This pervasive condition is greatly affected by the past—the nonpartisan reforms begun a century ago and now widely effected in American local government. Zeigler and Jennings report that such reforms as nonpartisan ballots and at-large elections actually lower the degree of electoral school conflict, particularly in metropolitan areas. This is true whether conflict is measured by the degree of competition, office turnover, or incumbent defeat. Very little difference in this depressing effect found with nonpartisanship is explained by district size, frequency of elections, or the timing of board elections.

Rather, nonpartisanship has a more qualitative effect on the nature of school election competition in both city and rural districts. The nonpartisan approach and at-large elections affect the degree of competition however one measures it. Is competition measured by whether candidates are fighting over a major change in school policy, by the degree of differences among candidates over a range of policy issues, or by whether they differ about the board's role? None of these attributes of competition increases if there are nonpartisan ballots or at-large elections involved. Quite the contrary, the reforms reduce such measures of competition, and much the same depressing of competition occurs in metropolitan and nonmetropolitan districts.

In short, political scientists have found that what applies to nonpartisanship in other aspects of the local political scene is also true for school politics. Such reforms increase the cost of citizen participation, make the linkage between representative and citizen more difficult, and so muffle the expression of the full range of political interests within a community. Those so constrained inevitably tend to be of lower socioeconomic status, for structures of governance are not value free. Rather, these reforms actually encourage the access and satisfaction of middle-class and higher-status people. The rhetoric of Progressivism proclaimed the expansion of democracy—"the cure for the evils of democracy is more democracy" was their standard. The reality has been otherwise, screening out those who cannot use the cue of political party to decide among complicated public issues, including those of schooling. Such reforms ensure that —until recently at any rate—the game of school politics was played by few, and mostly those better favored by fortune.

The Zeigler-Jennings analysis advances considerably our earlier knowledge about the link of citizen demand to school boards via elections. The popularly accepted democratic theory of responsiveness and responsibility was earlier known to be a poor explanation of school elections. Now, however, we know more about the intervening effects of competition and other electoral conditions. We still see a tepid political environment, only occasionally upset by a raging electoral storm. Yet, when the actual conditions of democractic theory come about, these data show that the citizen-board link operates as it is supposed to. But that is not often, at least not during the 1960s, when the data were gathered. We still need to know how that linkage operates when we move from a normally consensual electoral condition to a normally conflictual one. Conditions of political turbulence in the 1970s already outlined seem to present a changed and charged electoral climate. Storms brewed from the discontent of lay and professional groups filled the empty arroyos with raging torrents that swept the old before them, and deposited new forms on the landscape of school governance.

An illustration of this metaphor is available in desegregation conflict. In a ten-year review of the issue in several score northern cities, Rossell demonstrated that desegregation generated a truly conflictual electoral politics for school boards.[18] Thus she found that the issue generated much higher voter turnout. In turn, this surge of electoral interest led to increased defeat of incumbents, usually those identified with support of the issue, especially in higher-status school districts. Moreover, her findings support propositions not discussed before in this research. For example:

1. Low turnout does not necessarily mean the absence of conflict, and high turnout is not a consistent measure of electoral conflict in local elections dealing with single issues. There are other measures of electoral dissent than high turnout.

2. The stage of the issue affects the participation rate; general controversy in the early stages increases the turnout more than the implementation of a specific desegregation policy in later stages does. But implementation generates more electoral dissent if local decision makers must work with something forced on them rather than something they voluntarily adopt.
3. Citizen perceptions of when to use the ballot to "throw the rascals out" is quite discriminating; incumbents are more likely to be defeated when they try to implement desegregation than when there is general controversy over citizen demands.

OTHER PLACES, OTHER MANNERS

Such research findings agree that the citizen-board linkage in elections is not simple but must be differentiated for different issues, times, and communities. What issue enters the election, whether its entrance occurs in a period of high or low conflict throughout education, and what the constituency characteristics are all suggest varying conditions for the electoral connection. The Zeigler-Jennings study alluded to such distinctions occurring even in a period of consensual school politics; the city or rural context makes a difference in many matters, as do distinctions in how the election is structured. Several research efforts in the last decade have sought to show the effect of these differences.

Community Status and Electoral Turnout

Implicit in much analysis of competition's role in democracy is an assumption that greater social variety in a community engenders greater competition. Clearly the variety of city lifestyles can be contrasted with the conformity of nonurban life. The first generates more political conflict because there are more opposing social and economic bases for making demands on the local political system. Hence an urban setting generates greater competition and greater turnout in elections. On the other hand, the rural setting provides only a limited basis for either. The same is reported for the 1940s, the 1950s, and the 1970s.[19]

While this thesis may be correct for city-rural differences in a social context, the evidence for different electoral behavior is much less certain. Outside the South, rural turnout rates in general elections are actually quite high, certainly more so than in the city. The figures for board elections are less studied, yet it is demonstrable that the urban population's greater social complexity generates a greater concentration or intensity of organizational life. Measures of the latter in the eighty-eight-school-district study found them closely associated with metropolitan or nonmetropolitan status (beta = .44) and with population size (.35). This is not simply a matter of the absence or presence of political parties as a major social organization that mobilizes school concerns. There might well be an argument that boards should be partisan, but the best evidence finds that party influence appears only where there are other pressure groups highly active.[20]

Another way to look at the influence of community context is to compare the status differences of districts. Some scholars had proposed that people with the same distinctive status, class, or occupational qualities generate the same kind of demands on political systems. But the evidence has told different stories at different times after World War II. Conventional wisdom prior to the 1960s[21] found the politics of working-class schools to be associated with low intensity and low election turnouts; upper middle-class politics were the reverse. It seemed that workers were less interested in school politics and that interest increased as one moved up the social scale. Then comparative studies by Minar of working-class and middle-class suburbs around Chicago, based on data gathered around 1960, found quite the reverse.[22] There, competition varied inversely with status; working-class school politics turned out to be quite contentious, its election turnout high, and its challenge to the superintendent frequent. Conversely, middle-class suburban school politics was low keyed and hardly visible, with few voters and limited challenge to the professionals. Minar argued that the difference resulted from workers' propensities to challenge school decision making by professionals of higher status and from middle-class voters' tendencies to leave such matters to the "experts," a status they quite often shared.

Almost a decade later, the Zeigler-Jennings research came to a third conclusion—status showed minor impact on the electoral competition for these boards.[23] However, status does strengthen the explanation of how certain electoral arrangements affect competition. The differences between the studies may lie, the authors noted, in a broader measure of what constitutes competition and in the greater variation in lifestyles found in the larger sample of districts; Minar's were from Chicago, theirs from around the nation.

However, another national sample about the same time but composed of northern cities facing desegregation did not reach the same result. Rather, Rossell found what the first researchers had: high-status groups participated more in elections in which desegregation was central. Rossell suggests that her differences with Minar lie in the fact that his high-status citizens let professionals handle elections because their decisions were not threatening, whereas the decision to desegregate did generate greater concern about racial and other threats.[24]

These recent studies suggest a much richer perspective on what citizens are doing when they vote in board elections than previous research did. The turbulence of the last decade or more has clearly generated a new kind of electoral process. Where there are few issues to agitate the local political system—which could be most of them in the small districts outside the city—the old pattern may prevail. Elections there have low visibility and little heat, with low turnout facilitating school support by middle-class voters. But even one hotly contested issue changes all this, for then the arroyo becomes a gullywasher. High-visibility, high-turnout elections, with the social strata sharply opposed to one another and the professional educators under strong criticism yield another kind of electoral process.

The exact nature of the status alignments in voting may depend upon the particular issue. No one has yet tried to classify board elections in such terms, a modification of the Lowi concept that different policies generate different kind of politics.[25] Rossell's work on desegregation suggests that at least this policy rearranges electoral coalitions. At the other extreme and during the same time period as desegregation, the politics of sex education has been an area in which professionals have changed the curriculum without much controversy.[26] Education about American society, however, seems to generate fierce status conflicts between ideologues, who also come into conflict even over science.[27] But then financial reform conflict seems to unite all status levels as in the Proposition 13 mood of the late 1970s. A theoretical analysis of various policy effects has yet to be done, but there is a rich diversity to study and draw from in the recent turbulence of school politics.

Citizen Participation

During the period after the mid-1960s, many called for more participation in school decision making. This ran beyond calling for greater voter turnout in board and referenda elections. Rather, this movement sought a qualitative change in the process of policy making by expanding the number who sit on the boards. This could be done directly, as in the New York City decentralization movement of the 1970s which created thirty-three neighborhood school boards instead of the single one. Or else it could be arranged by the attachment of "citizen advisory councils" to existing boards or local school sites. This movement has not been restricted to the United States either; it recently surfaced in France, Italy, England, Sweden, West Germany, and China.[28]

There were several purposes for making such changes. Some sought increased participation for instrumental reasons, for example, to increase the chances of specific policy changes. Thus it was urged that more Black or Hispanic parents be put on such councils, where they could influence the system to be less racist in some particular— more sensitive teachers and administrators, a multicultural curriculum, and so on. A second purpose for greater citizen participation was psychological, that is, the process itself would improve the participant's sense of value as a person. There might not be much policy change, but participation would stimulate others and so permit the emergence of a "community will."

Salisbury has recently traced the origins of these different purposes for participation (rooted in classical political theory) as a way of understanding why citizens today engage in this special civic act.[29] His subjects were citizen participants in the schools of six St. Louis suburbs during the middle and late 1970s. Different kinds of communities were studied to determine the intervening effects of social differences upon participation. The findings are complex, but a few of them suggest how the simple act of participation is altered by social context.

Social context is everywhere important in defining who participates and what participation means. Mothers with children, those deeply rooted in the community, the upper social strata—not all in these categories participate, but persons having these characteristics are more predisposed to participate than those who do not share these qualities. The amount of participation does not seem to be very influenced by family background and socialization, but having children in school is important, and participation leads to more intensive participation. Participation has traceable but highly complex effects upon one's personal development, level of information, social interaction, and subsequent civic involvement.[30]

Participants in school politics are more distinguished by *what* they do rather than *how much* they do. Some just regularly go to meetings, some specialize in contacting public officials, while others talk to fellow citizens about school matters, and still others work primarily in school elections. There are three types of participants in voluntary groups distinguished by the substance of their acts—members, active members, and officers. All work through different institutions in their efforts at participation—family and neighbors, political parties, voluntary organizations, the election system, and school officials. Those who participate remain positive in their support of public education, with trust in the honesty and effectiveness of its administrators; they are also sanguine about their own ability to influence school policy in their communities. As Salisbury notes:

There is broad support in these findings for the ancient view that the active citizen would also be the confident and effective citizen. And there is broad support also for the view that suburban school-centered participation bears little relationship to the larger and more cynical world of national politics.... The central finding is that . . . the more people participate, the greater will be the impact on them, and the greater the impact, the more likely it will take the form of enhanced personal growth and development.[31]

All this occurs in a school politics that is dynamic—constantly changing in its actors, participants, issues, and conflicts. The changes that accrue from such participation are not dramatically large and abrupt; rather they are small and incremental. But over time, as Lindblom and others have noted, such small changes add up to massive changes in the amount and quality of a policy service, such as the education provided.[32] Those entering the policy world expecting immediate major changes are doomed to frustration. No system, by definition, changes in this way short of violent revolution—and not even then, as the Soviet system illustrates. However, those entering the school policy world with a sense of developing capabilities and generating pressures for some change are much more likely to have effects, small though they may be. Over time, as the American experience has shown, they can transform an institution and thus benefit their children.

NONLOCAL PARTICIPATION

To this point, we have only focused on the channel of input demands to the school board's authority on the local level. Yet, partisan elections in higher state and federal office can also have consequences for the local schools because of the resources transmitted to schools. Increasingly, the budget fight in the state legislature over the amount of the subvention for local schools becomes an annual political drama in every state. Governors and legislators, therefore, have a direct bearing upon school quality, and, as we will see in a later chapter, that state role makes "local control" more imaginary than real. Further, what the legislature says about the taxing authority of local units is vital to the operation of the schools and the pocketbooks of most citizens.

There is one other nonlocal channel for popular participation: the elections of congressmen and the president. If the range of issues facing political authorities is extensive at the state level, the reach becomes enormous nationally. This should mean that the saliency of schol issues becomes reduced for most voters at the higher governmental levels. That is, concern over school taxes or what is taught becomes reduced when compared with issues of war and peace or the national economy. However, citizens follow national affairs more closely than local affairs, and state affairs least—that is, when they pay any attention to public affairs at all.[33] As yet we have little information on citizen use of resources to affect national authorities on school policy. Citizens may have *opinions* on Washington's policies, as we shall see, but the gap between popular opinion and action on many issues is enormous. And then citizen demands or even attitudes on federal policy may be so diffuse as to be nonexistent.

Some input is provided, however, through party channels in the form of issue stands. Rather consistently in the past, those identifying with the Democratic Party have been stronger supporters of federal aid to education than have Republican identifiers. The professional politicians of either party were even more widely separated on these issues than average party members.[34] After 1965, as federal funds became increasingly available to local school budgets already straining under an overloaded property tax, this partisan difference began to disappear. It reemerged in the Carter Administration, however, over creation of the Department of Education. In 1980 Ronald Reagan campaigned for its abolition and sought that end after his election, including cutting federal funds for schooling.

In short, diffuse attitudes about federal school policy can sharply crystallize under some circumstances. Thus, there was very strong support for the GI bill after World War II; to oppose this was to oppose the soldiers' efforts in that war. In another example, during the late 1960s national attitudes coalesced in intense opposition to school busing during the desegregation controversy. Citizen attitudinal input into national arenas deals little with educational policy, however, and there is little evidence that it flavors the decisions of voters in federal elections. Yet it could be that under some circumstances—such as a perceived threat to a closely held value—opinions themselves can crystallize to have electoral impact. Some of the support for Ronald Reagan was of this kind, from foes of busing.

In summary, then, although elections in the United States serve as potential channels for citizens to have school outputs in a fashion that is rare among the nations of the world, they seem very little used. Board elections are barometers, normally reflecting little pressure from the environment but subject to sudden change because of hidden disturbances. Indeed, additional examination of the disastrous weather changes that produce "rancorous conflict" would be immensely valuable.[35] Such analyses would have several uses. Practically they would describe the conditions under which professional administration of the schools excites public concerns, and theoretically they would help develop an understanding of the links betwen private wants and public outputs under stress conditions. These practical and theoretical concerns generate interesting questions. Practically, how much can the superintendent support external demands for quality from the profession when community standards reject or resist them? Does the frequency of superintendent turnover—chronic in the profession and especially so in larger cities—inhibit or enhance this schoolperson's efforts at financing, curriculum and staff improvement, or desegregation?[36]

Any theoretical questions are posed in contrast to the available evidence that American schools receive a minimum of significant input through the direct channel of elections. Yet from this, one must *not* conclude that the wants of citizens are ignored by the political authorities of School or State. Rather it suggests that elections—whether viewed as channels or barometers—are little used for exchanging demands across the boundary between the community and the school's political system. The possibility always remains, however, that a school issue which deeply agitates the community or the nation could suddenly focus on the channel of elections, overturning the old and bringing on the new, much as for other public policies. After the extensive rhetoric on local control of schools, this phenomenon may not amount to much, though professionals cannot ignore it.

COMMUNITY POWER STRUCTURE AND SCHOOL POLICY

Another exchange mechanism, less visible and formal than elections, is community groups with special influence upon school policy. Nations, for example, have been and are dominated by a particular subsystem—the military, clergy, wealthy, aristocracy—which in turn dominates the political system. In the last several decades, researchers have studied how power is organized in communities to make public decisions. Termed "community power studies," many have appeared; often the research pits sociologists against political scientists, who debate whether local power is hierarchical ("elitist") or segmented ("pluralist"). This literature is in part theoretical, methodological, and normative, although the distinctions among these modes of knowledge have not always been clear. We do not propose to detail this search for community power but to summarize its contours as a preface to noting its relationship to schools.[37]

Four Queries in Community Power Studies

We suggest that the complex intellectual debate on this subject centers around four questions: What is meant by *power?* How is its presence and arrangement discovered in the community? What accounts for the differences in power arrangements that exist among

American communities? What differences in terms of community life stem from these different power arrangements?[38]

Despite their enormous fascination with power, social scientists share little agreement on its meaning, except that it involves the capacity to cause or inhibit change in behavior impossible to effect without it. This modest consensus falls far short of being a theoretical statement that can help explain and predict the outcome of social conflict. As March's survey of the term's meanings concluded, "On the whole, however, power is a disappointing concept. It gives us surprisingly little purchase in reasonable models of complex systems of social choice."[39] Much of the conflict in the whole field could stem from this vagueness at the heart of the inquiry.

Given the indefinite meaning of the term, the measurements of power have been equally varied. Most research has dealt with the problem of how to detect community power and, once certain methods were justified, with what was found. It may be too strong to say that much of this work was trivial compared to the larger scholarly questions in this list, and perhaps the problem of method had to be tested in research before we could arrive at the present situation. However, for a decade after the publication of Hunter's *Community Power Structure* in 1953, the pages of the journals of sociology and political science were the forum for a strong, even bitter, clash over methods—positional, reputational, decisional, combinational. Part of this may have reflected a bias stemming from disciplinary training for such research.[40] By the mid-1960s it was clear that no one method was sufficient; judicious combinations were needed to accurately trace the dimensions of community decision making.

The third query—on what accounts for differences among community power arrangements—required collecting a pool of comparable data. That task has been slow to accomplish. One approach was to compare a small number of communities within the same methodological framework; thus, in the mid-1960s Agger et al. developed a theoretical and conceptual framework for the study of four communities. Another approach was to compare what was known about existing case studies, in order to test hypotheses about different power arrangements arising under different conditions. But the limited-sample approach was not a sample, so generalizations were limited; at best they were a modest advance over the host of independent case studies. On the other hand, analysis of pooled case studies faced the problem of the varying methodologies used and the research questions that motivated each study. By the end of the 1960s, the third approach was getting under way; this involved working with a large number of communities to which unified theory, concept, and hypothesis were applied. The announcement of a "permanent community sample" of fifty-one American towns with resident community analysts opened a new possibility; here was a more established data base from which to raise research questions about policy outcomes and decisional arrangements.[41]

The final query is one that has often been implicit in all this research: what difference does it make for the community whether power arrangements are elitist, pluralist, amorphous, and so on? Far too often, of course, each analyst dealt with only a single town in answering that question, hardly the basis for meaningful generalization. Nevertheless, the first major works on community power, the Lynds' *Middletown* and *Middletown in Transition*, were critical of the quality of life they found in a community dominated by one family. Many later writers never quite abandoned this normative approach. Much research has had an implicit criticism of the arrangements found (particularly the elitist) for what these meant to democratic values and the way people lived. For the researchers, even the somewhat less narrow power arrangements found in pluralist studies were criticized for seeming to justify a status quo that defeated the democratic promise.[42] The emergence of new federal programs and their resources for those who were formerly resourceless attracted the attention of scholars concerned about whether this development might rearrange power at the local level.[43] In this development, it was thought that the "mobilization of bias," which locally works to the advantage of the few who set the local agenda and mobilize maximum resources to achieve their ends, could be overcome and power returned to the people. The overtones of Populism and Progressivism are recognizable in such programs and in the scholars they attract to study them.

What Difference Does It Make Who Governs?

Even this highly condensed description of a complex problem in social research may seem inordinately long and vague to one unfamiliar with the subject. For one new to the field, a question of greater importance might be what is the significance of this research for schools? Its utility is like that of any knowledge of the community.

A fuller picture of the ties between school and community enables teachers and administrators to carry out their professional tasks better. A little less generally, one could note the queries of a leading school administration textbook: "For example, does the administrator become subservient to the power structure when elements of it are known to him? Or is he then in the position to become manipulator? Or in a better position to provide constructive leadership?"[44]

We can illustrate some of what is implied here. If the community is dominated by one small group that shares the same values, for example is elite, then school professionals wishing to pursue new educational programs must know what the group is whose support they must enlist. Educational innovation that proceeds with no notion of community values, of the guardians of this orthodoxy, and of their resources is an empty exercise. If, however, the community has a number of groups, each important in shaping policy in one domain, or has shifting coalitions that form temporary majorities on each issue area, another strategy is needed. In this case, one has a better chance of finding bases of support in the community by seeking coalitions of power. In sum, given that the school is part of the community, power research provides information about that relationship and suggests strategies for working with it.

Oddly, before 1970 the scholarly debate on community power research did not deal very much with the schools. The four works that mark the major developments of this controversy—by the Lynds, Hunter, Dahl, and Agger et al.—illustrate this neglect.[45] A review of the hundreds of research studies in this field yields further support for this finding; not even the recent aggregate, comparative studies prior to 1970 showed interest in this policy area.[46] An exception was Alford's study of the political cultures of four Wisconsin cities.[47] Among these four, different degrees of bureaucratization (that is, professionalism) and citizen participation were at work, but there was no evidence of any elitist control—other than the educational interest group of administrators and PTAs. In this work, schools are clearly seen as a proper policy concern for the analyst due to the size of the resources they expend and the occasional flash flood of citizen concern about school actions.

The relevance of such study for schools has been drawn primarily by educational administration scholars, a handful of whom have provided a bridge to other disciplines. Not much of even educational scholars' work is available, however, and little of it is comparative, even after 1970. In 1967 a listing of community power studies provided merely 10 out of 310 citations that were clearly related to educational policy; two of these had the same author, and four were unpublished dissertations.[48] The theoretical perspective in these earlier studies was limited, most found elitist arrangements, and all urged their results upon superintendents so they could better fulfill their jobs.[49]

The comparative phase was ushered in by the little-noted 1956 study of three small towns in Wyoming, one delightfully named Wideroad.[50] Utilizing reputational techniques and opinion surveys from samples in each town, Webb discovered that community control rested in the hands of a few people who were mostly unknown to the average citizen and to the school administrators. The work has a limited theoretical basis, yet its comparative aspects are a considerable advance.

Some years followed in which case studies still prevailed in the limited research on schools and power structures. One study of two towns showed that economic elite dominance did not exhaust all the possibilities, but the work was primarily descriptive.[51] But then in 1963–1964, a freshet of publications appeared whose quality was much improved. These emphasized the comparative method, their theory and concepts were well developed, and the consequent hypotheses and empirical grounding brought the research up to another level entirely. Most still cited the utilitarian value of such research, reflecting the incessant and unnecessary pleading of scholars to their audience of professional administrators that learning has practical applications.

What Difference for School Policy?

Yet to be faced was this question: What differences for school outputs did a specific form of local power make? A research orientation like this guided the Syracuse volumes of the early 1960s. Chief among these is an analysis of our New York suburbs. This "study of values, influence and tax effort," while theoretically oriented, also sought to help those who wanted to learn how to raise school taxes. Although the power arrangements in these suburbs were quite similar, they "displayed major differences in their levels of relative expenditure and tax effort." Hence, there was little consequence for school policy from administrators and teachers establishing friendship lines into the business and civic clubs. The critical variable seemed to be the distinctive attitudes in each community about school programs and needs, although specification of that relationship is quite complex.[52] This was a forerunner of the understanding that in suburbs community context makes a difference, a subject treated in the next chapter.

Whereas the Syracuse studies of 1963 found power arrangements irrelevant to financial differences, a year later Kimbrough found that they controlled many school matters in four southern counties. This volume makes a strong plea by an educational scholar to administrators on the differences that such knowledge can have for their job performance.[53] The two studies contrast sharply in their findings, possibly because the southern communities were so alike whereas the Syracuse suburbs were so unlike in their cultures. The Kimbrough work has been widely cited in education literature as showing the intervention effect of covert groups upon the entry and determination of inputs before the school board.[54] One way in which such groups can have an effect is upon the superintendent's tenure; McCarty has suggested that much of the variation in their tenures is explained by just such variations in local power arrangements.[55]

The theoretical complexities of school and power arrangements increased in the mid-1960s. A collection of essays edited by Cahill and Hencley contained a wealth of research strategies, questions, typologies, hypotheses, and interactional analyses.[56] The theoretical and practical utilities of comparative study are also seen in Crain's examination of school desegregation, first in nine major cities and later in over ninety.[57] The complex conclusions here challenged the popular belief in the power of a "civic elite," at least in the desegregation process. However, this elite seemed to set the "political style" of each city; it indirectly influenced the appointments to school boards; and it demonstrated a North-South distinction on the extent of elitism. In another of those ironies that our conflicting basic values occasionally thrust upon us, desegregation proceeded more smoothly if the board was more independent of the general public.

A major comparative study on the ties between power structures and school policy, the largest of its kind then and now, appeared in the work of Johns and Kimbrough in 1968.[58] The policy studied was community effort to reform school finances over a seventeen-year period after World War II in 122 school districts in Illinois, Kentucky, Georgia, and Florida. In 24 of these communities, in-depth studies of their power structures developed two "open" and two "closed" types. As hypothesized, closed systems were associated much more often with reduced financial efforts for schools.

In light of our concern with the degree to which power structures provide open and closed channels to the political system of the schools, one set of findings is particularly meaningful. If a system is closed and noncompetitive, we would expect to find citizens less participative but expect them to be more participative if the system extends them more opportunities to be so. This was indeed the case, whether participation was measured by proportions of voter registration, voting, or organizational membership and activity. Citizens tended to drastically misperceive the power arrangement in their communities, tending to see more competition than actually existed. But if they perceived that they lived in a competitive system, they felt more efficacious. Moreover, the type of power structure showed little relationship to the civic, economic, and educational beliefs of major community influentials, teachers, and registered voters. The authors found that the best explanation for why a district had a given pattern of financial effort or expenditure was whether it had employed that pattern in the past.[59]

Therefore, the independent effect of such community forces as the power structure, superintendent's role or influence, and citizens' values was grossly limited. These findings stand in stark contrast to the limited case studies of the past, even though the authors caution against generalizing too far from their work. Note that the taxpayer revolt that occurred since this study was made would tend to confirm the lack of relationship between the type of power structure and financial effort. With all districts swept up in the fervor of this revolt, few qualities of community life seem to make a difference in tax cutting.

Finance is not the only issue studied in relationship to local power. That local power structures can also have relevance for school governance was highlighted by McCarty and Ramsey in a 1971 study of fifty-one small, rural to large, central-size cities.[60] Again, no single pattern emerges of an elite that controls local power. Rather what was found varied from place to place. There was often an association between the kind of power structure in the community and on the school board, with important consequences for the superintendent's role. Thus, if the structure in the community and on the board was elite, the superintendent was limited to being a "functionary." If the structure in community and board was bifactional, the superintendent was a "strategist" maneuvering between the two. But if the context in both places was pluralistic—power varying with the school issue—the school official appeared as a "professional advisor" serving all factions equally and fairly. If, however, a community and board lacked any structure of power or was unpatterned, then the superintendent could define his or her role as "decision maker" and did so.

This is a far cry from the situation popularly ascribed to this professional as dominating the board across a range of school matters; certainly the subsequent national study by Zeigler and Jennings argued emphatically for this popular view. Boyd has also pointed out certain limitations of the McCarty-Ramsey findings, challenging the degree of pluralism they thought they found and, by implication, the impact of power structures upon school policy making.[61] In the next chapter we will review this debate over whether the board or the superintendent controls school policy making.

From such works, the concept of community power study and its relevance to school decisions slowly made its way into the training in social foundations of educational administrators.[62] That professionals should relate to their communities is not a new idea, of course, but now the emphasis has shifted to the uses of knowing that á few influential people can shape community outputs by controlling the access of demands to the school system. Similarly, this training more explicitly adopted the pressure-group approach to policy making. Whether these forces were valuable or not for the administrator's tasks was not clear, for some writers rejected the impact of lay pressures, while others insisted they were a necessary and inescapable part of the job.[63] No matter how slowly this facet of school politics was working itself into the cognition of administrators, scholars were well ahead of them, as the studies analyzed in this section demonstrate.

These scholarly concerns may be somewhat belated, for the findings of most studies are time bound in a society that is changing enormously. A reanalysis of power structures in 166 communities shows that political processes are changing, tending to become more pluralistic: "power . . . is less and less in the hands of a privileged few and is increasingly dependent upon the broker, be he elected official or not, who can bring together (to the extent he can bring together) the various elements in the community."[64] There is also the strong possibility that the intervention of major forces from outside into local communities may be rearranging power all over the nation.[65] We have also mentioned the more recent nationalizing force of federal school laws following on the older nationalizing forces of professionalism. Such intrusion into the school scene could not only diminish the weight of any local elite in decision making, but it could also narrow the options for decision by *any* power form.

The Vertical Axis of Local Control

These changes suggest the metaphor of a "vertical axis of power" that now runs through all school districts, that is, influences from outside their boundaries. School boards are faced with extramural pressures they cannot control and which powerfully shape what they can do. Thus changes in the shape of the economy—a boom or a bust—can drastically affect the size of the school budget. The oil crisis after 1973 engendered by the OPEC nations has seriously reallocated school budgets away from strictly educational purposes to cover rising energy costs. Similarly, the expansion of the controls over these boards by state and federal laws occasioned a storm of complaints during the 1970s, as Cronin's widely circulated declaration notes.[66] Perhaps an even greater outside influence stemmed from the state as it expanded its constitutional prerogatives under political pressures. Too, the rise of strong teacher organizations represents a local sign of what is in essence a national development. This group's influence in a big city's schools like Chicago has led one analyst to label it "union rule in Chicago."[67] If the state continues to extend its control and take up its share of local costs in the 1980s, teacher groups may well escalate their pressure upon state legislatures to reach decisions that are binding upon local districts.[68]

These influences working upon the school scene are only a part of a national pattern evident in the total urban setting. Changes in the economy, the growth of state and federal controls, the emergence of national professional groups—all afflict mayors and city councils as well as schools. Just as schools face desegregation problems, so city halls face affirmative action orders. When schools budget a third or more of their financial resources for fuel oil, urban bureaucracies must do the same with their budgets. If the state capitol mandates drug abuse curricula on the local school, it also mandates more training courses for city service employees—and both local authorities face increased reporting requirements. When local teachers strike for higher pay, police or fireworkers may well be out on the line just down the street. As Long's persuasive book traces, urban Americans live in an "unwalled city," and a close examination by Wirt of a major city like San Francisco shows just how these centralizing influences work upon city and school governance.[69]

The result has been an increase in the number of groups that seek to influence local school governance, the kinds of issues that get on the school agenda, and the kinds of resources brought to bear upon the school board. As recently as 1960—in some cases 1970—the agenda before almost all school boards did *not* include: slashing budgets, facing organized teacher demands, grappling with desegregation, assuring congruence with federal guidelines on a range of program services, meeting court requirements about treatment of minorities and students, finding ways to cut energy uses and costs, meeting state laws on accountability, incorporating parents into decision making, and so on. In 1980 some or all of these appear on all school board agendas in districts across the nation. That is why Cistone, editing a series of close studies of school board problems in the mid-1970s, characterized the present

... as a time when the external environment of the school board, as of virtually all social organizations, has been undergoing rapid and profound transformation. . . . The insularity, the selective responsiveness, that once characterized school board decision-making is being eroded under the powerful impact of social, economic, cultural, and political pressures. . . . The need to respond and adapt to the external situation is precipitating changes in the personality and character of the school board itself.[70]

Just as recent work challenges any simplistic notion of boards being dominated by narrow local elites, so this phenomenon of the vertical power axis counters the notion of the great influence of local structures. It may be that as this external axis works on local power structures of any kind, local groups are not doing much of any significance. That would be the case if basic decisions are being made for local power structures at other power centers, public and private, outside the district. What the locals can do, however, is work with the residue of decisions left them by others. Peterson's influential 1974 review of the literature concluded that pursuit of the question Who controls? in local schools, despite the voluminous writing, was empty of meaning when the evidence of *any* control locally was absent.[71]

Preoccupation with marginal matters does have its value; Salisbury has shown how citizens working with such margins are enhanced in spirit and mind. Also, this does not mean there are no independent courses left for administrators or boards. When the blizzard of 1977 struck Columbus and Cincinnati with the same fearful blows, each school system reacted differently in response to differences in each one's organizational ethos.[72]

What all this does mean, as van Geel has documented in detail, is that the authority to control school programs has always been altering, in accordance with numerous and sometimes conflicting principles of school and society.[73] The newest model of local control clearly emphasizes extensive sharing—not autonomy—in school board authority. Given that condition, the independent power of even the most elite local power structure is quite limited.

DEMOCRACY AND SCHOOL POLICY

In these last two chapters, we have sought to trace the various access channels for demands into the schools. One finding seems rather consistent: relatively few citizens use whatever channels are available to register their educational needs. Popular participation is episodic, providing spasms rather than a steady flow of demands. When finally aroused, it does not focus upon broad policies but upon specific aspects. Of late, this involvement has taken the form of an increasing failure to pass local school levies, from almost two-thirds passing in the mid-1960s to only one-third by 1980. Alongside this flood of dissatisfaction with public schools by an apathetic public, there are occasional waves aroused by a sex education course, a too-liberal textbook, student dress regulations, and other specific causes.

Interest groups may thus be the most frequent form of participation, but few citizens belong to them; the difficulties PTAs have in getting members enrolled and turned out are well known. Even groups seeking wider popular authority over local schools through "community control" programs have had great difficulty in getting "the community" to participate. As for board elections, they are rarely enticing enough to attract more than a small minority; they are dominated by the success of incumbents, and the competition is negligible. The potential does exist for sweeping the "school rascals" out of office and replacing them with members who have different ideas. Elections can operate in this fashion—but usually they do not. Community power structures in different forms probably exist in every community, but we know very little about the frequency of different kinds occurring. The Johns-Kimbrough study found that closed systems were more frequent, and the greater their frequency, the less effective public participation was in school decisions.

Yet to say that relatively few participate is not to say that this frees the school authorities to do whatever they wish. The power of one parent with a complaint raised against a perceived injustice is enough to agitate adminstrators and can, if not met, escalate into a flash flood from the community. After all, in the late 1970s, only a few objected to the MACOS* curriculum in Charlestown, West Virginia, schools, but that few disrupted schools greatly. The bombing of the district's central office symbolizes the potency of this frustrated minority. While the day-to-day life of official or teacher in the school system is filled with simply administering past directives from the public and profession, the potential exists for new waves of citizen inputs. At any given moment, the school system can be caught between the forces of popular participation and bureaucratization, as Alford has noted.[74] Over time, the latter prevails, but also through time the influence of citizen participation may be felt as pressure to relieve unsatisfied old demands or to achieve just-realized new ones. This does not mean that school authorities live in a constant quivering sensitivity to community and group demands—far from it, if one accepts the continuous criticism of school bureaucracy. Nor does it mean that the authorities are so inertia bound that they cannot be changed in their course—the history of educational reform belies that charge.

Under some conditions, then, demands do enter the political system of the school and do make their way through to policy outputs. The conditions under which this takes place at the local and state levels are the subjects of the next chapters.

---

*"Man: A Course of Study" is a social science curriculum package developed by scholars with U.S. Office of Education funding support.

NOTES

1. David Easton, *A Framework for Political Analysis* (Engelwood Cliffs, N.J.: Prentice-Hall, 1965), p. 122.

2. H. M. Hamlin, "Organized Citizen Participation in the Public Schools," *Review of Educational Research* 23 (1953): 346–52. Compare this with the study fifteen years later by Otis A. Crosby, "How to Prepare Winning Bond Issues," *Nation's Schools* 81 (1968): 81–84.

3. Richard J. Brown, "Party Platforms and Public Education," *Social Studies* (1961): 206–10.

4. Roald F. Campbell et al., *The Organization and Control of American Schools* (Columbus, Ohio: Charles E. Merrill, 1965); Peter J. Cistone, ed., *Understanding School Boards: Problems and Prospects* (Lexington, Mass.: Lexington Books, 1975); Tyll van Geel, *Authority to Control the School Program* (Lexington, Mass.: Lexington Books, 1976).

5. Charles R. Adrian and Charles Press, *Governing Urban America,* 3d ed. (New York: McGraw-Hill, 1968), p. 434.

6. The Detroit reference is Marilyn Gittell et al., "Fiscal Status and School Policy Making in Six Large School Districts," in *The Politics of Education,* Michael W. Kirst, ed. (Berkeley: McCutchan, 1970), p. 63. The influence of partisan groups or affiliation is found in Willis D. Hawley, *Nonpartisan Urban Politics* (New York: Wiley, 1972).

7. Robert L. Crain et al., *The Politics of School Desegregation* (Garden City, N.Y.: Doubleday-Anchor, 1969), and David Kirby et al., *Political Strategies in Northern School Desegregation* (Lexington, Mass.: Lexington Books, 1973).

8. Lester G. Seligman, *Political Recruitment* (Boston: Little, Brown & Co., 1972).

9. Peter J. Cistone, "The Recruitment and Socialization of School Board Members," in Cistone, *Understanding School Boards,* chap. 3, and Cistone, "The Ecological Basis of School Board Member Recruitment," *Education and Urban Society* 4 (1974): 428–50.

10. George S. Counts, *The Social Composition of Boards of Education* (Chicago: University of Chicago, 1927), Supplementary Educational Monographs, No. 33; National School Boards Association, *Women on School Boards* (Evanston, Ill.: NSBA, 1974).

11. L. Harmon Zeigler, M. Kent Jennings, and G. Wayne Peak, *Governing American Schools: Political Interaction in Local School Districts* (North Scituate, Mass.: Duxbury, 1974). Chapter 2 provides the following information.

12. Howard D. Hamilton and Sylvan H. Cohen, *Policy Making by Plebiscite: School Referenda* (Lexington, Mass.: Lexington Books, 1974).

13. This felicitous phrase is from Edith K. Mosher, "The School Board in the Family of Governments," in Cistone, *Understanding School Boards,* chap. 5.

14. William Boyd, "The Public, the Professionals, and Educational Policy-Making: Who Governs," *Teachers College Record* 77 (1976): 539–77.

15. Zeigler et al., *Governing American Schools,* p. 25.

16. Ibid., chap. 3.

17. Hawley, *Nonpartisan Urban Politics,* analyzes this outcome throughout California.

18. Christine H. Rossell, "School Desegregation and Electoral Conflict," in *The*

Polity of the School, Frederick M. Wirt, ed. (Lexington, Mass.: Lexington Books, 1975), chap. 4.

19. H. Lloyd Warner et al., *Democracy in Jonesville* (New York: Harper & Row, 1949); Arthur J. Vidich and Joseph Bensman, *Small Town in Mass Society* (Princeton: Princeton University Press, 1958); and Alan Peshkin, *Growing Up American* (Chicago: University of Chicago Press, 1979).

20. On the association between complexity and social organizations, see Zeigler et al., *Governing American Schools*, p. 100; on party and pressure groups, see ibid., pp. 104–5; on an argument for boards to be a matter for political parties, see Michael D. McCaffrey, "Politics in the School: A Case for Partisan School Boards," *Education Administration Quarterly* 7, no. 3 (1971): 51–63.

21. Richard F. Carter, *Voters and Their Schools* (Stanford: Institute for Communications Research, 1962).

22. David W. Minar, "The Community Basis of Conflict in School System Politics," *American Sociological Review* 31 (1966): 822–34. Enhancement of this work is found in William L. Boyd, *Community Status and Conflict in Suburban School Politics* (Beverly Hills, Calif.: Sage, 1975).

23. Zeigler et al., *Governing American Schools*, pp. 60–62.

24. See Rossell, "School Desegregation." Note that she used yet another measure of competition—dissent—based on the defeat of incumbents.

25. Theodore Lowi, "American Business, Public Policy, Case Studies and Political Theory," *World Politics* 16 (1964): 677–715.

26. James Hottois and Neal A. Milner, *The Sex Education Controversy: A Study of Politics, Education, and Morality* (Lexington, Mass.: Lexington Books, 1974).

27. Paul Goldstein, *Changing the American Schoolbook* (Lexington, Mass.: Lexington Books, 1978).

28. Fred S. Coombs and Richard L. Merritt, "The Public's Role in Educational Policy Making: An International View," *Education and Urban Society* 9 (1977): 169–96.

29. The following paragraphs rely upon Robert H. Salisbury, *Citizen Participation in the Public Schools* (Lexington, Mass.: Lexington Books, 1980).

30. For reviews of the literature on the impact of participation on the participant, see David H. Smith and Richard D. Reddy, "The Impact of Voluntary Action upon the Voluntary Participant," in *Voluntary Action Research, 1973,* David H. Smith, ed. (Lexington, Mass.: Lexington Books, 1973), pp. 169–239; and Dale Mann, *The Politics of Administrative Representation* (Lexington, Mass.: Lexington Books, 1976), chap. 5.

31. Salisbury, *Citizen Participation,* pp. 177, 199.

32. Charles E. Lindblom, *The Policy-Making Process.* (Englewood Cliffs, N.J.: Prentice-Hall, 1968). For particular evidence of the proposition as it applies to changes in education, see Diane Ravitch, *The Revisionists Revised: A Critique of the Radical Attack on Schools.* (New York: Basic Books, 1978); and Frederick M. Wirt, "Neoconservatism and National School Policy," *Educational Evaluation and Policy Analysis* 2, no. 6 (1980): 5–18.

33. M. Kent Jennings and Harmon Zeigler, "The Salience of American State Politics," *American Political Science Review* 64 (1970): 524–27.

34. Herbert McClosky et al., "Issue Conflict and Consensus Among Party Leaders and Followers," ibid. 54 (1960): 413; Thomas A. Flinn and Frederick M. Wirt, "Local

Party Leaders: Groups of Like Minded Men," *Midwest Journal of Political Science* 9 (1965): 82.

35. William Gamson, *Power and Discontent* (Homewood, Ill.: Dorsey Press, 1968), although the focus here is not upon school issues.

36. Joseph M. Cronin, *The Control of Urban Schools* (New York: Free Press, 1972); and Larry Cuban, *Urban School Chiefs Under Fire* (Chicago: University of Chicago Press, 1976).

37. For a review of this debate, see Willis D. Hawley and Frederick M. Wirt, eds., *The Search for Community Power*, 2d ed. (Englewood Cliffs, N.J.: Prentice-Hall, 1974). For illustrations of the level of analytical thinking, see Terry N. Clark, ed., *Community Structure and Decision-Making: Comparative Analysis* (San Francisco: Chandler, 1968); for an illustration of comparative research, see Terry N. Clark, "Community Structure, Decision-Making, Budget Expenditures, and Urban Renewal in 51 American Communities," *American Sociological Review* 33 (1968): 576–93.

38. We have been informed on these queries by Willis D. Hawley from an unpublished paper. For a biliography, see Hawley and Wirt, *Search for Community Power*, 1st ed., pp. 367–79; and Willis D. Hawley and James H. Svara, *The Study of Community Power—A Bibliographic Review* (Santa Barbara, Calif.: ABC-Clio, 1972).

39. James G. March, "The Power of Power," in *Varieties of Political Theory*, David Easton, ed. (Englewood Cliffs, N.J.: Prentice-Hall, 1966), pp. 39–70.

40. See the articles by John Walton, "Discipline, Method and Community Power: A Note on the Sociology of Knowledge," *American Sociological Review* 31 (1966): 684–89; and "Substance and Artifact: The Current Status of Research on Community Power Structure," *American Journal of Sociology* 71 (1966): 430–38; Terry Clark et al., "Discipline, Method, Community Structure, and Decision-Making: The Role and Limitations of the Sociology of Knowledge," *American Sociologist* 3 (1968): 214–17.

41. The first approach is illustrated in Robert E. Agger et al., *The Rulers and the Ruled* (New York: Wiley, 1964); and William V. D'Antonio and William H. Form, *Influentials in Two Border Cities* (South Bend, Ind.: University of Notre Dame Press, 1965). The second is illustrated in Walton, "Discipline, Method" and "Substance and Artifact" and in Claire W. Gilbert, "Some Trends in Community Politics: A Secondary Analysis of Power Structure Data from 166 Communities," *Southwestern Social Science Quarterly* 48 (1967): 373–81. The third approach is seen in T. Clark, *Community Structure and Decision Making*. The "sample" is reported in Peter H. Rossi and Robert Crain, "The NORC Permanent Community Sample," *Public Opinion Quarterly* 32 (1968): 261–72.

42. Peter Bachrach, *The Theory of Democratic Elitism* (Boston: Little, Brown & Co., 1967).

43. Nicholas Masters et al., *Politics, Poverty and Education: An Analysis of Decision-making Structures* (Washington, D.C.: Office of Economic Opportunity, 1968); Roland W. Warren, ed., *Politics and the Ghettos* (New York: Atherton, 1969); and Paul E. Peterson, "Forms of Representation: Participation of the Poor in the Community Action Program," *American Political Science Review* 64 (1970): 491–507.

44. Edgar L. Morphet, Roe L. Johns, and Theodore L. Reller, *Educational Organization and Administration,* 2d ed. (Englewood Cliffs, N.J.: Prentice-Hall, 1967), p. 194.

45. Robert S. and Helen M. Lynd, *Middletown*, pt. 2 (New York: Harcourt Brace

Jovanovich, 1929); and *Middletown in Transition* (New York: Harcourt Brace Jovanovich, 1937), chap. 6. For a more thorough critique of the Lynds for imputing power to this family, see Nelson W. Polsby, *Community Power and Political Theory* (New Haven: Yale University Press, 1963), pp. 14–24; Floyd Hunter, *Community Power Structure* (Chapel Hill: University of North Carolina Press, 1953), pp. 214–15, 223; Robert A. Dahl, *Who Governs?* (New Haven: Yale University Press, 1960), chap. 11; Agger et al., *Rulers and Ruled,* chap. 4.

46. For articles on this power and the policies of transportation, defense, contracts, poverty programs, and Japanese communities—but none on schools—see the entire issue of *Southwestern Social Science Quarterly* 48 no. 3 (December, 1967). An aggregate study omitting this is Clark, "Community Structure, Decision-Making, Budget Expenditures."

47. Robert R. Alford, *Bureaucracy and Participation: Political Culture in Four Wisconsin Cities* (Chicago: Rand McNally, 1969).

48. See the Pellegrin bibliography in *Southwestern Social Science Quarterly* 48 (1967), and especially the reference to Agger, Bloomberg et al.

49. See Leland C. Wilson, "Community Power Controls Related to the Administration of Education" (Ph.D. diss., Peabody College, 1952); Theodore J. Jensen, "Identification and Utilization of Opinion Leaders in School District Reorganization" (Ph.D. diss., University of Wisconsin, 1952); Keith Goldhammer, "The Roles of School District Officials in Policy-Determination in an Oregon Community" (Ph.D. diss., University of Oregon, 1954); Keith Goldhammer, "Community Power Structure and School Board Membership," *American School Board Journal* 130 (1955): 23–25; Donald E. Tope, "Northwest C.P.E.A.—Aims and Results," *The School Executive* 74 (1955): 74–76; Vincent Ostrom, "Who Forms School Policy?" ibid., 77–79.

50. Harold V. Webb, *Community Power Structure Related to School Administration* (Laramie: Curriculum and Research Center, College of Education, University of Wyoming, 1956).

51. John M. Foskett, "A Comparative Study of Community Influence," in *The Social Sciences View School Administration,* Donald Tope et al. (Englewood Cliffs, N.J.: Prentice-Hall, 1965), pp. 115–30.

52. Warner Bloomberg et al., *Suburban Power Structures and Public Education* (Syracuse: Syracuse University Press, 1963), pp. 88 ff., 168; In a related study from the same series, see Jesse Burkhead, *Public School Finance: Economics and Politics.*

53. Ralph B. Kimbrough, *Political Power and Educational Decision-Making* (Chicago: Rand McNally, 1964), esp. chaps. 4–5, 10–11.

54. This interest has stimulated a number of dissertations at the University of Florida. Compare ibid.; Kimbrough, "Development of a Concept of Social Power," in *The Politics of Education in the Local Community,* Robert S. Cahill and Stephen P. Hencley, eds. (Danville, Ill.: Interstate Printers & Publishers, 1964), chap. 5; and Appendix H in n. 58.

55. Donald J. McCarty, "How Community Power Structures Influence Administrative Tenure," *American School Board Journal* 148 (1964): 11–13, offers some hypotheses in a highly researchable area.

56. Cahill and Hencley, *Politics of Education,* p. 75.

57. See sources in note 7.

58. Roe L. Johns and Ralph B. Kimbrough, *The Relationship of Socio-economic Factors, Educational Leadership Patterns, and Elements of Community Power Structure to Local School Fiscal Policy* (Washington, D.C.: Bureau of Research, Office of Education, HEW, 1968). The first edition of our book has a more detailed analysis of this study.

59. This phenomenon has been reported for many other kinds of expenditures; that is, what has been spent in the past determines current expenditures more than other potential explanatory variables. See Ira Sharkansky, "Economic and Political Correlates of State Government Expenditures: General Tendencies and Deviant Cases," *Midwest Journal of Political Science* 11 (1967): 173–92; and Ira Sharkansky, *Spending in the American States* (Chicago: Rand McNally, 1968). This research found that this explanation was most true for general government and next for education among state expenditures. The data for education are found in Frederick M. Wirt, "Education Politics and Policies," in *Politics in the American States: A Comparative Analysis*, 3d ed. (Boston: Little, Brown & Co., 1976), pp. 326–330.

60. Donald J. McCarty and Charles E. Ramsey, *The School Managers* (Westport, Conn.: Greenwood, 1971).

61. William L. Boyd, "The Public, the Professionals, and Educational Policy-Making: Who Governs?" *Teachers College Record* 77 (1976): 56.

62. A clear signal in an important training journal is Russell T. Gregg, "Political Dimensions of Educational Leadership," *Teachers College Record* 67 (1965): 118–28. Illustrative of texts' use of the concept is Morphet et al., *Educational Organization*, pp. 75–76; and Thomas J. Sergiovanni et al., *Educational Governance and Administration* (Englewood Cliffs, N.J.: Prentice-Hall, 1980), pp. 112–14.

63. John H. Bunzel, "Pressure Groups in Politics and Education," *National Elementary Principal* 43 (1964): 12–16, is typical of the political science approval, while Neal Gross, *Who Runs Our Schools?* (New York: Wiley, 1958), typifies the educational scholar's disapproval.

64. Gilbert, "Trends in Community Politics," p. 381.

65. John Walton, "The Vertical Axis of Community Organization and the Structure of Power," *Southwestern Social Science Quarterly* 48 (1967): 353–68, and Roland L. Warren, *The Community in America* (Chicago: Rand McNally, 1963).

66. Joseph M. Cronin, "Federal Takeover: Should the Junior Partner Run the Firm?" *Phi Delta Kappan* 57 (1976): 499–501.

67. William J. Grimshaw, *Union Rule in the Schools: Big City Politics in Transition* (Lexington, Mass.: Lexington Books, 1979).

68. See the possibility in James W. Guthrie and Patricia A. Craig, *Teachers and Politics* (Bloomington, Ind.: Phi Delta Kappa Educational Foundation, 1973). For evolution of teacher power, see Jack Culbertson et al., *Preparing Educational Leaders for the Seventies* (Columbus, Ohio: University Council for Educational Administration, 1969), chap. 7.

69. Norton Long, *The Unwalled City* (New York: Basic Books, 1972); Frederick M. Wirt, *Power in the City: Decision Making in San Francisco* (Berkeley: University of California Press, 1974). For a set of case studies showing extramual influences on schools from government, see Mary F. Williams, ed., *Government in the Classroom: Dollars and Power in Education* (New York: The Academy of Political Science, 1978).

70. Cistone, ed., *Understanding School Boards*, pp. xiii–xiv.

71. Paul Peterson, "The Politics of American Education," in *Review of Research in Education II,* Fred Kerlinger and John Carroll, eds. (Itasca, Ill.: Peacock, 1974), pp. 348–89.

72. David K. Wiles, *Energy, Winter, and Schools: Crisis and Decision Theory* (Lexington, Mass.: Lexington Books, 1979).

73. These developments are treated in detail in van Geel, *Authority to Control.*

74. Alford, *Bureaucracy and Participation.*

6

The Local
Conversion Process

PART A
BOARDS, SUPERINTENDENTS,
AND THE COMMUNITY

Through the channels and agents already described, environmental demands move into the political system of the schools. Some are rejected, but others are converted into outputs—laws, ordinances, court decisions, guidelines, and so forth. This conversion process involves interaction with state and national political authorities, but it is primarily acted out among forces within the local community— school board, superintendent, bureaucracy, teachers, voters, and so on. These contribute to what Easton terms *withinputs*: "the effect that events and conditions both within and without a system may have upon its persistence [whose study] sensitizes us to the value of looking within the system as well as the environment to find the major influences that may lead to stress."[1] This set of interactions at the local level is what concerns us in this chapter.

The term *withinputs* may be new, but the concept is a familiar one. Scholarly interest in the internal dynamics of policy making is not new; what is new is the broadening intellectual perspective that relates internal to external factors in that process. Part A of this chapter

127

explores the relationship of the community to the formal subsystems of the school system—board, superintendent, and principals—in which most conversion activity is enacted on a day-to-day basis. As with people in any organizations, the thrust of their work is to routinize activity in order to rationalize objectives and economize resources; as a consequence, such effort inherently maximizes system persistence. But such decision making also has differing consequences for different groups. A second major local force—voter influence—provides episodic inputs to the school system, as described in the preceeding chapter. That force is best conceptualized as generating a set of potential constraints on school authorities—a relationship that is not altogether clear. In this chapter, then, we move from the environment to the interior of the political system of American schools. In many respects, however, the view is similar to that observed within any other unit of governance—in city hall, the state capitol, or Washington, D.C.

COMPOSITION AND HISTORY

The school board and professional educators authoritatively allocate values in formulating and administering public policy for the schools. Service on the board was once an extremely low-profile, low-conflict position, but in the last two decades, board members have been thrust into the middle of all those politically turbulent issues described in the Introduction. In the process their roles changed; some became champions of lay groups, but others supported the professional groups. A board member now needs to know and judge issues in finance, discrimination, textbook values, teacher demands, and so on—a lengthy list of crucial and excruciating claims on school resources. Board membership has become exciting in terms of the ancient Chinese *curse* we mentioned, "May you live in exciting times."

But the board, whether meeting or blocking a demand, is not static nor are its members value free. They modify, regulate, innovate, or refuse political demands in response to a variety of value preferences. On the one hand, they are not uncontrolled in this conversion function; subsystem elements may conflict within the system, higher system levels can constrain, and voters might always disrupt. In short, board members and administrators are not "passive transmitters of things taken into the system, digesting them in some sluggish way, and sending them along as output."[2] Rather, they reflect a very personal element in the interplay of school politics. Policy output, then, depends in part upon the feelings and values, failures and successes of human beings. Consequently, it is important to know something about what school board members are like.

Their social characteristics have changed very little since the famous Counts survey of 1927.[3] Most are still owners, officials, and managers of businesses, or else they are professionals. Their income is well above average, only a fraction are women, and even fewer are workers. The reforms that began over a century ago resulted in the replacement of one class—workers—by others—middle class and professionals—who had generated those reforms. Their motives are a mixture of orientations to self, group, and community. As stated, however, few evidence much interest in higher office;[4] few actually move up politically. Only rarely does a President Jimmy Carter or Senator Richard Lugar (Rep.-Ind.) launch a national career from such boards.

The meaning of the social qualities of this governing agency cannot be understood without some sense of its political function. A historical sketch will help set the framework for understanding the school board's current role.[5]

The Local Conversion Process

When public schools began, no administrators intervened between teachers and board, as the board itself was an administrative body. Each member undertook reponsibility for a special school task, much as the commission form of local government operates today. The growing details of the board's administrative job, which accompanied the growth of enrollments, and the growing expertise of the new professionals, transformed the board into a legislative body. Its major function became to set broad policy guidelines and act as watchdogs over their administration. Yet even that function was transformed in this century with the increased control over local schools exercised through state and national laws and the increased power of professional administrators and teachers' unions.

Prior to the mid-1960s, a description of the board's function would be something like this. School boards most often mediated major policy conflicts, leaving determination of important policy issues to the professional staff or to higher external levels if there was no evidence of community concern—and even in mediating they might do very little. In the process, they legitimated the proposals of the professional staff, making only marginal changes, rather than represented citizens. Board members spent the bulk of their time on managerial details.

Beginning in the 1960s, the board found that even this picture of low conflict was disrupted, but many believe the school board still cannot do much. As noted earlier, the board is increasingly hemmed in by state and federal statutes, confronted by teachers threatening strikes, and pelted by community demands that an inadequate financial base or tenure provisions will not permit it to satisfy. As one observer remarked:

It must be plain from all that has gone before that in three major aspects, all vital to public education (integration, teacher militancy, and finances), the American school board has reached a point where what was mere inadequacy has come close to total helplessness, where decline and fall are no longer easily distinguished.[6]

This picture of an extremely beleaguered board is true enough as far as it goes. What is missing is an explanation of how the board usually operates in its relationship to the community and to the professionals. It must represent both, and yet it must control both. A pivot between community notions of schooling and professional standards of service, the board must be seen in some larger perspective than leading an exciting, cursed life.

BOARD SUPPORT FROM THE COMMUNITY

We need a broader conceptual framework for understanding boards as small political systems. One possibility is to conceive of their processes as reflecting the ever-present tension in a democracy between the demands of equality and the demands of merit. Mann's analysis[7] has pointed out that we expect education to be decided by and responsive to people in general but also, and simultaneously, to be technically advanced and thus determined by standards of excellence. Despite fervent wishes to the contrary, the two expectations do not always coincide. More, as Mann demonstrates, the board is caught up in an ideology of an informed citizenry participating in democratic decision making.

In fact, citizens are poorly informed on such matters, seemingly disinterested in acquiring such information, and hence participate little. But even if this is an accurate description of citizen inattention and inactivity, this does not mean that they do not affect schools. For, it is argued by some, this lack of citizen participation and information have generated a massive public loss of support for schools that is potentially devastating. Actually, the evidence can support both the pessimist as well as the optimist on this matter.[8] Pessimists can point to Gallup polls that show declines in the high rating of schools, especially on the coasts and in their big cities; decreasing votes for tax and bond referenda; and evidence from other nations of criticism, disenchantment, and loss of funding for public schools. Optimists can point to failure to evaluate confidence in schools or achievement records over long enough periods of time; growing funding for schools; education's relative vote of confidence compared to other American institutions (in 1980, much better than for big business, news media, Congress, organized labor, and a bit better than for the Supreme Court); high support for maintaining or increasing current service levels by those also voting to limit taxes and expenditures; and impressive movement of Blacks into college and of more people into adult education.

One must understand the school board's role partly in terms of this system support for education as a whole. By 1981, the signals being transmitted to all boards were charges of failure, inefficiency, inequity, and the rest of the pessimist perspective. Media fastened on evidence of "failure" or "crisis" and accentuated—some even charge stimulated—this perception of breakdown. This signal did not jibe with many boards' perceptions of their problems; a comparison done of citizen concerns about schools and those of board members showed very little correlation.[9] Citizens were most concerned about discipline (only fifth on board members' lists) and least about declining enrollment (but first for board members). So there are serious problems of support for some aspects of schools, particularly in an era when the public is far more critical about everything in public life and uninterested in looking for success in that area.

However, there may be strong evidence that our schools have done a better job with more people, compared to earlier eras and other nations,[10] but in politics, what is important is what citizens *think* is reality—not what reality is. The 1970s has been, as the 1980s will be, a period of skeptical challenge to boards and professional educators for the job they are doing. What can occur is that the usually dry arroyos of community-board linkage will become flooded by protests over a perceived disparity between expectations and reality in school services.

What are the consequences of this gap for the school board, the system's authoritative local agency? There is evidence of what Lutz and Iannaccone have termed "the dissatisfaction theory of democracy." Their study is unusual for its effort to modify theory by testing it in successive analyses in different contexts and locales.[11] It asserts that voters' dissatisfaction rises as the gap between their values and demands and those of board members and superintendent increases. In districts characterized by rapid demographic change—either expanding or contracting in size—dissatisfaction is particularly strong. Newcomers' values, expectations, and demands differ sharply from those of older residents. At some point, the dissidents become strong enough to defeat board incumbents and then a new board replaces the superintendent.

Rare in its use of longitudinal research, this study presents convincing evidence from over fifteen years of testing this thesis, leading to a strong affirmation that school boards are indeed democratic. As Lutz has argued, it depends on the question put to the system. Such an affirmation is not possible from answers to the research question, Who governs? or Do the products of administrator actions coincide with citizen preferences? Rather, the critical question may be, Who has access to modify the governance, under what conditions, and how?[12] If that is the critical question, it seems likely that once the public knows, it can redirect governance to meet certain conditions, one of which is a redefinition of the needs they want the school system to meet. One can read today the conflicting winds of evidence in different ways over the question of whether such a major citizen shift is under way nationally, generating a storm against local school boards. It is much clearer that continued dissatisfaction with board efforts to meet these new needs can produce not simply changes in board membership but also new agendas, new constituents, new resources, and in time even new structures of governance. Certainly that is what happened in the nineteenth century as a result of the challenge to machine rule.

THE BOARD AND STATUS POLITICS

Another conceptualization of the community-board linkage stems from status differences in the former that affect the latter. If a community were homogeneous in status, the board member's tasks would be simple—just consult one's own preferences, which will largely reflect the community's. Studies of small town school politics show such congruence between citizens and their boards. This can also be seen in the pervasive role of the high school within the Black community, where the high school embodies most aspects of the latter; among whites, the school is only one aspect of institutional community life.[13]

American community life is becoming much more varied than this, however, so boards face competing demands arising from needs that reflect diverse community statuses. The historical record of such a process is clear, although there is debate about which groups were favored or not as a result. The shift from working class to middle class and business domination in board composition has already been noted. For some scholars, this was evidence of industrialists controlling schools in order to provide a trained manpower pool; for others, this was evidence of capitalists foisting education on a proletariat in order to control them. But Peterson's current historical analysis of this shift in board role demonstrates something else: the spread of professionalization in the schools was actually encouraged by trade unions, it attracted the middle class to the schools, and at least in the case of three major regional cities, it was welcomed, not resisted, by the middle class.[14] In the past, this status context underlay the control of schools in our cities. Reformers focused upon changing the structures of power, for these are never value free but rather dispense differential rewards to different groups. Certainly this was what the business groups who supported such reform believed.[15]

In the contemporary period, this status orientation to understanding school conflict undergirds the work of Minar and Boyd, among others.[16] The role behaviors of superintendents differ in working-class, as opposed to middle-class, suburbs and are associated with different political turbulence. With qualifications, the findings show that before the 1970s the higher-status districts had fewer political conflicts (that is, votes for losing candidates), lower electoral participation in board elections, and less challenge to superintendents' administrative decisions than did lower-status districts. Associated with these differences were dissimilar cultural norms about citizen involvement with schools and school professionals. A similar tie in between status and school politics was found in a national sample of districts done in the late 1960s.[17] There was a strong correlation between high interest-group activity among districts within the metropolis (a heterogeneous set), but there was much lower interest-group intensity in districts outside the metropolis.

However, these findings, set in less turbulent days than described in the Introduction, were qualified by later events. Thus when an issue becomes significant to the traditionally low-conflict, higher-status community, its members can become very active in challenging boards and school professionals. This has been the case in northern cities in the matter of desegregation, where higher-status elements became just as vocal as South Boston working-class citizens.[18] Both status groups were protecting their social neighborhoods, on racial grounds in this case, although it could have been for other incursions, such as freeways, low-income housing, or heavy-industry location.[19]

Further, there is some evidence that the status of the district affects the "board culture" of that school.[20] Homogeneous districts develop a board style of "elite" councils—small in size, seeing themselves as guardians of the public but separate from it, making decisions privately, consensually, and in limited range and exhibiting administrative, judicial, and legislative functions. On the other hand, "arena" councils exhibit the opposite qualities, many of which reflect a heterogeneous community. This elite cultural system has usually prevailed, modifying inputs from different ethnic, religious, and status groups so as to subordinate them.

The Special Stimulus of Consolidation

Consolidation is a factor that has enormously increased not only the volume but also the conflict of status demands on boards. What was once an archipelago of districts in America, each island homogeneous with board and community in harmony, has been fused together into larger, more varied districts. The 89,000 districts of 1948 became 55,000 five years later, 31,000 by 1961, and 16,000 by 1979. During the 1970s, on any given day, three districts disappeared forever between breakfast and the cocktail hour. But in the 1960s that many had evaporated between breakfast and the morning coffee break, with another seven gone by the cocktail hour, so changes were slowing by the 1970s.[21] Not only are there now more diverse values, reflecting different status bases, confronting board members, but there are also fewer board members to handle this increased input. By the early 1970s, as Guthrie calculated, "Where a school board member

once represented about 200 people, today each . . . must speak for
approximately 3,000 constituents.[22]

This problem in the accommodation of increasingly divergent
views underlies the Lutz-Iannaccone dissatisfaction theory of democracy noted earlier. Evidence of this mixing of districts is suggested by
the finding that there is a greater rate of interest groups coming to
board attention in metropolitan areas and a lesser rate in nonmetropolitan districts.[23] We will return to this shortly.

The Mosaic of Status Politics

No agreed-upon picture of the board's link to the community
appears from the preceding mainly because the literature spans
different periods and issues. However, the view that a board's openness to its community is a variable does emerge. That is, the linkage
should be different under conditions of low versus high community
dissent over school policies. We could expect, and a national sample
study validates,[24] that when there is little conflict, boards are less
receptive to community input. When there is more intense community
conflict, however, the board becomes more receptive to challenging
established policies. This seems less true for racial school conflict,[25]
but at least by 1970, this linkage appeared in four possible styles of
board politics. These are illustrated in table 6.1.

Like all typologies, this is a still life that covers many communities,
but it also hints at a more dynamic process. That is, the four board
styles shown here represent different stages of the Lutz-Iannaccone

Table 6.1
Styles of School Board Politics

Skills of Opposition	Numbers in Conflict	
	High	Low
High	I. Reform ideal of citizen democracy	II. Challenge by takeover group
Low	III. All-Out Battle	IV. Continuity under traditional ruling group

Source: Leigh Stelzer, "Institutionalizing Conflict Response: The Case of Schoolboards," Social Science Quarterly 55 (1974), reprinted in The Polity of the School, Frederick Wirt, ed. (Lexington, Mass.: Lexington Books, D.C. Heath and Company. Copyright, 1975, D.C. Heath and Company), p. 81. Reprinted by permission of the publisher.

model of longitudinal school conflict. Both typology and model have their respective uses, although the more dynamic model is capable of generating more powerful hypotheses. However, a proposition about school politics that should not be overlooked is evident in both constructs. That is, boards do not merely transmit what the community says, for often it says very little; nor do boards dictatorially block off any signals not on their wave lengths. Rather, when issues heat up the local environment, there is considerable evidence that boards become much more receptive to citizen inputs and more willing to oppose the traditional direction of school policy. There is a particularly political quality to this response of school boards, best caught in the aphorism of V. O. Key: "Public opinion is that opinion which politicians find it prudent to pay attention to." In this and other respects, board members are truly politicians.

THE BOARD AS A DECISION-MAKING AGENCY

A question that is separate analytically from the role of community inputs is how boards make decisions, although the two merge in reality. Several older models of this process were characterized by their naivete. One was that the school board necessarily reflected the social composition of its members. As we have just seen, that is inadequate as an explanation of who governs and, as we will see shortly, it does not answer the further question, How does it govern? Another naive model was found in education administration literature for a long time. This described the board as the maker of school policy and the superintendent as the administrator of that policy, with a clear separation of function. Empirically, that has not been the case, for the two reciprocally stimulate and hence affect each other. Thus, in 1981, when a national sample of superintendents was asked by Wirt to indicate whether their policy involvement had recently become greater or lesser, two-thirds answered that it was greater, and one-half reported that their professional judgments were increasingly accepted by their boards. Similar results were found for city managers and planning directors.

Multiple Currents of Decision Making

Another, more sophisticated way of conceptualizing board decision making is to see it as different processes for different kinds of issues. In

Figure 6.1
Models of Decision Making in a Political System

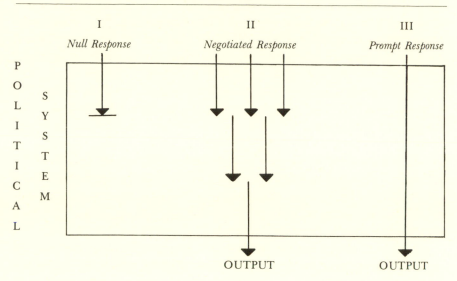

figure 6.1 we see that any naive model of decision making is confounded by a more varied reality. In the null response model, we are looking at what happens to most environmental demands made upon a political agency—the agency does not respond. The blocked arrow symbolizes this process, and extensive evidence validates this model. Thus only a small fraction of proposed bills ever become laws in legislatures at any level of American government; only a fraction of appellate court appeals are ever accepted for hearing and decision. As for the school board, its time is primarily spent elsewhere, as noted below.

Under special conditions, the negotiated response model of figure 6.1 describes other board decision making. The several arrows in this model indicate the flow of competing demands into the political system over an emerging issue; in time these become narrowed as alternatives are formulated and a decision is authorized in the form of board policy (output). Here, the board member's role is that of negotiator among competing community groups, "working out things" over time, seeking compromise solutions that can produce a coalition majority. Such action, however, is episodic, an occasional burst of pressured decision making rather than a regular agenda.

The third model, prompt response, moves us to two quite different occasions when the political system responds to community demands. One of these occasions occurs during a *crisis*, a sudden combination of threats either to the school system or its constituents. The crisis might arise from physical causes—buildings burned, flooded, or blown away—or from social causes that generate conflict over values the schools serve and the resources they distribute. There is a curious quality to a crisis in that most political actors must agree there is a crisis or else the third model does not describe what happens. The danger must be clear to all, whether those helped or those helping, and the remedy must be relatively simple, understood, and accepted by all. If not, then some group or board member will question the necessity of taking fast action. Much of the conflict in local school politics arises from some claiming that a "crisis" exists while opponents are denying it and then redefining the situation in terms compatible with their own interests.

There is a second and quite different aspect to the prompt response model in which action involves *routines*. These include filling in the details of major policy decisions and are found in reports received and acted on, procedures for implementing a given policy, budgetary support for accepted programs, and so on. The unusual aspect of this context is that there are so many outputs of this kind. Indeed, much political decision making, not simply board actions, consists of routines as measured by the volume of personnel, funds, paperwork, and so forth issuing from a political agency. One study of board members found that they spent over 80 percent of their time on managerial details, not on deciding broad issues of general importance.[26]

As noted earlier, in every typology there is a longitudinal model crying to get out, and so it is with figure 6.1. If these three models are seen as a sequence, they form a rough chronology of policy evolution. That is, many demands begin as the unthinkable of the first model, supported by only a few "crackpots" and ignored by the political system. An illustration would be Blacks seeking equal resources for their segregated schools decades ago in the South. Then at a later time, the second model starts to work. New combinations of societal events generate more support for the now possible idea so that its opponents must exert large energies to block it; over time, however, opposing sides move toward resolution and a new output. Under Supreme

Court threat southern school systems first moved to deny discrimination, then to equalize resources for Black education without desegregating, and then reluctantly and under pressure to accommodate external pressures by desegregating. A nationwide example is the pattern of invasion of city folk into rural areas where they succeeded in developing new suburban school systems after World War II.[27] Given enough time, resolution of conflict moves toward opinion closure, in which the once unthinkable is now conventional, and one can roam schools in the South and suburbia and see little sign of former raging conflicts. At this stage, the third model of routines dominates decision making.

RATIONAL AND OTHER DECISION MAKING

There is another conceptual framework for analyzing the decision making of school boards; this focuses on the degree to which officials use "rational" versus other methods of arriving at decisions.[28] During the 1970s, this became a major inquiry about public policy, but there has only been one scholarly study of school boards done from this analytical base.

Peterson's powerful analysis of three major decisions by the Chicago school board over several decades employs competitive analytical concepts; he transferred these concepts from the study of national security policy to use them at the local level. Alternative perspectives are featured in this study, which are set out in table 6.2. That is, depending on the issue, decision making could take the form of bargaining among members, which could be of two kinds. One is protecting or promoting relatively narrow organizational or electoral interests ("pluralist bargaining"); the other involves broader interests rooted in protection of race, class, or a regime ("ideological bargaining"). Alternatively, decision making could take different forms within a policy-making body with a presumed unity, that is, a "unitary" model, as found in organizational theory or in assuming rationality in decision making. In this last, Peterson made a highly useful adaptation to an intense debate over the possibility of "rational" policy. He modified the definition of rationality in terms that are more realistic: that is, "board members agreed on certain objectives, that reference to these objectives was made during the course of policy making, and that policy outcomes were consistent with these objectives."[29] Prior to

Table 6.2
Models of School Board Decision Making

Pluralist

Theme: Decisions are the result of a contest among groups lacking much common
      interests.

  1. *Pluralist:* decision the result of a contest among board members representing
     narrow-purpose groups and designed to defend and enhance as many group
     interests as possible, for example, budgetary contests among curriculum
     interests.
  2. *Ideological:* decision the result of a contest among board members representing
     broad-purpose groups designed to defend and enhance interests of a class or
     a race, for example, affirmative action policy on teacher promotions or prin-
     ciple appointments.

Unitary

Theme: Decisions are the result of interactions among groups that share some qualities
      which presume an overreaching unity among them.

  1. *Organizational:* decision the result of board members motivated by desires to
     promote objectives of the school organization, for example, maintenance of
     professional standards against challenges by laypersons.
  2. *Rational:* decision the result of board members agreed on a set of educational
     objectives, which are referred to in decisional debate and which are consistent
     with the decision itself.

Source: Abstracted from Paul E. Peterson, *School Politics Chicago Style* (Chicago: University of
Chicago Press, 1976).

this, any discussion of rationality was so bounded by empirical
requirements which were unrealistic that no decision could be termed
rational; yet thousands of board members thought they were, in fact,
acting rationally.

Such models of decision making provide alternative perspectives of
a complex process without dictating which is "correct." Further, they
provide the means for testing competing causal theories. Such variety,
laid across that sketched in preceding typologies of board actions,
provides a rich pool of analytical constructs to work amid the mosaic
of thousands of boards in differing conditions.

THE PROFESSIONAL AS DECISION MAKER

If the community is only occasionally active and if the board has
strong limitations on its political efficacy, school professionals should

retain a greater influence on policy issues. Professional educators have their resources too. They define alternatives, produce research, provide specific policy recommendations, and recommend the formal agenda. Using these resources, professionals generate pressures and information that can shape the board's deliberations and policy decisions. In Easton's framework, the school superintendent and his or her staff provide withinputs to the school board and the bureaucracy. Many specific policy issues, however, may never reach the school board if the superintendent and his or her staff act under broad discretion from the school board. Consequently, both board and superintendent are authorities seeking to gain support from the community through the use of appropriate outputs in the form of budget, curriculum, teacher selection, and so on.

The professional staff does operate under certain constraints, however. They must anticipate reactions of board members to their actions because the board does have the basic power to fire them.[30] They also learn that the ultimate power of a provoked electorate is to remove them by changing the board composition, as noted earlier. It is further likely that the superintendent would act in accordance with the school board's wishes on many issues even *without* the threat of removal from office. It is also natural to assume that board members would hire a person whose values were similar to their own. An example of this is the low rate of turnover in smaller districts, which tend to be more homogeneous in their values.[31] In effect, the board's impact on specific decisions may be more indirect than direct, but it is nevertheless real.

A major research question during the 1970s was whether superintendents molded school boards into suppliant agents under professional control in policy making. One way this was thought to occur was the socialization of the newcomer to professional values. A two-suburb study rooted in the 1960s argued that this was the case, and a six-suburb sample in one state about the same time confirmed the finding. Community elites closest to the school professionals deferred more to their judgments and values than elites more removed. But a large sample of Canadian board members during the 1970s sharply challenged whether the process existed, much less had an effect.[32]

The question about who controlled whom received much national attention among education administrators with the publication of the Zeigler and Jennings study of eighty-eight school districts.[33] The authors focused their analysis on whether democratic principles were being served in the interaction between board and superintendent, and their answer was an emphatic no, although there were numerous qualifying conditions. In summary, they found:

1. Board demands on and opposition to the superintendent increases and board victory decreases as one moves from small town to suburb to city school district.
2. Board dependence upon the superintendent for educational information and board opposition to him are *positively* correlated in city districts, but board victory is not likely. The two factors are *negatively* correlated in suburban districts but show null relations in small towns (although in neither locale does this interaction affect the chances of board victory).
3. Superintendent interaction with the board is positively related to board opposition to him or her in city and suburban sites but much less so in rural locales.
4. The superintendent's socialization of board members reduces board opposition in both urban and small-town places, but both these interaction and socialization effects have limited association with board victories against the superintendent in smaller districts, although high association in urban districts.
5. Support-seeking by the professional is inversely associated with board opposition in urban and suburban schools, but no relationship exists in small-town locales, and only in suburban locales is there any sizable relationship between this action and board victory.
6. The degree of congruency between board and superintendent on a number of issues, including their role definitions, is conditioned by the metropolitan status of the district.

Here, then, is considerable evidence that board behavior with the professional is sharply affected by size of the district. These findings support the thesis that the more diverse urban social context generates more potential conflict over school decisions and more likely places the board in opposition to the superintendent. But due to the board's own divisiveness, it is less likely to overcome the superintendent. Ironically, then, Zeigler and Jennings found that effective opposition to professional influence by the board occurred in small districts with their limited political conflict and consensual elite board. Urban boards, on the other hand, were more contentious but had only limited effect against professional power.

Yet, the recent political turbulence has turned boards more from "spokesman *for* the superintendent *to* the community," as Zeigler and Jennings conclude, more into activist agencies responding to such demands for change. As other studies demonstrate,[34] these new currents raise the consciousness of policy makers to the sharpness of the issue and thereby alter their behavior; this is more the case for board members than for administrators. In all the research reported here, the distinction between urban board behavior and values and those in other locales—while more sharp on some issues and in some contexts than others—can be seen to work against board dominance by the professional.

But there was an immediate and powerful critique of this finding of superintendent dominance. Boyd pointed out that administrator control over the board was highly contingent on other matters.[35] It varied with the kind of policy at issue and with the size and homogeneity of the district. Administrative power is increasingly circumscribed by new constituencies and the rulings of external governments as noted previously. Criticism of the undemocratic and unresponsive nature of this professional control in education assumes that it is worse than in other local policy areas. But the fragmentation of delivery systems for local transportation, welfare, or pollution control makes citizen access to any of these a feat just slightly less difficult than the many labors of Hercules. At least a citizen knows where to go to register a complaint against the local school, although few do so.[36] School officials may seem more unresponsive because their greater accessibility, compared to other services, makes them more "public." An early 1970s study of nine major cities and six public agencies found that education ranked highest on responsiveness and innovation compared to the others (except for the War on Poverty agencies especially designed to maximize client input).[37]

In all this, Boyd noted, one factor of the board-administrator relation that was not tapped in research is the force of the "law of anticipated reaction." This is the capacity of the administrator to estimate the limits within which she or he could act without board concern—the "zone of tolerance" in organizational theory. In other words, superintendents inhibit their own behavior due to awareness of the controls these boards exert. Subtle and hard to measure, this is nevertheless a reality that superintendents detail in endless anecdotes.

THE PROFESSIONAL AS REPRESENTATIVE

Much research has put the professional at odds with the community,[38] the antihero of school democracy; but it is instructive to consider an alternative perspective. This conceives of the professional role as being a representative of something other than the profession.

To begin with, many of the participatory factors set out in this book have had major consequences for other professions besides education. A "revolt of the client" appears not only in education but also in law, medicine, among the clergy, and in other areas. This is not only happening here but in other English-speaking nations as well.[39] A consequence of this tension between the professional and a resentful client is that training schools have begun to redefine the professional role so that upcoming professionals are more sensitive to citizen needs. One aspect of this development in schools of education is the growing attention to defining the "political" role that the educator must play. The traditional apolitical myth still holds for many, but future school administrators are increasingly being taught that they operate in a web of external demands they must respond to and balance in some fashion.[40]

Along these lines, Cuban's clinical study of how social and political forces reshape superintendent roles in our big cities reaches some significant conclusions.[41] Role definitions change in times of external challenges by pressure groups, as with school consolidation around World War I and the urban crisis of the last two decades. One consequence of this is increased turnover in these positions; in the early 1970s, twenty-two out of twenty-five urban superintendents were replaced. Another obvious consequence is that old role concepts become outmoded. Under such political turbulence, adopting the role of "negotiator-statesman" is more effective than any notion of being a neutral technician. Then, conflict is seen as inevitable in human affairs, and interest group demands are regarded as legitimate. They must be dealt with and reconciled as part of the job. The superintendent is not just a leaf floating along helplessly on the flood of turbulent politics. Yet note how far this concept brings us from that of the school administrator as an omnipotent, insensitive figure that many critics posit. One can see in the actual careers of many superintendents—for example, the late Marcus Foster of the Oakland, California, schools—that one achieves success in some instances, while yielding to insuperable organizational and resource obstacles in others.[42]

One can go a step further in reconceptualizing the role of school administrator, so that he or she is not stolidly unresponsive to the community but still acting so as to represent it. This approach requires defining democracy not as some plebiscite on a range of issues but as one in which agents act in the interest of those represented ("substantive representation"[43]). In a range of districts Mann found many principals who defined their role in primarily these terms ("trustee"). A minority went further and claimed their role was to act only as the community rquired ("delegate"), and a scattering exhibited mixed roles depending on the occasion ("politicos"). Mann went on to urge the trustee role as a desirable norm, so long as the administrator used specified techniques for encouraging community involvement.[44]

This differing representative role can be illustrated by principals acting differently. The contrast in school site politics is striking. As one superintendent in a West Coast suburb put it:

In some schools, changing the location of a bicycle rack will cause parents to call the principal. In other schools, we can cut the school day from seven periods to six periods without neighborhood reaction.

Principals also act differently toward the central administrative office depending upon the presence or absence of neighborhood groups other than parents.[45] Principals can see themselves as neighborhood emissaries; some neighbors generate strong demands on them, others make minimal or no demands. So the evidence is that the school site context helps shape this representational role and not necessarily the administrator alone. But as the next part shows, other professionals play a role in school governance.

PART B
BUREAUCRACY, TEACHERS, AND POLICY MAKING

The local school bureaucracy has expanded substantially in the past twenty years. Some of the causes include the growth of federal and state categorical programs, increased court and legal activity, expansion of collective bargaining, more aggressive community interest groups, and increase in functions schools perform such as environmental and bilingual education. These causes are individually analyzed in various chapters throughout this book, but one result has been a proliferation in central office subunits and a more complex administrative structure. Despite this central office expansion, however, previous pressure for decentralization has recently waned.

CHANGING SCHOOL GOVERNANCE STRUCTURES

One result of the debate over how local school policy is to be made has been structural changes. We have noted that the present structure that excludes school boards from city council jurisdiction is an adaptation to the machine era's governance structure. School consolidation represents another structural accommodation to changes in educational policy making that resulted in part from the great population movements around World Wars I and II. These structural changes had policy consequences. Thus at the end of almost a century of the nonpartisan reform effort, a sixty-seven-city study showed that such structures, independent of a district's economic and environmental characteristics, played a part in school expenditures.[46] The direction of the effect was negative; that is, the more that reform elements existed in the school governance, such as nonpartisanship and independence from the mayor, the less it spent. But the more that school governance featured the older political structures—ward elections and so on—the more schools were open to influence from nonprofessional groups.

In recent decades the push for structural changes has been termed "community control." The first edition of this book paid much attention to this drive in its formative stages. Now, a decade later, many of its supporters have faded, though some changes were effected. Community control seeks to create several subsystems within one school system, relocating decision making from the center to several new community-based school boards of lay members.[47] Particularly favored by minority groups who lacked the resources to influence the central administrators, this new concept envisioned a neighborhood board able to remove personnel hired by the old centralized board and with complete discretion to reallocate budget priorities. Little support for this existed among school professionals.

Decentralization, on the other hand, was supported by teachers, principals, and administrators in the individual schools who found the present centralized system cumbersome. They complained they could not get supplies and personnel from the central office and were prevented by overall regulations from making curricula and teaching reforms. The assumption was that better education would be possible if more locally based, professional educators had more decision-making power. In effect, field administrators would gain authority from central administrators, something like an army command situation. Under community control, however, lay board members and citizens (particularly minorities) would ostensibly gain more influence than when—as at present—they confront all the professionals as well as citywide voting constituencies. Looking at these two trends in structural changes, there has been very little community control but widespread decentralization in big city schools throughout the 1970s. This tells much about the weight of the professionals.[48]

The increasing complexity of school policy making tends to provide considerable influence to those who control detailed information and analyses of policy alternatives. The control of information highlights the role of the school bureaucracy vis-à-vis the superintendent. At this point, our research in rural districts has not progressed far enough to differentiate the influence of the superintendent from his or her own staff. We do, however, know a lot about this pattern in the urban schools. There, the central office staff has accumulated so vast a decision-making authority in such areas as curriculum, personnel assignment, and facilities that the roles of outlying district administrators and building principals are restricted. Under present conditions the principal is too involved with day-to-day management of the school to participate effectively in broad policy making. District superintendents, in turn, are primarily concerned with assuring that policies set down by central headquarters are followed by the schools in their districts.[49]

The top officials at the central office are traditionally chosen from within the system by the superintendent or superintendent's committee. In some districts the board must ratify his or her recommendations, but a new superintendent cannot always bring in a new team of top administrators. Few incumbents are removed or fired from the district. The superintendent may not be able to implement policies through his or her administrative officers. For example, Rogers concluded that in the school desegregation program in New York the board and superintendent policies were emasculated by the contradictory or evasive directives and actions of some line administrative officers.[50] Indeed, the central office might make official policy statements, but the operation of the school system was highly decentralized with various bureaucrats ignoring the central desegregation policy and going off in conflicting directions.

Fragmented Centralization

The growth of federal and state categorical programs has led to fragmented centralization—no single office or program brings together separate categories and integrates them in a consistent way.[51] Instead, there are numerous separate special controls and funding subsystems each with its own specific purposes. Consequently, there are local education coordinators for compensatory, special, bilingual, vocational, environmental education, for desegregation, and so on. Sometimes these coordinators report through the state government to Washington, others report directly to the federal level. The federal system is not only fragmented by funding sources but also by its organizational or reporting structures. Some federal or state funding sources bypass intermediate levels of government and go directly to a particular school.

Each level of the educational system has to maintain administrative linkage, not only with higher levels but also with horizontal groups. Principals negotiate with parents and the central office. The local director of compensatory education deals with a local parent advisory committee, and the state office of compensatory education is charged with enforcing federal regulations. When these horizontal and vertical organizational relationships are multiplied at a rapid rate, the interaction effect can result in administrative overload and inconsistent policy. As Meyer observes:

Consider the practical situation of a school principal or superintendent. The state will provide extra funds for a special program for handicapped students. The federal government will provide further funds if there is no special program (i.e., for mainstreaming). The parents insist that funds be managed equitably within the school and district; but both state and federal governments provide special funds which must be spent only within a few schools, or even for a few students within a school.

What is the administrator to do? The answer is simple: have a differentiated subunit for each funding or authority program, let these subunits report as best they can in conformity with requirements, avoid having the subunits brought in contact with each other (so as to avoid explicit conflict or inconsistency), and remain in ignorance of the exact content of the various programs, reports, and budgets . . .[52]

All of these problems get magnified in large school districts that receive forty or more categorical programs and have eighty separate sources of income. For example, the state of California has over twenty large categorical programs of its own!

Fragmented centralization implies that the school site impact of categorical programs will be nonuniform, cumulative, and primarily indirect. Indeed, the major federal categories do not attempt to prescribe teaching methodologies or curriculum. Very few of the rules in these categorical programs specify and control the actual work processes by the teacher. Consequently, it is increasingly difficult to pinpoint the actual policy outputs that result from this welter of organizational fragmentation and complexity. Moreover, the superintendent and board are not clear how effective their central policy directives will be. Each organizational subunit can play numerous constituencies off against each other. The special education director can blame undesirable components of the program on state requirements or the mandated parent advisory committee. The state department of education (SDE) can increase its influence over local education agencies (LEAs) by claiming that federal coercion is responsible for the new pressures.

The historic pattern of educational leadership has changed and has become more reliant on negotiations and bargaining with a multitude of internal and external subunits. The building principal is confronted with an increased number of duties and role expectations. During periods of resource decline, competition for scarce funds becomes more intense. Local authorities discover that they cannot reduce administrators as rapidly as teachers due to external influences that require local project directors.

In a survey of how the principal's job has changed over five years, respondents reported they are now more constrained by rules, more subject to public scrutiny, and less in control of their own schedules.[53] Three specific activities increased the most: paperwork (in part caused by special programs), consultation with parents, and coping with students' noninstructional needs. A majority of the principals reported that they now spend less time supervising instruction. Interestingly, collective bargaining contracts take more of the principal's time, but contracts can be modified to fit unusual school site conditions. This flexibility depended on the particular relationship between the teachers and the principal, which confirms earlier studies which found that each school neighborhood had distinctive policies, depending on such things as the principal, community economic structure, and history of local activism.

Teacher Politics

At the local level *itself*, there are other groups that persist and have power over time and will compete with the bureaucratic structure for control of school policy. Grimshaw has recently made a strong argument that there has been a total system transformation in who rules local schools as a result of teacher unions.[54] Chicago's schools were first governed by political machine rule, then by a reform rule (which meant a professional education bureaucracy), and are now governed by union rule. These three models are distinguished in terms of structure, process, and actors. However, the union rule is characterized by a crucial political quality—lack of control by elected officials; not even the late Mayor Daley could cope with teacher union demands. A continuing question of the democratic polity, however, is What if Grimshaw is correct in saying, "Union rule bears hallmarks of an enduring form of urban government"?

Certainly their growing size alone makes them a local pressure group regularly confronting each district board and superintendent every few years with increasingly implacable force. By 1975, collective bargaining agreements covered 60 percent of all public schoolteachers. A Rand study of contracts in 1970 and 1975 shows many gains but also mixed results. These are summarized in table 6.3. Only four items on this list found acceptance in a majority of the contracts— grievance arbitration, maximum class hours, excluding disruptive students, and responding to teacher evaluation. The board usually accepted changes that affected local site management but not those affecting its own authority. However, it was the scope of negotiable items permitted by state law that influenced how much was worked into these agreements, unless local teacher groups were politically weak. In the main, teacher influence varied by district and school site,

Table 6.3
Teacher Contract Provisions, 1970 and 1975

Key Provision	Attained by 1970	Attained between 1970 and 1975
All grievances to be subject to arbitration	80%	10%
Minimum number of aides per classroom specified	12	14
Maximum class size specified	23	10
Maximum class hours specified	50	20
Teachers can exclude a disruptive pupil	32	18
An instructional policy committee to be established	18	11
Teachers can respond formally to evaluation	38	13
Teachers can refuse assignment	14	11
Only seniority and credentials to determine promotion	23	3
Involuntary transferees to be selected on specific criteria	26	10
Reduction-in-force procedures spelled out	13	31

Note: Based on a national random sample of 155 teacher contracts.
Source: Lorraine M. McDonnell and Anthony H. Pascal, "Organized Teachers and Local Schools," in Mary F. Williams, ed., Government in the Classroom: Dollars and Power in Education (Montpelier, Vt.: The Academy of Political Science, 1979), p. 36.

and rarely did teachers exercise a veto over school management. Teacher unions had the most difficulty enforcing such contract provisions as pupil discipline, building maintenance, and security because grievance procedures were less effective. Seniority and teacher transfer clauses were the most highly implemented. The unions' long-run influence, however, may come more from influencing decisions at state and federal levels that then percolate down to the local school system. As close students of this subject point out, there are serious potentials for rearranging traditional school governance by teacher lobbying in state capitals.[55]

There is also an entirely different way to view the teacher's role, and this occurs when we turn from their outward relationship with school authorities to their inward relationship with their students. We have seen in chapter 3 one aspect of this relationship in the teachers' role in political learning. But even in such a seemingly value-free subject as elementary school mathematics, the teacher is not simply an imple-mentor of educational policy. As scholars presenting this new per-spective have concluded:

In this semi-autonomous role, teachers are better understood as political brokers than as implementors. They enjoy considerable discretion, being influenced by their own notions of what schooling ought to be as well as persuaded by external pressures. . . . This view represents a middle ground in the classic sociological contrast between professional autonomy and bureaucratic subordination. It pictures teachers as more or less rational decision-makers who take higher-level policies and other pressures into consideration in their calculation of benefits and costs.[56]

In a real sense—by definitively allocating public resources in such matters as choosing which students will get what kind of curriculum content—the teacher takes on a political role. This parallels the similar political role of board and administrative decisions. Thus, decisions in elementary math about what will be taught, to whom, and for how long are matters that teachers usually decide. There are some pressures, however, from students (what has worked with them in the past predisposes its reuse) and from external sources. Externally, a varied urban environment with its ambiguous messages about instruction is much more likely to free the teacher to make such decisions compared to a small rural homogeneous setting. Centralized versus decentralized state requirements—for example, statewide text adoption by the state board—are another kind of external factor affecting teacher discretion. Within the school organization itself, Hawley has pointed to factors of organizational rigidity or receptivity that create expectations in teachers about how power is to be used.[57]

Much of the preceding suggests an organizational structure for schooling characterized by "loose coupling." This is the tendency of educational organizations to disconnect policies from outcomes, means from ends, and structure or rules from actual activity.[58] Such a nonstructure puts the teacher's behavior beyond the control of the formal authorities, who themselves have no chain of command with straight lines and precise directions for teaching policy. Within such disjointed relationships, one would not expect much impact from program innovations that originate outside the local unit.

In fact, scholars have just begun to probe this situation. By 1980 there was growing interest in evaluation studies from the bottom up rather than those from the top down, which had characterized the 1970s. Longitudinal studies were just beginning to come out, such as a thirteen-year impact analysis of ESEA Title I, which showed that over time federal efforts to target more dollars to participating students were indeed successful. Federal objectives were gradually incorporated into district standard procedures, and so the potential for teacher impact existed. If evidence of this impact is found, it would suggest that the loosely coupled system is not completely uncoupled. A survey of the history of classroom reforms finds lasting results if the changes are structural, create new clientele, and are easily monitored.[59] Vocational education and driver training are good examples of this.

Thus the role of teachers in local governance is much more than just trade union politics. We need more knowledge of the teacher as a significant screen between external influences and the student and the teacher as a political agent within the classroom in both manifest and latent terms. Then we will better understand how teachers function as one set of local actors in the conversion of private needs into public policy, how they operate in the essentially political nature of this conversion process.

CURRICULUM POLICY: AN EXAMPLE OF NEW FACTORS IN SCHOOL GOVERNANCE

The external factors that currently penetrate the local school district dramatically affect the traditional mode of local governance. As an overall consistent finding, the more the channels to the board and administrator are swept by regular floods of aroused school constituents, the more the board becomes responsive; the more it challenges traditional professional definitions of educational service, the less autonomy such professionals have. This diminution of local professional control has been a consistent theme in the political study of education, although it has proven impossible to precisely define the concept of local control.

Curriculum Conflict

Nevertheless, there are still strong demands for local control on some traditional matters such as the curriculum. Political conflict surrounding curriculum has escalated in the past decade. Efforts to ban books doubled in the first five years of the 1970s over the last five of the 1960s. A 1974 book-banning crusade exploded into life, threatening violence in Kanawha County, West Virginia. The American Library Association reported three to five episodes a week in 1981 ranging from the Idaho Falls banning of *One Flew Over the Cuckoo's Nest* to Anaheim, California, excising Richard Wright's *Black Boy*. After the Warsaw, Indiana, school board banned forty copies of *Values Clarifica-*

tions, the school board president posed the essential political question, "Who shall control the minds of the students?"[60]

One federal attempt to take a role in influencing local curriculum was rebuffed in the 1970s. Congress eliminated the federal curriculum development role in large part because of a 1975 debate on the National Science Foundation's proposed social curriculum, "Man: A Course of Study" (MACOS). Typical of this pressure was the charge of Congressman John Conlan (Rep.-Arizona) that MACOS was a federal attempt to "use classrooms for conditioning, to mold a new generation of Americans toward a repudiation of traditional values, behavior, and patriotic beliefs."[61] Yet twenty years earlier the federal government had entered the curriculum and text development field because critics alleged that schoolbooks were outdated, inaccurate, dull, and lacking in diversity. The value conflict over school curriculum intensified during the last decade, however. Boyd explains that the scholars and experts the federal and state governments rely on for curricular improvement have been criticized for trying to impose their own cosmopolitan and secular values. Curricular reform itself has been professionalized through government and foundation grants. No longer are perceived crises such as Sputnik required to generate curriculum change, for it has a self-starting capacity.[62]

Curricular conflict has many roots. Military threats or changes in public sentiment such as the women's movement generate value conflict about curriculum even though this is not why they were initiated. Other forces, such as court decisions favoring bilingual education or the pronouncements of influential individuals, can change the curriculum orientation without the direct development of new materials. In order to incorporate all these influences, the new process of textbook creation is "managed," whereby a writing team prepares a series of texts. The actual author is frequently the publisher's internal editor not the authors listed on the title page. Teachers are also contributors to textbook content through their instructional preferences.[63]

These skeletal concepts can be brought to life by the flesh of reality provided in a specific education issue. The reform of the mathematics curriculum in this country from the mid-1950s to the late 1970s nicely illustrates these multiple influences. It also shows the essentially political nature of curriculum decision making, even though professionals often regard curriculum as apolitical and something to be shielded from gross political concerns.

When educators regard the curriculum as a "professional" matter, this does not mean they are unaffected by the society in which it is taught. In the course of American history, curriculum has been made to relate to major matters in the larger society—religious training, literacy, Americanization, occupational training, and so on. When left to themselves, the criteria professionals use for deciding such matters vary—appeals to tradition, scientific testing, common social values, or individual judgment. But no broadly accepted criteria for such judgments have existed, although there has been rough agreement to teach English, history, science, mathematics, health, and somewhat less agreement on social studies and foreign languages. There is no agreement among the diverse states and LEAs, with their variegated populations and value orientations, on the required content and intellectual level of such accepted curricula, however.

Supporters and critics of existing curricula transmit conflicting signals into the education policy making system of any state. Traditional supporters have included:

1. School accrediting and testing agencies, which are private groups with public overtones.
2. Schools of education, often inertia bound to ongoing instruction in the traditional curriculum.
3. State boards of education (SBEs) and state departments of education (SDEs) discussed earlier, which must by law oversee a host of earlier policy decisions.

Those seeking curricula changes, however, have grown apace in recent years. Publishers invest a lot in maintaining their existing textbooks, so on the one hand, they are not agents of change, but they also invest in new instructional materials, which they try to sell to LEAs or states. They are swayed by intense pressure group activity, so they cannot impose just any values in their materials. The federal government has been another source of curriculum change. By the early 1970s, half the schools were using a new physics course instigated with federal research funding, and about two-thirds were using a new biology course. Private foundations also stimulate research that can eventuate in new curricula and teaching materials. Professional associations of scientists and other scholarly, business, and professional groups engage in such research as well. And always, university professors generate ideas about curriculum change. To further complicate our understanding the matrix of private groups, none of these speak with a single voice.

This picture of curriculum decision making becomes even fuzzier when we consider what happens at the local level. LEAs, teachers, administrators, boards, and parents may feel strongly about changing some part of the curriculum to fit prevailing local values. Despite central control of curriculum in some states (particularly the Southeast, LEAs can blunt these outside forces. There have been frequent emotional episodes of local opposition to teaching about evolution, the United Nations, the role of racial minorities, and the social nature of humankind. In each case, local people sought to block either state directives or professionally accepted norms of "good" curriculum.

There are also new ideas about instruction and its materials as part of the more general questioning of the once-unchallenged professional's dominance of school policy. For example, parents have demanded more homework and dress codes for their children or lobbied for alternative schools with more curricular electives. Despite such dramatic incidents, the larger picture is one of LEAs generally accepting what the professionals decide from their positions at the state or national level.[64] Nonetheless, powerful local forces such as advocates of the creation story can always intrude on this policy making system.[65]

The New Math Movement: Reform and Reaction

With this as background on the politics of curriculum, we can now illustrate the policy process model set forth earlier. The two-decade effort to introduce a new math curriculum in American schools is useful for that purpose because it shows both the power and limits of professional control.

The traditional methods of teaching mathematics in public schools are rooted in early nineteenth century pedagogy. But for some time mathematicians and school math teachers had been discontented with these methods. During this private-issue stage of policy making, discontent was not sufficient to generate anything other than a scattered questioning of the old ways. Some university professors were experimenting with a new approach to math instruction, but there was as yet no sense of urgency or resources to act.

The private-issue-transformation stage of policy making occurred at the confluence of several dramatic events in the late 1960s.

Americans were enormously shocked in the late 1950s by the Russian success in orbiting the first space vehicle, the Sputnik. Critics of the American schools were already charging educators with educating the modern generation poorly; they seized on Sputnik as an illustration of how this American "defeat" was attributable to "poor" schools. Thus external technological changes were used by initiator groups to call for curriculum improvements, particularly in language and mathematics training. The media appealed to university curriculum specialists for enlightenment; parents made demands for action on state and national policy makers; and, in short, the issue quickly became a public one and was placed on the political agenda.[66]

The crisis atmosphere of this issue's emergence illustrates how quickly the institutional agenda can be reached by a new, consensual issue. Congress legislated and the U.S. Office of Education implemented a new law to proved monies for improving the quality of math and language training and increasing the supply of such teachers. This National Defense Education Act (NDEA) of 1958 provided funds for developing new curricula in math, training employed teachers in the new math, and incorporating these changes into schools of education. In short, this policy output stage elevated the goal of providing students with better math training to national attention by redistributing federal money to teaching methods aimed at that goal.

The implementation stage was impressive in its thoroughness. Federal agencies fastened on a particular strategy of raising students' math comprehension. This involved a new way of thinking about math theoretically, which could be taught from the first grade onwards by methods that students could easily grasp. The traditional curriculum ladder (arithmetic, geometry, beginning and advanced algebra, trigonometry, and—in some schools—calculus) was abandoned almost everywhere. Instead, students were introduced sequentially to different levels and relevant applications of such concepts as set theory. Thus, to get across the concept of numbering, instead of using the traditional method of counting to the base of ten, students were taught to count from the base of seven or another number. The logic of numbering was sought rather than the rote learning of a multiplication table.

Federal funds underwrote eight-to-ten-week summer training institutes for many teachers. Special text materials were devised and disseminated; later, computer usages became available. States endorsed these innovations, providing additional funds to incorporate the new into the old math curriculum. Administrative state agencies beefed up their curriculum divisions relevant to math programs and assisted in the implementation of the changes. Local school boards were encouraged to participate by releasing their teachers for summer instruction and to graft the new onto the old. In time, if one's school system did not enjoy the new math, one felt left out of a national tide of change. Recall that such retraining and materials were provided for every level of schooling, and public and parochial schools alike were enlisted in moving the reform into the system and onto the students. This was all done in a remarkably few years.

The program-outcome stage produced several results, but one of them was unintended and eventually counterproductive. If one goal was to improve math training, then millions of students had been exposed to the new math concepts and understood them reasonably well. If another goal was to institutionalize the reform, then there were thousands of LEAs that had adopted the new curricular concept. But if the goal was to prepare students for the application of mathematics to life, some feedback that was quite critical developed. Parents (who often did not themselves understand the new math concepts despite efforts to give them a quick exposure) increasingly complained that their children could not use mathematics for everyday requirements such as multiplying or adding in preparing a bill or grocery list.

So widespread did this negative feedback become by the opening of the 1970s that state laws and regulations were altered. State text adoptions returned to the old math, and state tests changed accordingly. Signs that teachers were also reverting to the old math contributed to this reversal.[67] There was little evidence that students were learning mathematical principles any better. Indeed, in the widespread decline in math and English test scores across the nation in the mid-1970s, few curricula could claim much success, and the new math had no strong constituency within the school system nor lobby organization other than federal leadership through the National Science Foundation (NSF). It was not easy to monitor whether teachers stressed the new math, and the new math did not stimulate any addition or structural identity within the school bureaucracy. By the mid-1970s, the feedback cycle had resulted in a shift away from the new math with little permanent residue from what had been an aggressive national effort. Some teachers continued to partially implement their NSF summer institute new-math skills, but hostile external forces gradually diminished such content.

Coda

This chapter has assembled the array of contenders for control of decision making at the local level. The variety of the participants and the spread of issues addressed point clearly to the political turbulence of schools that is the theme of this second edition. But there are other levels of decision making involved, to which the following chapters now turn.

NOTES

1. David Easton, *A Framework for Political Analysis* (Englewood Cliffs, N.J.: Prentice-Hall, 1965), p. 114.

2. Ibid., pp. 132–33.

3. George S. Counts, *School and Society in Chicago* (New York: Harcourt, Brace, 1928).

4. L. Harmon Zeigler and M. Kent Jennings, *Governing American Schools* (North Scituate, Mass.: Duxbury, 1974), pp. 39–42. A similar finding exists for municipal councils.

5. For a recent review of this agency's functions, past and present, see Peter J. Cistone, ed., *Understanding School Boards* (Lexington, Mass.: Lexington Books, 1975).

6. Robert Bendiner, *The Politics of Schools* (New York: Harper & Row, 1969), p. 165.

7. Dale Mann, "Public Understanding and Education Decision-Making," *Educational Administration Quarterly* 10, no. 2 (1974): 1–18.

8. Michael W. Kirst, "Loss of Support for Public Secondary Schools: Some Causes and Solutions," *Daedalus* (September 1981), assembles the contrary evidence noted below.

9. For the poll data from both sources, see ibid.

10. See the evidence in Frederick M. Wirt, "Neoconservatism and National School Policy," *Educational Evaluation and Policy Analysis* 2, no. 6 (1980): 5–18, and Diane Ravitch, *The Revisionists Revised* (New York: Basic Books, 1978).

11. Frank W. Lutz and Laurence Iannaccone, eds., *Public Participation in Local School Districts* (Lexington, Mass.: Lexington Books, 1978).

12. Frank W. Lutz, "Methods and Conceptualizations of Political Power in Education," in *The Politics of Education*, 76th Yearbook of the National Society for the Study of Education (Chicago: University of Chicago Press, 1977), p. 32.

13. Frederick A. Rodgers, *The Black High School and Its Community* (Lexington, Mass.: Lexington Books, 1975).

14. Paul Peterson, "Urban Politics and Changing Schools: A Competitive View," and David W. Plank and Paul Peterson, "Does Urban Reform Imply Class Conflict?

The Case of Atlanta's Schools" (Papers under National Institute of Education contract, 1980).

15. Raymond E. Callahan, *Education and the Cult of Efficiency* (Chicago: University of Chicago Press, 1962).

16. David W. Minar, "The Community Basis of Conflict in School System Politics," *American Sociological Review* 31 (1966): 822–34; William L. Boyd, *"Community Status and Conflict in Suburban School Politics*, (Beverly Hills, Calif.: Sage, 1975), and "Educational Policy-Making in Declining Suburban School Districts" (Paper presented to the American Educational Research Association convention, 1978).

17. Zeigler and Jennings, *Governing American Schools,* chap. 6.

18. Christine Rossell, "School Desegregation and Community Social Change," *Law and Contemporary Problems* 42 (1978): 133–83.

19. Emmett H. Buell, Jr., *School Desegregation and Defended Neighborhoods: The Boston Controversy* (Lexington, Mass.: Lexington Books, 1981).

20. Boyd, *Community Status.*

21. Carol Mullins, "School District Consolidation: Odds Are 2–1 It'll Get You," *American School Board Journal* 11 (1973): 160.

22. James W. Guthrie, "Public Control of Public Schools: *Public Affairs Report* (University of California, Institute of Governmental Studies, 1974), p. 2.

23. See note 17.

24. Leigh Stelzer, "Institutionalizing Conflict Response: The Case of Schoolboards," *Social Science Quarterly* 55, no. 2 (1974).

25. David J. Kirby et al., *Political Strategies in Northern School Desegregation* (Lexington, Mass.: Lexington Books, 1973).

26. Keith Goldhammer, *The School Board* (New York: Center for Applied Research, 1964).

27. Frederick M. Wirt et al., *On the City's Rim: Politics and Policy in Suburbia* (Lexington, Mass.: Heath, 1972), pp. 161–66.

28. For an introduction to these concepts in an educational context, see Dale Mann, *Policy Decision-Making in Education* (New York: Teachers College Press, 1975).

29. Paul E. Peterson, *School Politics Chicago Style* (Chicago: University of Chicago Press, 1976), pp. 134–35.

30. William L. Boyd, "The Public, the Professionals, and Educational Policy-Making: Who Governs?" *Teachers College Record* 77 (1976): 556–58.

31. Based on several censuses of administrators conducted by Paul Salmon, American Association of School Administrators, Washington, D.C., mimeographed.

32. The sources, in order, are: Norman D. Kerr, "The School Board as an Agency of Legitimation," *Sociology of Education* 38 (1964):34–59; Michael P. Smith, "Elite Theory and Policy Analysis: The Politics of Education in Suburbia," *Journal of Politics* 36 (1974): 1006–32; Peter J. Cistone, "The Socialization of School Board Members," *Educational Administration Quarterly* 13, no. 2 (1977): 19–33.

33. Zeigler and Jennings, *Governing American Schools*, pt. III.

34. Seltzer, "Institutionalizing Conflict."

35. Boyd, "The Public, the Professionals."

36. M. Kent Jennings, "Parental Grievances and School Politics," *Public Opinion Quarterly* 32 (1968): 363–78.

37. Roland L. Warren, S. M. Rose, and A. F. Bergunder, *The Structure of Urban Reform* (Lexington, Mass.: Heath, 1974).

38. David Rogers, *110 Livingston Street* (New York: Random House, 1968).

39. Frederick M. Wirt, "Professionalism and Political Conflict: A Developmental Model," *Journal of Public Policy*, in press.

40. For example, Thomas J. Sergiovanni et al., *Educational Governance and Administration* (Englewood Cliffs, N.J.: Prentice-Hall, 1980).

41. Larry Cuban, *Urban School Chiefs Under Fire* (Chicago: University of Chicago Press, 1976).

42. Jesse J. McCorry, *Marcus Foster and the Oakland Public Schools* (Berkeley: University of California Press, 1978).

43. The seminal theoretical work is Hanna F. Pitkin, *The Concept of Representation* (Berkeley: University of California Press, 1967).

44. Dale Mann, *The Politics of Administrative Representation* (Lexington, Mass.: Lexington Books, 1976).

45. Harry L. Summerfield, *The Neighborhood-based Politics of Education* (Columbus, Ohio: Charles E. Merrill, 1971).

46. Brett Hawkins et al., "Good Government Reformism and School Spending in Cities," in *The Polity of the School,* Frederick M. Wirt, (Lexington, Mass.: Lexington Books, 1975), chap. 2.

47. Henry Levin, ed., *Community Control of Schools* (Washington, D.C.: Brookings Institution, 1972).

48. A six-city comparison is in George R. La Noue and Bruce L. Smith, *The Politics of School Decentralization* (Lexington, Mass.: Lexington Books, 1973).

49. Dale Mann, *The Politics of Administrative Representation* (Lexington, Mass.: Lexington Books, 1976).

50. For a good case, see Rogers, *110 Livingston Street.*

51. See John Meyer, "The Impact of Centralization" (Stanford: Institute of Educational Finance and Governance, 1979).

52. Ibid, pp. 16–17.

53. Paul Hill et al. *The Effects of Federal Education Programs on School Principals* (Santa Monica, Calif.: Rand, 1980). For analysis of school site politics, see Harry Z. Summerfeld, *The Neighborhood-based Politics of Education* (Columbus, Ohio: Charles E. Merrill, 1971).

54. William J. Grimshaw, *Union Rule in the Schools* (Lexington, Mass.: Lexington Books, 1979).

55. James Guthrie and Patricia Craig, *Teachers and Politics* (Bloomington, Ind.: Phi Delta Kappan, 1973).

56. A review of this emerging research is found in John Schwille et al., "Teachers as Policy Brokers in the Content of Elementary School Mathematics," (Paper prepared for the NIE Conference on Teaching and Educational Policy, February 1981), and John Schwille, Andrew Porter, and M. Gant, "Content Decision-Making and the Politics of Education," *Educational Administration Quarterly* 16 (1980): 21–40.

57. D. C. Lortie, "The Balance of Control and Autonomy in Elementary School Teaching," in *The Semi-Professions and Their Organization,* Amitai Etzioni, ed. (New York: Free Press, 1969); Alan Peshkin, *Growing Up American* (Chicago: University of Chicago

Press, 1979); Willis D. Hawley, "Dealing with Organizational Rigidity in Public Schools: A Theoretical Perspective," in *The Polity of the School,* Wirt, chap. 11; and Willis D. Hawley, "Horses Before Carts: Developing Adaptive Schools and the Limits of Innovation," in *Political Science and School Politics: The Princes & the Pundits,* eds, Samuel K. Gove and Frederick M. Wirt (Lexington, Mass.: Lexington Books, 1976), chap. 1.

58. Karl Weick, "Educational Organizations as Loosely Coupled Systems," *Administrative Science Quarterly* 21 (1976): 1–19.

59. Michael Kirst and Richard Jung, "The Utility of a Longitudinal Approach in Assessing Implementation: A Thirteen Year View of Title I, ESEA," *Educational Evaluation and Policy Analysis* 2 (1980): 17–34; and David Tyack, Michael Kirst, and Elisabeth Hansot, "Educational Reform: Retrospect and Prospect," *Teachers College Record,* 81 (1980).

60. *Time,* January 19, 1981.

61. Jon Schaffarzick and Gary Sykes, *Value Conflicts and Curriculum Issues* (Berkeley: McCutchan, 1979), p. 3.

62. William L. Boyd, "The Changing Politics of Curriculum Policy Making," in Schaffarzick and Sykes, *Value Conflicts,* pp. 73–138.

63. Paul Goldstein, *Changing the American Schoolbook* (Lexington, Mass.: Lexington Books, 1978).

64. See Tyll van Geel, *Authority to Control the School Program* (Lexington, Mass.: Lexington Books, 1976).

65. See James Holtois and Neal Milner, *The Sex Education Controversy* (Lexington, Mass.: Lexington Books, 1975).

66. R. J. Munger and Richard Fenno, *National Politics and Federal Aid to Education* (Syracuse, N.Y.: Syracuse University Press, 1962).

67. Larry Cuban, "Determinants of Curriculum Change and Stability," in Schaffarzick and Sykes, *Value Conflicts,* pp. 179–190.

7

Referenda in the Conversion Process

It is not only through school board elections that citizens seek to impress their preferences for school policies. Another channel is the referendum, by which citizens vote directly on such school policy matters as budgets, bonds, or levies. Viewed in another way, the referendum is a device for registering public support of schools. Unhappiness with excessive spending, insensitive teachers, lack of student discipline, objectionable curriculum, or even the losing football team can generate lack of support, and simply voting no is a convenient way of expressing this dissatisfaction. Of course, happiness with other facets of school policy can motivate a yes vote. Given the convenience of the device for voters, school boards and administrators have to pay much attention to this well of potential support. In short, they must become "political" by seeking to mobilize group support within the community for what they agree is necessary funding.

In recent years, however, school authorities have found that this support is drying up. Whether because parents are increasingly unhappy with schools or are squeezed by galloping inflation or whether there are simply fewer parents with children in the public schools, referenda have not gained public support as they once did. This development is another part of the current political turbulence in schools. In this chapter we examine this phenomenon in light of the extensive writing about referenda support. Moreover, we show how

163

present-day factors compel the school professional to adopt political strategies not unlike those of other actors who struggle for resources and values in the public arena.

BACKGROUND AND SIGNIFICANCE

By the end of the nineteenth century, many Americans were disgusted with their government. Legislative excesses had brought restraints and an expansion of executives' capacities to balance off corrupt assemblies. But as the century closed, neither political position received much praise. Political parties were everywhere seen as corrupt links between legislature and executive, the judiciary was equally tainted, and the beneficiaries of this degradation—in an era of rampant capitalism—were not only politicians but businessmen.

The political movement of Progressivism moved against this union of private and public greed. Reformers felt that more democracy must be a part of the operations of democracy, and citizens should have more control over the corrupters of the political and economic weal. To achieve these purposes, the initiative, referendum, and recall, among other devices, were adopted in many American states. It is hard to realize now how radical these practices were once thought to be. In our own time they have "become quaint; one thought of them, as one remembered Teddy Roosevelt's teeth, in a haze of mezzotint sentimentality."

Their promise of referendum control has not been matched by reality, for little evidence exists that they balanced interest-group power in state politics. Not many citizens consider them important enough to use. Aside from the occasional, controversial issue that precipitates a large turnout, most referenda attract far less than a majority. Yet the promise is not completely hollow. One reality policy makers have to keep in mind is that these devices *can* be resorted to if their actions become too offensive. Earlier advocates spoke of this power as "a shotgun behind the door"; today, political scientists speak of their potential for creating "anticipated reactions" in officials who will then ostensibly curb their excesses in anticipation of what the public will accept.[1]

The use of referenda to pass school budgets, levies, and bonds is an exception to the use of direct democracy to maximize citizen participation in policy making. As Hamilton and Cohen point out, school referenda were the handiwork of *conservatives* seeking to *prevent* passage of bond issues and to keep property tax rates down by state law. To obtain taxes and expenditures above the state limits, the school referendum was required, often open only to property owners and requiring extraordinary majorities to pass. Conservatives thought that few such efforts would succeed, given these barriers, but that is not what happened. The unintended consequences were that local revenue sources dried up and pressures on the state to bail out the locals escalated—a familiar ring in the educational finance politics of the 1970s. This in turn generated pressures for new state taxes and led to the widespread adoption of the sales tax and new grant and taxing arrangements for the local schools. Thus, "the tax limitation schemes begat fiscal policy centralization and a web of state-local fiscal relationships and interdependence."[2] In addition, local districts regularly use referenda to overcome the legal limitations imposed by the states.

The referendum, more significant for education than for other areas of public policy, is important in two respects. It is the necessary device for securing financial support of schools in all states except Alabama, Hawaii, and Indiana; however, some districts are exempt in fourteen other states. Also, it may be conceptualized as a conversion process at the local level that bypasses the school board and authoritatively allocates values. We must keep in mind that, unlike board elections, referenda are direct policy-making processes. Passage or defeat definitely allocates school system resources, in general for operating levies and in specific for bond issues. The act of voting for or against—or not voting at all—relates the individual citizen to the school in a direct and intimate way unparalleled for other major public policies.

The relationship can take several forms, however. Sweeping support of what school professionals offer citizens may reflect close correspondence between the preferences of the two. Ostensibly that condition arises when school authorities carefully anticipate the limits of the public's demands; beyond this point public support will drop off. Alternatively, the relationship may be closely divided but still united enough to provide a majority referenda support; this reflects community cleavage over policy issues. Here the school authorities have less room in which to anticipate the public's acceptable limits. A third possible relationship is when school authorities are defeated on the referenda they urge; here their anticipatory wisdom was poor.

Then adjustments will vary depending upon the size of the defeat; a narrow loss is worth another referendum effort, while a large defeat indicates considerable rearrangement of the school policies that the referenda funds were to support.

The Taxpayer Revolt

These conceptual distinctions are well illustrated by voting patterns for bond issues in recent decades. Figure 7.1 traces these dynamics over the turbulent years featured throughout this book. Here we can see the withdrawal of support in the record of total elections, the proportions that passed, and the dollar value of those passed. The early 1960s were the peak of an unusual time when Americans transmitted a large flow of economic resources into the political system of the schools. The general prosperity of the early 1960s and our loss of face over the scientific advances of the Russians most likely explain this result. Emboldened by such support, school boards submitted ever more bond issues in the peak years of 1962–1964. But after that there is a visible falling off in all indicators of citizen support, bottoming in 1968–1972. This remarkable turnabout is attributable to many factors, but note the sensitivity of school boards to this mood, reflected in their offering fewer and fewer bond issues. This is highly suggestive of the law of anticipated reactions, that is, authorities curbing their needs when they perceive that citizens would not meet them. There was a small resurgence in these indicators in the early 1970s, but a few years later they were all down again.

The record would undoubtedly be even more severe were figures available on levies and budget elections and if the dollar value approved was adjusted for this period. Whereas bond support fell as low as 46 percent in the 1970s, it has been suggested that the lowest for these other referenda is about 25 to 30 percent. Nonetheless, whatever indicators are used, they point to the importance of this electoral device as a form of policy making for American schools. The volatile nature of the public's moods is reflected in figure 7.1, pointing to the kind of voter dissatisfaction with schools that produced the political turbulence noted in the Introduction. Figure 7.1 also suggests the atmosphere of uncertainty surrounding harried boards and superintendents. The lines for total elections and percentage passed show the difficulty that authorities would have had in guessing what the electorate would accept. Decreasing the total submitted seemed not to

Figure 7.1
School Bond Election Approval, 1957–58 to 1976–77

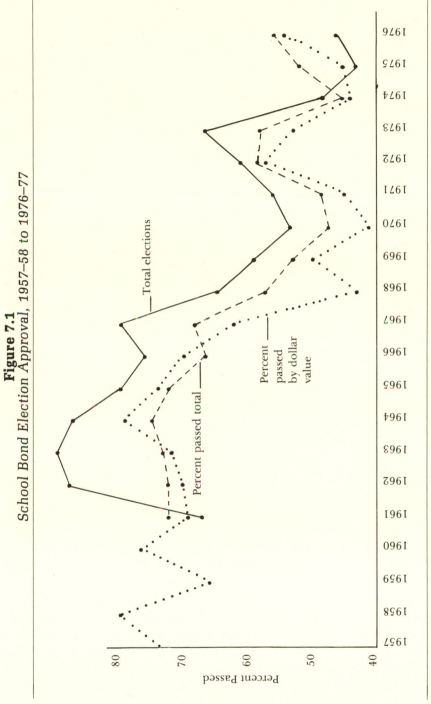

Source: Annual reports, National Center for Education Statistics, Bond Sales for Public School Purposes.

stabilize the approval rate in one period while increasing the totals in the early 1970s increased the approval rate. Of course in this figure we are not looking at a single political system or single set of authorities; these are aggregate records of a variety of local systems. Thus, we have not explored the regional variations.[3] Yet the parallelism of the lines and their correlations[4] point to a uniform public attitude about schools, whether in periods of high or low support. These match data drawn from polls cited in earlier chapters.

The collective study of these referenda can tell us much about the environment, demand inputs, and political system of American schools. In this chapter we explore what citizens are doing when they engage in or ignore school referenda.

Until the 1970s, it was possible to lament the surprisingly limited study of school referenda. After all, school districts were until quite recently the most numerous unit of governance in the country by far. The devouring force of consolidation noted in earlier chapters is starkly portrayed in the disappearance of 86 percent of these districts in just a third of a century. Today only one remains where seven once existed. Then there was a spate of research and rethinking about the time that the voter revolt against referenda appeared. One major volume evaluated the field so as to construct a propositional inventory of what the research showed, and another tested these propositions in several ways.[5]

LINKAGES AMONG VOTERS, TURNOUT, AND SUCCESS IN SCHOOL REFERENDA

When a citizen votes aye or nay on a secret ballot for a school budget, levy, or bond issue, no one is there to inquire what she or he has in mind. Yet this is an important query, both for school authorities who need to finely tune their public support if they are to mobilize sufficient financial resources and for scholars interested in the ties of the act of voting to its outcome. The importance for the authorities has long been known, and many professionals lament the time required to go about with a tin cup among the citizens, as they see it. Practical advice on the voter linkage has abounded for years—some based on singular, anecdotal evidence but some based on review of research.[6]

When scholars started to study these linkages, an extensive but complex body of knowledge emerged. We sketch these findings rather than itemize them. First it is important to discuss the underlying concepts about this linkage and then to fill in with some of the strongest evidence. Figure 7.2 sketches the basic paradigm of this research effort and details some of its components.

The primary concept of these linkages is this: (1) present policy events within the school system are affected by (2) previous voting outcomes on school referenda, (3) which in turn were a consequence of the turnout, and (4) the turnout was a product of characteristics of the voters, their district, or both, and (5) this action can be explained in several ways.

We can begin at the left side of the model. There has been much research on which *voter* characteristics are associated with a larger turnout or with voting for or against a referendum. These characteristics are usually measured by social and attitudinal qualities (status, ethnicity, ideology, attitudes toward schools). Partial theories rooted in the individual voter's motivations are offered as attempted explanations for these associations. The explanation could be economic; that is, one votes for a referendum if what one gains is more than what the tax will cost or votes against it if one loses more. Too, there are explanations based on whether the individual is oriented more to self or community. Explanations can also be based on psychological motivations, particularly the degree to which the voters are alienated from society or schools.

Another cluster of characteristics thought to be associated with good turnout and support are traced to *district* qualities. Districts differ in their demands for educational services, as measured by economic resources of the population or the proportion of school-age children. Explanation is then derived from quantitative analysis of these environmental attributes and can involve testing the propositions that high demand will increase voter turnout or tax support. Or it could be that districts are analyzed by qualifications for voting, size of the vote needed for referenda success, conditions under which financial matters may or must be submitted, and so on. These enable one to explore political explanations, such as rational decision making, models of legitimation, and so on. Finally, the degree of political turbulence in a district and the qualities of that history are district attributes that enable one to use community conflict theory as explanations.

These independent variables are much more detailed than the dependent variables whose explanation is sought. Thus, turnout is usually measured by the proportion of eligible adults that actually

Figure 7.2
Model of Research into Financial Referenda

Individual-Level Explanations → *Turnout* → *Voting Outcome* → *Subsequent Policy Events*

Voter Characteristics:

Variable
– status
– ethnicity
– ideology
– school attitudes

Individual-Level Explanations

Economic—optimization
Ethos—other-regarding
Psychological—alienation

Turnout

Percent of eligibles
Social composition

Voting Outcome

Size of support
Social composition of yeas and nays

Subsequent Policy Events

Future frequency of referenda
Results of future referenda
Amount of funds in future referenda
Board turnover
Superintendent turnover
Board policy (program changes)

District Characteristics:

Demand levels: resources
school age cohort
Structural requirements:
– voting
– majority for passage
– mandatory submission
Amount of politicization

System-Level Explanations

Environmental—macroanalysis
Political access—legitimation
Community conflict

turns out to vote and their social composition. Then the voting outcome is usually measured by the proportion of those voting for the referendum and by their social composition. Less studied but a logical next step is to measure what happens after the votes are counted. This would indicate the consequences that follow from passage or failure of a referendum—what happens now to future referenda (frequency, funding, results of votes), to the school authorities themselves, to school policies?

WHO VOTES AND WHY?

Research rather consistently paints a picture of those who turn out and support school referenda and those who do neither. This is crucial information for school authorities who must spend their time estimating where their support comes from. It is also significant for those testing propositions about citizen inputs to the political system of the schools. We only outline the main findings here: the literature is now fairly extensive and much of it is reinforcing.[7]

One quality of referendum voters has changed dramatically during the 1970s—they are no longer restricted to being taxpayers. In 1970, the Supreme Court struck down that requirement in the fourteen states that still required it.[8] The Court concluded that nontaxpayers were subtantially affected by such elections and also that the practice rested on a false assumption that only taxpayers pay property taxes when in fact renters pay them indirectly to landlords and commercial stores. Thus a practice that was widespread for all kinds of voting when our republic began finally vanished from our electoral system.

The Influence of Status

The largest volume of research has traditionally fastened on the status of those who turn out and those who support referenda. One clear finding about this cohort always appears—they are predominantly drawn from the middle and upper strata of the community. Attributes of this status can be measured by income, occupation, or education, but all show much the same thing, that is, a descending cascade of turnout and support from upper to lower statuses. Table 7.1 displays this characteristic using education as a status measure employed in nine studies from 1958 to 1970. Singly or combined, these status variables account for most of the variation in voting

Table 7.1

Percent Referenda Support by Education Level,
Selected Studies, 1958–70

Years of School	Bowling Green, Ohio 1966	Youngstown, Ohio 1968	Birmingham, Michigan 1961	Corning, New York 1957	Ithaca, New York 1958	Okemos, Michigan 1958	Austintown, Ohio 1970	State of Washington 1970
1–8	30	38						41
9–11	40	48	35	23	43	32	24	46
12	49	56					45	50
13–15	57		53	31	69	63		53
16+	88	71					73	79

Source: Howard D. Hamilton and Sylvan Cohen, *Policy Making by Plebiscite: School Referenda* (Lexington, Mass.: Lexington Books, D.C. Heath and Company. Copyright 1974, D.C. Heath and Company), p. 180. Reprinted by permission of the publisher.

behavior, and are therefore predictors of unusual power. Parental status and religious affiliation are also strong indicators; for example, parents and Protestants are much more likely supporters than non-parents and Roman Catholics.[9] Yet status accounts for much more of the differences between protagonists in school referenda.

Note that there is little evidence that voters actually see themselves in such status terms. Rather, each group sees itself and its opponents as groups motivated by self-interest. One study found that economic explanations permeated both sides. Proponents saw themselves as parents seeking to benefit their children, and the opponents (elderly, retirees, those on fixed income) sought to escape the economic bite of more taxes. The opposition, however, saw a different group context, although still economically motivated. They regarded themselves as homeowners and taxpayers (not opponents of children's welfare), while they felt the supporters (teachers and schoolpeople) were only seeking to improve their lot economically.[10]

Note that these studies of status and voting results rest on data from 1970 or before. Given the political turbulence of the 1970s in the schools, has anything changed in these relationships? A recent review found little change in such items as higher support for referenda among the younger, richer, and better educated voters. But there was evidence that people in professional and managerial occupations had become stronger supporters than those in other occupations.[11]

Influence of Ethnicity

Other factors confound the influence of status. Thus ethnicity has special importance in distinguishing among referenda voters; that is, within each income level, ethnic identity sorts out supporters and opponents. The scholarly revisionism of the 1960s found that alleged ethnic assimilation had not taken place. In Glazer and Moynihan's words, "The point about the melting pot is that it did not happen."[12] Thus in Chicago among the same status (low-income and middle-income voters), Irish and Polish voters were less supportive of a tax issue than Black voters were. Others noted the curious partnership of the poorest Black and wealthiest white precincts in giving high support for many school issues, including finances.[13]

The Blacks' main problem has been relatively low turnout in such elections, even though they support tax referenda more than urban whites do.[14] Explanation of voting behavior based solely on economics would have large numbers of the poorer Blacks turning out to support such referenda, for these measures tax others to provide Black children with greater educational resources. But clearly this is not the case when so few of this group turn out to vote. The political use of Black votes to secure control of urban school systems has been very little studied; Cleveland Blacks were capable of withholding their supporting votes from a school system slow to desegregate.[15] The use of votes by Black and Hispanic groups to control and direct the big-city schools needs more study in the 1980s, when they will increasingly constitute the majority in many urban districts.

It would be an error, however, to conceive of whites as a unified voting group. A survey designed to sort out the tie between ethnicity and referenda in the 1960s found quite different degrees of support among those of British versus European ancestry. Moreover, even when controlling for such powerful influences as status and parental type, this distinction did not disappear. In short, "Ethnicity was distinctly more potent than social class or parentage."[16]

Ethnicity may well have a distinct influence on referenda voting when the voting takes place in the absence of political parties. Indeed, the significance of ethnicity for referenda voting may actually arise from this very absence of party, for it is the party that, in other matters, provides cues to citizens on how to vote. In the absence of such cues, ethnicity may be employed by the voter instead, with one result being an increased social cleavage within districts. This is possible with school referenda, especially so as ethnic groups seem to differ on their views of the purposes of education.[17]

The Influence of Ideology

There are suggestions that in special school elections voters may develop and use a kind of ideology or ethos centered around the school as an institution in the society. Thus, ethnicity may be one of the ways by which people are socialized to a particular perception of the function and value of schooling. This approach was central to an effort by Banfield and Wilson to contrast two opposed sets of attitudes about government and public issues. One ethos ("public regarding") centered on an Anglo-Saxon Protestant group life, which emphasized belief in "the interest of the whole," public obligation, rule by the most qualified, and a government that is honest, impartial, and inefficient. The other ethos ("private regarding") was alleged to center on immigrant groups and on lower-class and working-class citizens. This latter group focused more on private interests of family and personal loyalties rather than the community at large, politics as an individual or family competition for advantage, or the party machine as the organization of governance in contrast to the nonpartisan governance of the first.[18]

While this overall concept has been strongly challenged, it has not been applied to school politics. Only Hamilton and Cohen tested it in school referenda attitude surveys. In a small Ohio town they found results that matched very well big-city studies that used ecological data. Here again is another focus for valuable research in the 1980s.

Another way of defining this private versus public orientation is found in how people vote their economic interests. Parents who have schoolchildren but voted against a school levy could be regarded as showing one sign of a private orientation. They may have decided that the cost of the levy was greater than what their children would gain, thereby ignoring any general (or public) commitment to the schools at large. Conversely, nonparents voting in favor of the levy could be seen as evidence of a public orientation; some such commitment to the community at large must explain why they agree to tax themselves. In several polls, these self-regarding and public-regarding types were found to be about equal in strength, each ranging from 15 to 25 percent of voters. But when other mixed types were thrown in, about half the voters were private-regarding and another one-quarter public-regarding. Clearly, self-interest looms large as a motivation for voting, but again other values can intervene.[19]

Influence of Attitudes Toward Schools

One of these intervening factors can be the voter's perceptions and sense of worth about educational institutions. There is evidence that the more one has children in schools and the greater the personal contact one has with school officials, the greater the credibility extended to schoolpeople. Parents with children in school but who lacked contact with school officials did not support a tax levy very much. In short, what the school system communicates to its public can generate support, and without this, potential supporters will fall away.[20]

Another perspective on schools that could influence the vote is a predisposition of voters to regard public expenditures as a "good thing" or to believe that government taxes are "bad things" by themselves, regardless of the particulars of the referendum in question. One study found these lines to be firmly drawn among substantial numbers of opposing voters. As the authors perceptively noted of these gross attitudes, "They . . . may be the principal devices used by voters for simplifying the problem, i.e., for coping with the information problem and reducing the decision-making burden."[21] But again there has been little research effort to trace such fixed constellations that voters use for steering the turbulent seas of school politics.

It may be difficult for advocates of public education to realize that there are voters with an engrained bias against supporting school finances. However, elections are channels for funneling many kinds of attitudes, and one with great relevance for schools is "alienation." This is the sense of being ignored by a society that is thought to be controlled by a conspiracy of persons quite different from one's self. Alienation has been found to be significant in referenda on fluoridation, metropolitan government reform, and open housing, so it should not be surprising to find it present among those voting against school referenda. We must not exaggerate the proportion of alienated people nor underestimate its role in defeating such measures. After all, if one believes there are no channels to the powerful or that they ignore one's wishes about public policy, the referendum device is well adapted to striking back at the "they" who are thought to run roughshod over "us." And striking back must mean a negative vote, as the only other alternative—voting yes—would please "them." Yet this attitude might be better understood as reinforcing other motives for opposition. Thus alienation and referenda opposition are correlated, but they are also inversely correlated with social status.[22]

This discussion of voter characteristics linked to turnout and support for school referenda points both to continuities and divergences. Scholars are clearly moving beyond the once-traditional research focus on only status correlates of districts or voters themselves. The fuzziness of the findings to date as well as the danger of "ecological fallacy"* require that future work should fasten on attitudinal and ideological maps of these voters. How voters see schools— obviously diverse perceptions—and how they feel about schools need to be related to basic predispositions about one's self, the political system, and society in general. We are far from any general knowledge about the *origins* of either these underlying or manifest attitudes and perceptions. Such knowledge would be particularly useful for school authorities trying to determine what their public will accept in taxes.

---

*Ecological fallacy is inferring the attitudes of individuals from gross demographic characteristics of the place where they live.

Knowledge of techniques of communicating and presenting educational programs to the public[23] are of little avail if they are not accompanied by an understanding of what voters feel and think about education in general.

WHAT DIFFERENCE DOES THE DISTRICT MAKE?

As figure 7.2 hinted, the generation and transmission of the public's views can be enhanced or inhibited by the distinctive characteristics of the district in which the action takes place. Sometimes termed "structural," these are attributes of the organizational life and community behavior of a locale. These attributes have been more studied because information on this aspect of school referenda is readily available.

Environmental Factors

The resources in a community, measured by census variables, have been regularly explored for their alleged effects on referenda results. Simple district size is not very predictive, however.[24] Rather it is the way that social life is influenced and structured inside the district that counts. The preceding chapter related how the community's structuring of the politics of board elections shaped numerous outcomes. That is, high-status suburbs do this differently than low-status suburbs do, suggestive of the self-regarding and public-regarding distinction noted above.[25] This situation represents the intersect of social, economic, and political factors. Partialling out these factors in twenty-two New York districts, figure 7.3 traces the effects of size, wealth, and employment upon operating expenditures. Not surprisingly it reveals that more of the first (size, etc.) is linked to more expenditures. Too, the relationship of expenditures to political mobilization (voter turnout) and political dissent (contested seats) is positively correlated with school budget election defeats. We see evidence here of the findings of Zeigler and Jennings in chapter 6 that there is greater politicization of school politics in metropolitan than in other districts.

Political Factors: Structures

Another structural factor of a district is the way in which it organizes school board selections and terms of office. The first edition of this book set out the qualities associated with successful referenda, as determined in a major study by Carter and Sutthoff during the

Figure 7.3

Social, Economic, and Political Linkages to Referenda Defeats,
New York Districts, 1965–1973

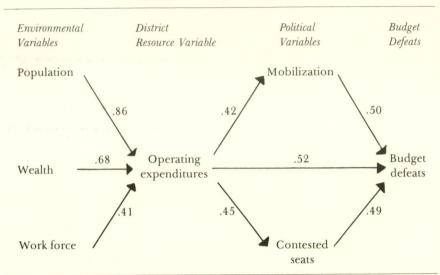

Source: Leigh Stelzer, "Public School Financing: A Theory of Popular Budget Decisions" (Paper delivered at Southwestern Political Science Association, 1974), p. 12.

1950s.[26] What was linked to success depended very much on whether it was a bond or a tax election under study; few structures were associated with success in both types, and none did so consistently. As this massive study was set in a much more tranquil era of school elections, even less association is likely to exist today between these structures and referenda outcomes. Indeed, pursuit of this possible linkage disappeared from the research field by the late 1970s.

What other district characteristics are relevant to election outcomes? Both earlier and more recent studies consistently find that a district's past record of success or failure is the best predictor of its present behavior. This finding implies that the divisions between school supporters and opponents—for whatever reasons— become institutionalized over time, including their stances on referenda. It is another matter, however, if that district's composition alters, as last chapter's discussion of the dissatisfaction theory of democracy set out. While figure 7.1 points to an overall shift in district voting on referenda, there must be some lag between this national trend and what happens in districts with records of either rarely or regularly passing referenda. Too, in recent years what is changing that is important is the size of the school-age cohort. As the baby boom passes through and out of the schools, the demand on educational resources that they represent expands and then shrinks. This reduction in demand in turn creates a larger cohort of parents without children in schools, hence a larger group inclined to "vote their pocketbook" and so oppose referenda. We will return to this consideration at the end of this book.

Political Factors: Strategy and Conflict

There are some overtly political qualities of districts that increasingly have been found to affect referenda. Although boards and administrators have long acted as if their efforts to mobilize referenda support were not political—in keeping with the traditional unitary myth of the profession[27]—this strategic repertoire can hardly be denied its political qualities. These have been set out in earlier textbooks for the fledgling superintendent, as well as by scholars urging the professional to use even more sophisticated techniques in analyzing the political process. If Democratic or Republican candidate for any office engaged in these techniques, we would instantly recognize the situation as typical voter mobilization, hence as being political. The fact that school professionals engage in the same act does not change its essential quality. This is not to deny the right of school authorities to employ such strategies. Rather, it is to suggest that school constituencies no longer accept a definition of such behavior as being nonpolitical, for often such constituencies are themselves deeply enmeshed in the politics of schools. Americans still today ask for the white or dark meat of a turkey dinner, using the same euphemisms that the Victorians of a century ago adopted in order to avoid offending tender sensibilities by speaking such words as "breast" and "leg." But, the meat is still the same, then and now.

We will not detail the strategic lore of winning school referenda; there is an enormous literature of anecdotes of this kind. But we do question whether much of that lore any longer applies to the current political situation and its turbulence. All of it rested on certain assumptions about the linkages between authorities and voters, that is, that this was low-visibility and low-conflict school politics. Little of the lore took into account the possibility that strategies would vary, given the differing social compositions of communities. But as Minar and Boyd have shown for the period when school politics was beginning to heat up, superintendents must adopt different "conflict management" styles in working-class and middle-class suburbs.[28] And, as shown in the preceding chapter, the size of the district (and the accompanying differences in heterogeneity) have major consequences for the political interaction of board and superintendent and for these authorities and the voters.

What is the value of traditional strategic lore when, as Cuban found, metropolitan superintendents were recently being replaced at a very high rate, for example, twenty-three of twenty-five in the early 1970s[29]; or when school officials in Youngstown, Ohio, in the late 1960s sought to pass a referendum seven times within a thirty-month period, including three within six months?[30] What is its value when curriculum dissidents dynamited the school's central offices in Kanawa County, West Virginia, in the early 1970s?

Care must be taken that the training of school authorities does not assume far too much about the steady-state nature of American communities, for what we have witnessed in the last two decades is a persistent conflictual community context. Coleman's classic essay on such conflict fully applies to school issues.[31] That is, school policy consists of a set of events that touch important aspects of the community and which citizens know they can do something about. The latter points to the importance of a referendum on a highly conflictual issue such as a school closing. What the referendum device does is provide an opportunity for direct inputs designed to reallocate the resources—and values—of the school's political system. In the process, conflict develops in a regular fashion. Thus the specific issue that starts the conflict develops into a general issue; new and different issues emerge from this, which in turn generate disagreements that escalate into hostility. These developments cause latent community cleavages—class, race, generations—that have little to do with the original referendum issue to surface. Then this in turn draws in groups usually uninvolved who are not really school supporters—for example, the alienated voter noted above.

All of this is an indication that referenda tell us much about the presence or absence of stress within a community. Comparative analysis of stress need not rely upon case studies detailing actors and actions. One rough macromeasure has been found in the size of voter turnout for referenda. Much evidence has shown that, traditionally, the greater the turnout the less chance of passage.[32] Yet evidence drawn from the more tumultuous 1970s suggests that this has become less certain. Increased turnout currently points to those groups noted above who are not usually school supporters or who are alienated entering into the decisional context.

A macromeasure that indicates community stress more directly is found in the relationship between the size of the tax or levy increase sought and the degree of voting support for it. The first edition of this book presented data on California tax elections in the late 1960s that substantiated this tie-in. Thus, of the referenda to *lower* the tax rate (N = 9), 78 percent passed; 97 percent of those also passed that sought the *same* rate (N = 79); but only 44 percent passed that sought an *increase* (N = 504). Too, as the size of the tax being sought increased, the proportion of successes fell off, from sixty cents or less tax increase (48 percent successful) to sixty-one to eighty cents (38 percent) to over eighty-one cents (33 percent).[33]

Probably the macromeasure most directly tapping community conflict over schools is the size of the vote supporting a referendum. When support is in the range of 45 to 55 percent, the district must be much more sharply divided over school policy than when support exceeds 55 percent. These marginal contests seem direct measures of high community cleavage, that stressful environment which, in Easton's concepts, the political system works to avoid or accommodate. By itself this analysis is insufficient to portray the complexities of such conflict, as Boyd's suburban studies demonstrate.[34] But it does permit generalizations in macrostudies of the American school mosaic, particularly in longitudinal research. Such measures allow differentiating districts based on their political qualities.

THE LOCAL CONVERSION PROCESS IN TRANSITION

This chapter has pointed to the dual interest in referenda—by the practitioner who must rely upon them in many states for continued sustenance and by the scholar of democratic politics. School officials are very unenthusiastic about the device, although they express little of that feeling publicly, but there is not evidence that it will be abolished any time soon.[35] Against the picture of public rejection of referenda presented here, we must not underestimate the influence of the professional. Whether due to skilled conflict management, wise anticipation of reactions, or convincing definitions of public policy, school authorities have traditionally kept disruptive public inputs to their system to a minimum. But recently, escalating conflict has threatened school authorities' control and the system's persistence. Low-key community relations used to be the norm, wherein the decisional forum withdrew somewhere into the crevices of the professionals' world, supporters both inside and outside the system were maintained and reinforced, and so on. Limited citizen control over schools was exceeded only occasionally by episodic events, but even these did not often go directly to major policy, focusing rather on peripheral and quite specific issues.

In this situation one sees much of both systems analysis and democratic theory in operation. As Minar concluded, "There is reason to believe that the reduction of public conflict is something of an ideal toward which school systems tend."[36] Here we see signs of system persistence, of coping with threatened stress by shaping the required referenda inputs, and of forestalling eruptive demands. All this is done to anticipate community demands. The result is an output reflecting both public and professional needs and wants.

We also see here the conflict of majoritarian and minoritarian values raised in an earlier chapter. Although the rhetoric of majority rule is strong in our school districts, the reality was actually minority decision making confirmed by referenda in all but a few communities. Much of this condition arose from the predominant influence of the school professionals who moved the system toward goals that they—and not often the community—defined. Board members' ties to the community were tenuous and ambiguous, while their control over the bureaucracy was limited and general. At best boards were adjudicators at the margins of school policy. When groups not satisfied with this minority control sought changes through official channels, they often found the professionals' control unassailable.

It is these conditions of system maintenance that students, ethnic members, parents, and teachers are currently attacking. Some permanent change by school authorities is likely in the face of these challenges; as we have noted, dissenters are presently finding some "give" in the structure. But it is highly unlikely that professional control will be abolished. The real, continuing authority to allocate school resources at the local level will remain where it has been since Americans entered into a covenant with school professionals that educational policy was not like other policies. The causes for system

maintenance are many, of course, but not least among them is the fact
that it is school professionals who oversee the administration of
policy—even if they do not always shape its origins—and hence they
can influence the outcome.

Yet the recent turbulence must have some effects on this traditional
system maintenance. Here we find the items listed in figure 7.2 under
Subsequent Policy Events. We have seen in the previous chapter how
there have been board and superintendent turnovers. We have noted
major policy changes of some persistence. Further, in the decline of
the total number of referenda offered, figure 7.1 shows the desperate
efforts of school authorities to anticipate the voters' zone of tolerance
in the 1970s. Too, the presence of increasingly institutionalized sets of
new actors at the local school level requires adaptation, and often new
training, in administrative roles.[37] There is some shift in training
administrators from an emphasis upon organizational theory as
explaining their decisional environment to an emphasis upon political
context.[38] Certainly the superintendent today needs to understand
much more than just the old notion of keeping the referenda campaign
low key in order to win. Partial theories of what goes on in voters'
minds in these elections abound: economic self-interest, status considerations, social distance attitudes, community ethos, influence and
persuasion channels, the newly politicized electorate, and so on.[39] The
professional needs to know much more about the politics of decision
making; and for this, one must grasp other political theories—
rational, incremental, implementation, and so on.[40]

Finally, whatever new role the professional adopts within this
current turbulence, he and she will have participated in the most
recent skirmish of our historic clash between participatory and meritocratic values. That clash reflects the ongoing tension between majoritarian and minoritarian impulses in a complex society, which we
discussed in chapter 4 on pressure groups. James Madison, Alexis de
Tocqueville, or Lord Bryce, brought back to life and observing the
events discussed in these last two chapters, would understand quite
well what they meant. They and many others grasped the basic,
underlying dynamic of American politics and policy making; that is,
the tension generated by a nation of diverse groups seeking to realize
their values through the subsystems of society, including the political.

In one slice of time, the meritocratic impulse may seem totally
dominant; pre-1960 writing about educational administration partakes much of this quality. More recently, though, one can see the

triumph of the participatory impulse in the success of new school constituencies. Somewhere between the two there may be long periods of accommodation to new and successful demands upon the educational policy system. Professionals in many areas have learned to adapt when compelled by such clientele pressures,[41] but the process does not end at any of these stages.

If the nature of school governance seems more unstructured today because of this flux of actors and events at the local level, the new forces generated outside the district are just as perturbing. What the state and national governments and allied interest groups have done is to become another new—often highly constricting—dimension of converting private needs into public policy at the local level of public schools. It is to the state influences that we next turn.

NOTES

1. On Progressivism and the quotation, see Eric F. Goldman, *Rendezvous with Destiny* (New York: Vintage Books, 1956), p. 338. For origins and results of direct legislation, see William Munro, ed., *The Initiative, Referendum and Recall* (New York: Macmillan, 1913), and Joseph G. LaPalombara and Charles B. Hagan, "Direct Legislation: An Appraisal and a Suggestion," *American Political Science Review* 45 (1951): 400–21.

2. Howard D. Hamilton and Sylvan H. Cohen, *Policy Making by Plebiscite: School Referenda* (Lexington, Mass.: Lexington Books, 1974), pp. 3–6.

3. Little was found for the 1960s in the figures reported in the first edition of this book, at chap. 17.

4. The Spearman rank coefficients are unusually high: percent approved by total and dollar value, rho = .988; total referenda and percent of total approved, rho = .899; and total referenda and percent approved by dollar value, rho = .821.

5. The volumes are Philip K. Piele and John S. Hall, *Budgets, Bonds, and Ballots* (Lexington, Mass.: Lexington Books, 1973) and Hamilton and Cohen, *Policy Making*.

6. For example, Michael Y. Nunnery and Ralph B. Kimbrough, *Politics, Power, Polls, and School Elections* (Berkeley: McCutchan, 1971).

7. Piele and Hall, *Budgets, Bonds, and Ballots*, provides the major review of this research.

8. *Phoenix* v. *Kolodziewski*, 399 U.S. 204 (1970).

9. Hamilton and Cohen, *Policy Making*, p. 213.

10. For this innovative conceptualization, see Hamilton and Cohen, *Policy Making*, pp. 197–202.

11. Philip K. Piele, "Voting Behavior in Local School Financial Referenda: An Update of Some Earlier Propositions," (Private manuscript, 1980).

12. Nathan Glazer and Daniel P. Moynihan, *Beyond the Melting Pot*, (Cambridge: MIT Press, 1963), p. 290.

13. James Q. Wilson and Edward C. Banfield, "Public Regardingness as a Value

Premise in Voting Behavior," *American Political Science Review* 58 (1964): 883; Piele and Hall, *Budgets, Bonds, and Ballots*, pp. 105–7.

14. For Detroit data to this effect, see first edition of this book at page 103. Piele's manuscript (see note 11 above) reported that no change had been found in Black support.

15. Louis Masotti, "Patterns of White and Nonwhite School Referenda Participation and Support: Cleveland, 1960–1964," in *Educating and Urban Population*, ed. Marilyn Gittel (Beverly Hills, Calif.: Sage, 1967), pp. 253, 255.

16. Hamilton and Cohen, *Policy Making*, pp. 207–8.

17. Gerald Pomper, "Ethnic and Group Voting in Nonpartisan Municipal Elections," *Public Opinion Quarterly* 30 (1966); J. Lieper Freeman, "Local Party Systems: Theoretical Considerations and a Case Analysis," *American Journal of Sociology* 64 (1958): 282–89. On ethnic attitudes toward schools, see Glazer and Moynihan, *Beyond the Melting Pot.*

18. Wilson and Banfield, "Public Regardingness."

19. Hamilton and Cohen, *Policy Making*, pp. 209–11; on economic motivations and status, see Piele and Hall, *Budgets, Bonds, and Ballots*, pp. 113–14, 143–46.

20. For example, Thomas A. McCain and Victor D. Wall, Jr., "A Communication Perspective of a School Bond Failure," *Education Administration Quarterly* 12, no. 2 (1974): 1–17; for a review of this aspect, see Piele and Hall, *Budgets, Bonds, and Ballots*, pp. 83–91, 130–34.

21. Hamilton and Cohen, *Policy Making*, p. 211.

22. See discussion of alienation research in Hamilton and Cohen, *Policy Making*, pp. 202–5, and Piele and Hall, *Budgets, Bonds, and Ballots*, pp. 128–30.

23. Nunnery and Kimbrough, *Politics, Power, Polls.*

24. Piele and Hall, *Budgets, Bonds, and Ballots*, p. 75.

25. David W. Minar, "The Community Basis of Conflict in School System Politics," *American Sociological Review* 31 (1966): 822–34; William L. Boyd, *Community Status and Conflict in Suburban School Politics* (Beverly Hills, Calif.: Sage, 1976).

26. Richard F. Carter and John Sutthoff, *Communities and Their Schools* (Stanford: Institute for Communication Research, 1960), chap. 4; these are summarized in the first edition of this book at page 99. See also Piele and Hall, *Budgets, Bonds, and Ballots*, pp. 75–77.

27. Robert H. Salisbury, "Schools and Politics in the Big City," *Harvard Educational Review* 37 (1967): 408–24.

28. Minar "Community Basis of Conflict"; Boyd, *Community Status and Conflict.*

29. Larry Cuban, *Urban School Chiefs Under Fire* (Chicago: University of Chicago Press, 1976), chap. 6.

30. For an account, see Hamilton and Cohen, *Policy Making*, pp. 164–67.

31. James S. Coleman, *Community Conflict* (Glencoe, Ill.: Free Press, 1957); for research using this framework, see Hamilton and Cohen, *Policy Making*, chap. 7, and Piele and Hall, *Budgets, Bonds, and Ballots*, chap 4.

32. Piele and Hall, *Budgets, Bonds, and Ballots*, chap. 4.

33. Calculated from the first edition of this book at page 105, table 6.6.

34. Boyd, *Community Status and Conflict.*

35. Hamilton and Cohen, *Policy Making*, pp. 271–73.

36. Minar, "Community Basis of Conflict," p. 825.

37. Cuban, *Urban School Chiefs Under Fire,* app. 2.

38. For a review of this shift, see Norman Boyan, "Follow the Leader: Commentary on Research in Educational Administration," *Educational Researcher* 12 (1981): 6–13. For an analysis of the recent contributions of social science to administrators' knowledge and training, see the essays in Glenn L. Immegart and William L. Boyd, eds., *Problem Finding in Educational Administration* (Lexington, Mass.: Heath, 1979), and Jack Culbertson et al., *Preparing Educational Leaders for the Seventies* (Columbus, Ohio: University Council for Educational Administration, 1969).

39. Piele and Hall, *Budgets, Bonds, and Ballots*, chap. 8.

40. Dale Mann, *Policy Decision-Making in Education* (New York: Teachers College Press, 1975); Paul E. Peterson, *School Politics Chicago Style* (Chicago: University of Chicago Press, 1976); and on the referendum, Hamilton and Cohen, *Policy Making*, chap 11.

41. Frederick M. Wirt, "Professionalism and Political Conflict: A Developmental Model," *Journal of Public Policy* 1 (1981): 61–93.

8

The State
Conversion Process

INTRODUCTION

Variety and Individualism

If variety is the spice of life, educational decision making in the fifty American states is a veritable spice cabinet. It is quite reminiscent of Kipling's aphorism that there are a thousand ways to worship God, and they are all correct. This variety is the key to understanding much about the basic value of individualism in the American system. We need not rely merely on assertions about this variety. Table 8.1 sets forth the patterns of selecting and staffing chief administrative positions for education in the fifty states. Not only are there differences between the state board and chief administrator in such matters, but also within either office. Moreover, the ranges are truly impressive. School board members may serve from three to fifteen years, although four to six are most common; the board size may consist of from three to twenty-four (Texas is the latter), although seven to nine is the norm; and the number of state employees ranges from 47 to 1706, averaging 350.

Such variety reflects a pluralism of views on how to express the taproot political value of individualism. That value has been reflected through a prism of diverse historical experiences (for example, the impact of losing versus winning the Civil War), different natural re-

Table 8.1
Variety in American State Education Organization, 1972

	State Board	Chief Administrator	State Department
Selection Methods			
Elected:			
Party label	8†	13	
No party label	4	6	
Other	3	–	
Governor appoints	32	5	
Ex officio	2	–	
State board appoints	–	26	
No such office	1	–	
	50	50	
Term of Office			
Five years or less	23	27	
Six to ten years	24	–	
Over ten years	2	–	
At other's pleasure	–	23	
	50	50	
Number of Board Members			
7 or less	14		
8–10	20		
Over 10	15		
	50		
Size of Staff			
Under 200			18
200–399			13
400–599			12
Over 600			7
			50

Source: Calculated from Roald Campbell and Tim Mazzoni, eds., *State Policy Making for the Public Schools* (Berkeley, McCutchan, 1976), tables IX 2, 4.
†Number of states.

sources (for example, the poverty of the South versus the richness of the Northeast), demographic mixes (rural homogeneity versus urban heterogeneity), and so on. Through this tangle of past and present, the creation of institutions had to take various forms. The very basis of democratic life—the political institutions of party, pressure group, and voting—took different forms from region to region as a result of these combinations of events, resources, and population.[1] We should not be surprised, therefore, that the evolution of educational institutions also took different forms. For one thing, ideas about how to organize and provide schooling were affected by varied historical experiences. As we will see, the New England states' violent opposition to George III instilled in them a fear of state-centralized services, including schools, which remains even today. Meanwhile, the southern states of the old Confederacy were so devastated by the Union troops' destruction of property that county institutions were wiped out. State control and moneys had to be provided in large amounts, then and ever since.

Even the precise meaning of something that all states agreed to in principle—compulsory schooling—was affected by this intervening individualism. Massachusetts was the first state requiring school attendance in 1852. By 1900, thirty-five states had so acted, but the last state, Mississippi, did not adopt such legislation until 1918.[2] In short, it took two-thirds of a century to institutionalize acceptance of an idea that had wide popular support. Even today, however, it is not clear what the meaning of this adoption is; differing political, economic, sociological, and organizational explanations can be provided.[3] Underlying this variety is a long-standing thirst for education. From its beginnings, schooling has been thought to serve major purposes. When it first emerged in the colonial period, education was religiously oriented to help the child "delude Satan." Later, education was designed to enable the young to live a better life, however defined. But then and now, education was a means of salvation, whether of the soul or one's economic future.

Exactly how the goal was to be achieved was never easily agreed upon. A century ago there was conflict over such school policies as establishing free public education, racial equity, popular control, moral purpose and financial support—just as there has been in our time. The continuity of issues is surprising.[4] This is because laypersons and professionals alike recognized that schools taught moral, political, and social lessons, and various groups differed on what they felt these lessons should be.

Professional Dominance and Recent Challenge

This atmosphere of conflict was diluted for many decades until after World War II. This dilution occurred because, as noted earlier, professionals were able to convince citizens that they alone possessed the scientifically based, value-free knowledge necessary to provide the "best" education. Such an apolitical myth was highly useful to school-people who could use it to fend politicians off their preserve. Professionals and their elected school boards consequently assumed the authority for making educational decisions relatively free from local and state officials, despite some lip service to democracy.[5] Beginning in the 1950s, however, this immunity from the participatory impulse of democracy crumbled under attacks from many constituencies.[6] Within the web of federalism, constituencies defeated by the professional structure on one level could turn to higher levels to compel changes in local resources, structures, and policy services. State and federal legislatures and courts echoed with demands as pressure groups mobilized into national coalitions. Rarely has the federal structure demonstrated its sensitivity to the multifaceted demands of the population so well as in this area.

In the process, the state took on a new and expanded role in education. As we shall see, the legislatures in particular became the center of such policy making, but administrative agencies also expanded their involvement in the daily work of local education authorities (LEA) in order to implement the new changes. Interventions took the forms of requiring minimum levels of service, mandating required services, rearranging tax and spending requirements, specifying new curricula, redefining the qualifications of the professionals, and so on. The analysis that follows sketches the patterns of these changes that have given the state role a new vigor in educational decision making. Much is still in flux, and the dust has not yet settled to reveal a clear picture of the state role. What is quite evident is that the state is everywhere much more active in school policy making and services—and in many other policy areas as well. As clearly, we see in this transformation a new adaptation of the way in which Americans work out the diverse meanings of individualism.

SOCIOECONOMIC DIMENSIONS OF VARIETY

Multiple Responses to Systematic Problems

Understanding a state's politics of education requires a grasp of its societal background. In the case of the fifty American states, such a demonstration quickly overloads the interest of even eager students in the field because of the varied and many dimensions for categorizing or evaluating units of government. The fifty states and their sixteen thousand LEAs vary along all the traditional dimensions of demography—age composition; size of school age population; parents' education, occupation, and income; economic resources; and so on in an almost endless list. Districts run from behemoth with a million students in New York City to a rural hamlet with a dozen in the graduating class. Their economics range from extremely wealthy suburbs to poor farm villages. Their resources vary just as much, from a multiple-building high school in a California suburb to a one-room schoolhouse on the Nebraska prairie.

This variety means that the total school system will adjust differentially to nationwide events that affect it. For example, a decreasing birthrate develops due to changes in contraceptive methods, new roles for women in the economy, more working married women in an inflationary economy, and new values about deferred child rearing. These factors combine to provide fewer children in the schools. Nationally, from 1969 to 1985, the enrollments in elementary school (grades K–6) will have dropped from 36.8 to 31.7 million and in secondary schools (grades 7–12) from 15.7 to 13.3 million. Yet the reactions of various school systems differ from place to place because some districts are growing, others are holding steady, and others are declining. The Southwest states are still growing, much as the rest of America was during the two decades after World War II. But in most states, the school districts of many large cities, rural areas, and even some of the older suburbs are being hit hard. Population decline causes districts to be consolidated under state law, with attendant local fury at losing conveniently placed schools. By 1980, most states were just beginning to face up to the ten-year decline in students that all states would soon know. There has been, however, no single reaction to this social phenomenon.

The Dimension of School Finances

School financing is another useful illustration of the variety of local implementation, for money plays such a large part in the American politics of education, as we will see. Schools have traditionally been heavily financed by local taxes, with the states providing only a small share, and the federal government the tiny remainder. That commonality aside, however, there has been almost total variation in school financing. A particular state's contribution has varied with its own resources, traditions, and values, as well as with the general intervening economic effects of wars and depressions. While the overall state share has increased between 1900 and 1981 from about 20 to 50 percent, variations among the states are huge. Thus in 1974, Hawaii, rooted in a royal tradition of centralism, provided 90 percent, while Nebraska provided only about 5 percent. Typically, in 1978, the state expenditure per pupil varied from $2,944 in New York to $1,347 in Arkansas, with the national average at $2,002.[7] This means an interstate differential in which an Arkansan child got only $1 of state money for schooling compared with $2.18 for a New Yorker. Characteristically, the poorer states are in the old Confederacy, a curious sign of the Civil War's effects lingering from a century ago. The wealthier states cluster among the industrial and small states of the East Coast and Great Lakes.

Though greater disparities exist among the LEAs within each state, there is still much stability in the ways states react to local needs.[8] Relatively rich and poor states remain very much the same over long periods of time; thus, the amounts of state aid or the patterns of other policies demonstrate little shift in these states' *relative* standings on such matters.[9] For example, from 1900 to 1966, state standings are highly correlated on such matters as the proportion of state support (rho = 0.60). In shorter periods, even higher stability is evinced; for example, average teacher salaries between the very dynamic years of 1963 and 1973 showed almost no shift in these states' rankings (rho = 0.90). (The reasons, other than the condition of each state's resources, will be explored later.) The pattern is both one of stability and variety among the American states. There is no socioeconomic dimension conceivable on which the states do not show much variation. Even the constitutional position of education in these states reveals this pluralism.

POLITICAL BACKGROUND

Education and Constitutionalism

The authority for public education in the United States does not stem from our national Constitution, but rather it is a "reserved" power remaining in the states.[10] This arises from the Tenth Amendment, which reserves to the states those powers neither expressly given the national government nor denied the state government. The national Constitution has never mentioned education, and until very recently, federal action for education has remained very limited.

If authority for public education is the state's, most have not exercised it directly until recent decades. The relative roles of state and local levels is expressed in the familiar saying, "Education is a state authority locally administered." That is, everywhere except Hawaii (where there is *no* local authority), the state constitutions expressly indicate that the LEA is, in law, an agent of the state. But for most of the last century states have used this authority only for setting broad goals and general guidelines for meeting those goals—and providing some moneys in support. In those decades, schooling was primarily in the hands of a huge number of LEAs (127,000 in 1931, now consolidated to about 16,000). Such initial decentralization has meant that schooling had a nature multifaceted beyond comprehension, reflecting a society that was also varied.

Then and now, LEAs govern different spans of education. Where once the rural township was common, covering all grades, we can now find districts that cover only elementary or only secondary schooling (or both), as well as separate vocational or special education schools (for gifted students or for mentally or physically handicapped students). Above these levels, the state's legal authority is vested in education committees of the legislature, the legislature as a whole, a chief state school officer, a state board of education, a state agency for higher education, a state department of education, and a governor. We will return shortly to examine their political roles in educational policy making. Add to this list the voters themselves, who in some states directly participate in policy making by use of referenda. Then there is often a quasi-official agency, the state university's school of education, which certifies the credentials of the professions by setting out course requirements (often fixed in the state constitution itself). The nineteenth-century reform wars, which removed the political party from school policy making, ended up enmeshed in peace treaties of state constitutions and laws. These schools of education thereafter ensured the victory by certifying the competence of the professional novitiate seeking entry.[11]

Growth in State Responsibilities

The shift in the state role has been drastic, and the rate of involvement has dramatically increased. In the original thirteen states' constitution, there was no mention of education. Today all states refer to education, sometimes briefly (Connecticut's schools rested on three paragraphs until well into this century) and sometimes at length (for example, Michigan's 1964 revision). State involvement started at the end of the last century, with school reforms that introduced more professionalism. The authorization of LEAs and limits on their taxing appeared everywhere at that time. Consolidation also emerged pervasively around World War I. By 1925, one-third of the states already had state supervision set out in detailed, minimum standards for such matters as local sites, buildings, lighting, heating, outdoor and indoor equipment (including even the size of a globe), academic and professional qualifications of teachers, length and kinds of courses, requirements for hygiene, and community relations programs.[12]

One significant example of this centralizing process is seen in the number of states requiring a university degree to teach. In 1900, no state required a degree for elementary teaching, and only two did so for secondary education. By 1920 the figures were still only zero and ten; but by 1940 they were ten and forty, and by 1965 all states required a degree for secondary and forty-five required it for elementary teaching. In 1969, a monumental survey of the state's role provided innumerable examples of this growth in state function.[13]

A brief but informative new presentation of the range and variety of state power is seen in table 8.2. Most states do certain things such as keeping records on pupils, for example, but only a few states do other things, such as guidance and counseling. A clearer picture of this variation emerges when we consider these differing policies as reflections of the "system maintenance" capacities of professions to assure control over the functions they deem most vital.[14] A later chapter will show that on such matters, all the states maintain very strong control.

In other words, the *potential* for state intervention in local schools, once remote but always possible, has today become a pervasive reality. This constitutional position does not, however, exhaust the political aspects of schools. We may now turn to more direct evidence of schools' political nature.

Increasing State Control over the LEA

Just as no political action takes place without different effects on different groups' values, policy making for education is contentious because some win and some lose. Recall that in chapter 1 we noted

Table 8.2
State-Mandated Education Policies, 1974

Policy	States	Policy	States
Pupil records	44	Teacher-pupil	
Teacher-pupil ratio	37	load standards	23
High school graduation		State-approved textbook	22
requirements	36	Pupil transport	21
Organization of		State-required curriculum	20
grade levels	33	Automatic teacher	
Salary schedules	32	tenure	19
Kindergarten	28	In-service training	18
Attendance agent	27	Extracurricular	
Safety/health	27	activities	15
High school book		Adult education in LEA	13
collection	26	School calendar	13
Guidance/counseling	26	Pupil promotion standard	7

Source: Abstracted from Lawyer's Committee for Civil Rights under Law, *A Study of State Legal Standards for the Provisions of Public Education* (Washington, D.C.: National Institute of Education, 1974), chap. 11.

that politics is not only conflict over the distribution of resources, but also and more basically it is conflict over the distribution of group values. This concept leads us to expect that the basic interactions among schools, the political system, and society are over who and what will be valued in the educational process. That is, schools are caught up in a competition for resources, status, and value satisfaction just like any other institution of our society. In previous chapters, we have seen the working of this concept in the *local* politics of education.

Central to this situation is the value of local control. It is this value that permits individualism to take the manifold forms so characteristic of American education. State control—constitutionally given—has worked in tension with this passion for local control.[15] State controls—summarized in table 8.2—take several forms: service minimums the LEA cannot fall below; encouragement of LEAs to exceed minimums (for example, by cost-sharing a new goal); organizational requirements; emphasis on efficiency methods, and so on. These controls assume that the state can provide equality better than the LEA through the standardization of instruction and resources. However, advocates of local control assert that greater payoffs will flow from a more flexible, hence more decentralized, system of schooling.

Thus, this state-local clash has been between two major values—equality versus freedom of choice (as discussed in chapter 4). More recently, states have introduced a third value—efficiency—by placing more controls over planning, budgeting, evaluation, and so on. The best assessment of this competition is that today equality and efficiency are more stressed by state action, and choice has been reduced. This is seen in the recent dramatic increase of state control in such areas as state administration of federal grants, state role in education finance, state requirements for accountability, state programs for children with special needs, and state efforts to stimulate experimentation.

An example from just one of these will demonstrate. "Accountability mandates" is a method of assuring parental influences and school responsibility for pupils' growth in achievement. Between 1966 and 1976, thirty-five states passed such laws, with fourteen adopting a comprehensive system. Some four thousand pieces of writing about this were published. Laws were enacted that dealt with budget format, teacher evaluation, curricula assessment to meet state standards, LEA objective setting, and minimum competency standards for high school graduation. In Florida

State assessment tests in certain subjects are publicized through school-based parent councils. Statewide tests are also used for high school graduation. Students must score in the 70th percentile statewide to obtain a diploma. Student test scores are related to teacher evaluations. School districts fear the adverse publicity that can come with publication of test scores lower than other districts.[16]

As this analyst concludes, "These various accountability techniques interact to enhance state control."

This capsule account highlights the point generally accepted by students of education, namely, that local control as a value and operational fact has declined to the vanishing point.[17] In this process, other values have gained prominence. If concern for equality could not be met by independent LEAs pursuing their separate ways, it was thought that state mandating of equal education programs backed by state resouces could do so. Reducing racially based educational inequalities beginning in the mid-1950s, restructuring fiscal relations in the late 1960s to reduce resource inequities, providing more for handicapped children in the mid-1970s—all involve state and federal governments writing the meaning of school equality. Then by 1980, concern over high taxes and heavy inflation had heightened interest in more efficient schools. Thus it is that the pursuit of equality and

Table 8.3

The Presence of Centralism-Localism Among the American States, 1970

	School Centralism by Regions	
Area	Mean SCS†	Number of States
All states	3.59	50
Northeast:	3.27	11
New England	3.00	6
Middle Atlantic	3.59	5
Southeast	3.87	12
Midwest:	3.52	12
Great Lakes	3.67	5
Plains	3.41	7
West:	3.65	15
Southwest	3.65	4
Mountain	3.16	5
Far West	3.79	4
Pacific	4.69	2

Source: Abstracted from Frederick M. Wirt, "School Policy Culture and State Decentralization" in Jay Scribner, ed., *The Politics of Education 1977* (Chicago: National Society for the Study of Education, 1977), pp. 164–87.

†The SCS ranges from 0.00 to 6.00, from low to high state control of the LEA. The score is derived from summarizing each state's laws on thirty-six school policies.

efficiency have overridden the longstanding concern for local choice in American education.

Interstate Variations in State Control

The picture is not one of entire state control, however, for states vary in this as in other matters. If we compute a state centralization score (SCS) using state education laws and cluster the fifty states by major historical regions, we find that important distinctions emerge. As table 8.3 shows, New England's history as the champion of localism appears as the lowest SCS, while the Southeast's old Confederacy appears with the highest SCS, reflecting the history sketched earlier. Other regions are usually mixtures, just as their population was mixed from both the Northeast and the Southeast a century ago. Similar signs of differing localism appear in table 8.4, where central-

Table 8.4
State Share of Local School Costs and Localism Culture

Culture Type	100–50 percent	49–30 percent	20–5 percent	Number of States
Highly centralized	12	4	–	16
Centralism dominant, localism present	3	8	4	15
Localism dominant, centralism present	3	7	4	14
Highly Localist	–	2	3	5
Number of states	18	21	11	50

Source: Calculated from Frederick M. Wirt, "Education Politics and Policy" in Herbert Jacob and Kenneth Vines, eds., *Politics in the American States: A Comparative Analysis* (Boston: Little, Brown, & Co., 1976), p. 322. The localist-centralism labeling is drawn from Daniel Elazar, *American Federalism: A View from the States,* 2d ed. (New York: Crowell, 1972), p. 202.

ized states have a larger state share of local costs, while the localist states have less state shares.[18]

The prime concern of localists is not opposition to better education but opposition to a greater state role in education. These New Englanders have on their side

300 years of tradition as well as the support and intensity of their own parochial mode of living. Occupied for the most part as farmers or as primary extractors of natural wealth, they are tied to fixed locations and bound by their own local preoccupations. Their legislative frame of reference begins—and all too often ends—with considerations of their own community's advantage. Since their rooted existence, if not their manner of enterprise, is akin to that of the 18th century, they can speak to modern legislatures with the hallowed tones of their forefathers, venerable and well-tested.[19]

Such values work themselves out into institutions and policies. In localist New England, school programs and budgets must be approved by meetings of an LEA's voters. The feared state is not permitted to pay much school costs. In 1966, before financial reform began, these states ranked quite low (27, 28, 30, 34, 46, and 47) in the state percentage paid of local costs.[20] Sometimes a state could itself be divided on localist-centralist lines. Arizona's southern half was once staunchly segregationist and the northern half less so, supposedly because of the influence of two different railroads, emanating from New Orleans and Chicago, respectively. Recently big cities have seen the state as the source of programs and funds needed for their many poor and minority children, but the suburbs and rural areas have been less positive about the state role because these are not their particular needs.

Conflicting Currents in the Gates of State Control

This section suggests that school policy making is an arena of competing values which produce different results within and among the states. Historically given values, including the role of state or local government, infuse institutions. The result of such institutionalization may be thought of as leaving a policy dam gate in each state: in one state the angle is regularly wide open; in another it is regularly narrow. Over time, political pressures to adopt new programs, reflecting new values, must work their way through differing angles of fifty-state educational policy systems. Some programs and funds get through more easily in some than in other states. As a result, comparison of the relative ranking of these states over time shows a high correlation, as the state institutions consistently let either a trickle or a torrent of state policy through.

By 1980, however, the size of this flow of money, whether from state or local sources, had overwhelmed citizens, generating new concerns over excessive expenditures and inadequate services in schools and other policy areas. This concern for efficiency led to a sudden nationwide movement for cutting taxes, expenditures, or both. Whereas eleven states refused to adopt such restraints in 1976, by 1978, twelve of sixteen states had adopted referenda measures to that effect.[21] A national poll found that 71 percent of the public did not believe they were getting good value for their money from their tax dollars. A network of interest groups, feeding on such widespread concern, moved the nation toward a national convention to adopt a constitutional amendment limiting federal expenditures or taxes. By 1981, thirty of the thirty-four state legislatures needed to call such a convention had taken this stand.

The New Role of Washington

The American federal government has had no direct constitutional responsibility in education, but since 1965 it has found ways to take on that role. Between 1862 and 1963, Congress considered federal aid to education thirty-six times but always rejected it. There were thirty-five federal laws prior to 1965 providing national resources in support of education, but rarely did funds go from Washington directly to the LEA's general budget. The Elementary and Secondary Act of 1965 (ESEA) changed all that; in the next ten years, thirty-eight new education laws appeared. By 1974, some fifty-two programs had been funded for about $6 billion, covering about 7 percent of all school costs.[22] Today then, about one out of every eleven dollars spent for American public schooling comes from Washington. This legislative effort was designed to cause LEAs to develop needed programs, yet the first broad-scope analysis of these results shows that the federal stimulus has been diffused—reform is adopted only if the local people welcome it.[23]

Federal funds coming into the states are affected by state political cultures. If Washington's money was tightly tied in amounts and objects of expenditures to a formula, the money got on target. But if it was given to states without clear objectives or subsequent oversight, the state legislatures used the federal money the way they did their own. A six-state study found such moneys going disproportionately to rural and suburban areas—which also had more votes in the state legislature—than to central cities where the biggest educational problems existed.[24] Thus state policy systems are not simply captives of Washington.

School desegregation has been a more publicized federal effort, which is developed more fully in chapter 11. This reform movement stemmed from the classic Supreme Court decision of *Brown* v. *Topeka Board of Education*. In the intervening twenty-five years since this case, this policy has followed a tortuous path. In the first ten years after *Brown*, nothing happened in the South where the greatest school segregation existed. In the next decade and after the 1964 Civil Rights Act and 1965 ESEA, federal courts consistently overturned all dual school systems resting on state law.

The courts also began to tackle the difficult problem of northern segregation rooted in privately segregated housing.[25] Much of the southern segregation had disappeared under strong federal pressures; where Washington was strong, segregation vanished.[26] But in the North, segregation has grown so that many central cities in metropolitan areas were mostly Black or Hispanic by 1979. Desegregating the entire metropolis was possible (Florida pioneered successfully),[27] but the Supreme Court drew a line at this remedy (*Milliken* v. *Bradley*, 1974).

In the traumatic policy change of desegregation, the states have played either a passive or negative roll. First, in the South the legislatures threw up a battery of statutes to obstruct the federal initiative; these techniques reached a nadir in Mississippi, which abolished compulsory school attendance in 1955. However, none of these obstructions was ever effective in court challenges. After the initial changes, southern state legislatures and governors, now representing new Black voters and more often persons with more enlightened views, helped ease the transition. Then-Governor Jimmy Carter of Georgia was one such political figure. Second, in the North only one state—Massachusetts—passed legislation forbidding segregation in schools, but its enforcement was ineffective. Elsewhere, states either did nothing or else continued to support legislation on zoning, land use, and building codes that excluded low-income residents (who were also often racial minorities) from areas outside the central city.[28] In this federal effort, we see once again that the state is not in thrall to Washington, although the latter can eventually compel compliance if it wishes to pay the price.

Summary

In looking at this political background we can see the patterns of cooperation and conflict that characterize federal systems. Control over American education has escalated from the local to the state level, but LEAs still have buffers against outside influences. The federal government now has powerful coercive influence on limited matters, but it also provides extensive financial and other support to state schooling policy. About 90 percent of the federal government's grants are with this state level; fewer federal ties exist with the LEAs, and these range from the popular school lunch grant program to the greatly resisted experimental schools program.[29] The former was earnestly sought by the LEAs, but the latter was not. This demonstrates that no matter how uncertain the constitutional basis of local control is, adherents of local control can still be effective in diluting outside mandates.

From the legal and political background it is possible to turn to a closer examination of how this politics is transformed into policy. In the next section, political agencies in state school policy making are reviewed to flesh out the picture outlined above.

STATE INTEREST GROUPS: BEFORE 1970

In political systems, policy making is always shared by formal and informal agencies. Formally, the legislatures, executives, bureaucracies, and courts have constitutionally given responsibilities. Informally, interest groups, political parties, communications media, and others exert pressures from within and outside the formal system. Of course, both sets are part of the "constitutional" system. In this and succeeding sections, these agencies of policy making are reviewed roughly in the sequence they appear in the policy process: lobbies, legislators, governors, bureaucrats. Whether phrased in the ancient *vox populi, vox Dei* or in contemporary "systems analysis" terms, democratic theory posits private groups seeking their interests in appeals to legislatures. The boundary between private and public has never been clear in life or in theory, so a useful point of departure for this section is the role of private pressure groups. There is a major difference between these groups' activities before and after 1970. We begin with the earlier evidence.

Classifying Lobby Types

Among the many factors that could influence a state's pressure matrix, major ones are variations in party competition, party cohesion in the legislature, and the socioeconomic context.[30] Two basic mixes of these factors are found among the American states. One pattern consists of strong lobbies, weak legislative parties, and a population that is low on urbanism, income, and industrialism. In the second pattern, lobbies are weak to moderate in influence, parties are competitive, and the economy is urban and industrial. In effect then:

> The long-assumed notion that pressure groups do not thrive in states with cohesive political parties has some validity, but in many cases peaceful coexistence and mutually beneficial agencies direct pressure away from the individual legislator and perhaps reduce the salience of pressure politics for the rank and file.[31]

What emerges from these two concepts is no single pressure pattern but rather four. The first is an *alliance of dominant groups*, much like the strong-lobby syndrome noted above; the southern states are a good example of this. Second, a *single dominant interest* pattern emerges in states with undiversified economies, two-party competition, and some legislative cohesion; the roles of a copper corporation in Montana or oil companies in Texas are illustrative.

Third, a pattern of *conflict between two dominant groups* is visible where a diversified economic base generates differences that the two-party system expresses: for example, auto manufacturers versus auto trade unions in Michigan. Fourth, a *triumph of many interests* appears where lobbies can freely interact in a legislature unbound by party control; thus in California, a highly diversified economy generates multiple interest and shifting legislative coalitions.[32] Clearly, lobbying over-represents the business and professional strata of society; about three in five registered state lobbyists act for corporations or trade groups.

However, the chief lobby for education has been the professional, particularly the teachers. Chapter 4 sketched this lobby's evolution in the National Education Association (NEA) as an umbrella organization for teachers, principals, superintendents, school board members, and others.[33] We also noted that, beginning in the 1950s, events led to a much more militant teacher movement, climaxing in successful collective bargaining drives in most states. This focus upon the interest of only one of its constituents—teachers—weakened the cohesion of the NEA, which came to take a more aggressive stance similar to its challenger, the American Federation of Teachers (AFT). As competition for shrinking financial resources grew in the 1970s, the unitary myth, which once bound different kinds of professionals, was split apart. No longer did teacher and administrator believe they shared a unity in the goal of educating the young.

In contemporary school lobbying in the legislature, we must once again resort to diverse models of action. Iannaccone's very influential typology of school lobbies may be used profitably here.[34] He conceptualizes the linkages between the lobbies and the legislature as taking four possible forms.

The *locally based disparate* linkage emphasizes local schoolpeople making contact with their state legislators; local legislators and professionals are the major interactors. Second, the *statewide monolithic* coalitions can form among state-level school interests who then speak with one voice to the legislature; here, interinterest differences are resolved before proposals are put to the lawmakers. Third, in the *statewide fragment* type, the state interests fail to unify, and so they press their individual needs upon the legislature. Finally, the *statewide syndical* coalition is institutionalized directly in a government body, which resolves group interests before presenting them to the lawmakers.

The attributes of these types are sketched in table 8.5. In each, the style of politics varies, as do the lobby's power to prevent or initiate

Table 8.5

A Typology of State Education Interest Groups

Attributes	Local Disparate	Statewide Monolithic	Statewide Fragmented	Statewide Syndical
Elite types	Squirearchy	Oligarchy	Polyarchy	Synarchy
Political styles	Entrepreneurial	Cooptational	Competitive	Coalitional
Lobby power:				
Prevention	Yes	Yes	Yes and no	Yes
Initiation	No	Yes	Yes and no	Yes
Legislator sentiment	Warm, paternal to teachers	Warm, undifferentiated	Differentiated: critical of administrators, warm to teachers	Warm, not critical
Focus of interest accommodation	Legislature	Apex of the monolith	Legislature	The group of syndics
Information:				
Quantity	Small	Large	Very large	Large
Nature	Unscientific	Precise, predictable	Scientific, but not predictable	Precise and predictable
Control	Personal	Monopolistic	Competitive	Monopolistic

Source: Abstracted from Laurence Iannaccone, *Politics in Education* (New York: Center for Applied Research in Education, 1967), chap. 3.

legislation, the legislators' reactions, the focus of adjusting interest group conflicts, and the qualities of information available to these groups. Moreover, Iannaccone saw these types as part of a developmental model. That is, (a) school lobbies began as locally based disparate, then (b) evolved into statewide monoliths as professionals saw their common interests, but then (c) altered into statewide fragments when their conflicting interests grew in importance, and finally, (d) statewide syndicalism could emerge if lawmakers tired of this conflict.

Changes in Lobby Types

What types best describe that which exists in the fifty states? In research up to the mid-1960s, Iannaccone found that the statewide monolith was most prevalent. But a decade later, a study of twelve states' politics of education reported a major shift to the statewide fragmented type in nine of these states.[35] These were the more northern industrialized systems, which shared a common history of a collapse of the old NEA umbrella that once overlay the statewide monolith. Coalitions of schoolpeople had once written education law in their private councils and then issued an agreed proposal to the legislature, which then usually went along because education was hard to be against and would reap the legislators little reward in any case. But in a few decades this pattern had been broken by growing conflicts of interests between teachers and administrators or between professionals and lay school boards.

What the twelve-state study revealed, moreover, was a system more complex than even Iannaccone's typology suggested. Added complexity came from those centrifugal forces that were making school policy systems everywhere more pluralistic and open. Indeed, the nature of the policy process seemed to vary with the issue in focus. The openness the study found was a major shift from earlier decades when professionals kept policy making a closed shop.[36]

When school lobbies sought success in the legislature, what were their resources and strategies? They possessed numbers and money (teachers) and high status (administrators and school boards). They transformed these resources into power by different means. All used professional staffs, but teachers relied more on their campaign money and votes, while administrators and school boards relied more on their information resources and local legislator contacts. Unlike the other two, teachers were much more likely to campaign, transforming their prime resource of size directly into votes. This activity marks a sharp break with the traditional apolitical stance of teachers.

As a result of such uses of power, school lobbies came to be viewed by their own leaders and legislators as among the most powerful pressure groups in the state. Legislators gave highest marks to the teacher associations, while administrators received the worst. They found teacher associations generally the more effective of the school lobbies and administrators the more efficient (obtaining the most for their fewer numbers and less money); the smaller teacher federations inconsistent; labor-management relations the dominant issue of such politics; and former school coalitions increasingly crippled by splits over this issue. So long as schooling issues were regarded as "educational," school boards and administrators were more influential because they could rely on their higher status to be heard. But when teacher groups changed the criteria for deciding issues to the "political," the teachers benefited from their greater numbers and money. Very likely they will continue to grow in power.

The pressure group matrix that emerges from this research, then, is one of open access, multiple participants and shifting coalitions of school groups. We should also find that the transition from a statewide monolithic to a statewide fragmented system enhances the role of the state legislature.

STATE INTEREST GROUPS: POST 1970

Within the last fifteen years, state policy initiatives have transformed somnolent state legislative committees into beleaguered arbiters armed with competent professional staffs. In addition, public education's fall from grace has generated an awesome volume of reform proposals of both the "quick fix" and cheap (PPBS*) and the comprehensive and expensive (bilingual education) varieties. In order to winnow the plausible from the preposterous, state legislative staffs have had to develop programmatic expertise as well. Today the state legislature is increasingly inclined to exercise its prerogatives to oversee all the state educational matters listed in table 8.2. The increased specialization in such matters has also made it much harder for interest groups to get anything through the legislature.

* Program planning budgeting system.

Interest Groups and Enrollment Decline

Public education is in most, if not all, states the largest single budget item. Current trends in school finance reform, inadequate local property-tax-based revenue, and the extensive federal education funds that flow through the states increase the influence of state governments in educational politics. The states have responded to these conditions with enhanced legislative involvement and expanded professional staffs in both the legislative and executive branches.

No longer can unified educational interest groups count on the docile accession to their demands they once could. For example, the school boards realized that the costs of maintaining unity would exceed the benefits to be gained from a more independent and skeptical state government. Accordingly, they splintered. In addition to the old-line groups who were flourishing on their own in this period of plenty for education, federal and state categorical programs inspired the proliferation of new single-focus interest groups. It became truly a time for the "triumph of many interests" noted earlier.

In at least one state, Illinois, the highly conflictual splintering of educational interest groups generated such an array of competing demands that the state felt compelled to resurrect the old monolithic structure in a new guise. The Illinois School Problems Commission— a formal body composed of the primary educational interests and state executive and legislative officials—embodied Iannaccone's state-wide syndical model. It achieved internal consensus, thus freeing the legislature from the debilitating task of arbitrating conflicts, but it generated other internal divisions and so by the mid-1970s broke apart.

Iannaccone articulated his developmental construct in the midst of an education boom in this country. His implicit prediction, that movement by many states toward the syndical type would continue, has not been fulfilled. There are two possible explanations for this. Either he and his predecessors had not anticipated the effects of educational decline, or they did not attempt to benefit from political theory. Unfortunately, his followers have not done so with any determination either. We will review their efforts after considering how educational decline may have rendered these constructs obsolete.

The phrase *educational decline* covers several trends. Often, dramatic decreases in enrollment are exacerbated by dwindling public confidence in the schools. Decline has also been compounded by the drastic upsets inherent in school finance reform. A major trade-off of the reform mandates has been increased state assumption of educational funding in order to redistribute resources. Local property tax bases, which prompt local board rejections and statewide taxpayer revolts such as Proposition 13, ensure further state assumption of authority. What do these factors mean along with the simultaneous intervention of federal and state courts and agency mandates to meet the needs of the disadvantaged for state educational interest group structures?

It seems clear that contemporary conditions surpass Iannaccone's framework. He and later analysts, such as Usdan, did not account for increased state assumption and the proliferation of special focus groups.[37] The former trend enhances the utility of cooperation by school boards and teacher unions at the state level. The latter militates against it because there are so many more groups to unify. The fragmentation model of interest groups in table 8.5 is counterproductive to efforts to augment state general aid, while the locally based model is clearly anachronistic. Moreover, the monolith model is irretrievable due to deep-seated labor-management conflicts and general aid versus categorical program conflicts; and the syndical model appears as a transient aberration during the 1960s in Illinois, unattainable elsewhere. To be sure, we are indebted to Iannaccone for compelling students to think more systematically about a dynamic and complex phenomenon, but it is necessary to update this conception of state educational politics.

The State Educational Interest Groups

Our review of Iannaccone's developmental construct suggested the gradual diminution of the authority of state education lobbies. However, Kirst and Sommers provide an alternative conceptual tool for differentiating among these lobbies,[38] dividing them into "general focus" and "special focus" groups. The former, typified by teacher, administrator, and school board organizations, are broad based and must, therefore, represent the full spectrum of educational interests. Given their size and resources, they are often assumed "to have more political clout than they actually have." Their resources are scattered over a wide range of issues and political levels, being differentially knit associations of locally based organizations. In spite of formal operating procedures and often sophisticated state leadership, power is essentially decentralized. They are "characterized by a strong 'bottom-up' flow of power wherein there is a continuous and taxing necessity of building coalitions among significantly autonomous locals." This is especially true of the management associations, whose independent-minded membership is reluctant to cede authority to state executives. Consistent with Olson's interest group theory of collective action, discussed in chapter 4, the costs of organizing large-member groups are high, and group cohesion around specific policy goals is low.

In contrast, the small-member group with a single "special focus" finds it easier to reach optimal effectiveness and outmaneuver the larger associations. The special focus groups can be divided into two kinds. One is the functional, such as those representing special education, and the other is the geographic, such as the big-city school district. Because of their narrow interests and concentrated power bases, these organizations are becoming increasingly influential in state politics.

The functional generally concentrates primarily on the source of its special funding, which for many categorical programs is the federal level, and then on the state administrative unit that dispenses the funds. A typical arrangement of a few governmental officials develops, as most state policy actors never enter the narrow realm of the special interest. Thus, in Michigan, the directors of the respective special and compensatory education units within the state department were reported to be among the most powerful individuals in state educational politics. They are able to mobilize the highly motivated and frequently volatile constituents and practitioners who support the causes of handicapped and compensatory education.[39]

In fact, these interest groups or significant individuals within them often serve as part of the formal governing apparatus for their programs, such as the Title I ESEA Advisory Committee. A specialized version of Iannaccone's syndical arrangement, this overlap between special interest advocacy and formal function constitutes the "institutional interest group." These are entities that perform formal political or social functions while simultaneously pursuing their own interests.

The highly effective geographically based special interests are even better embodiments of the institutional interest group. School districts in a given locale form natural alliances with other local and state government agencies, and they employ groups to augment their gains in the allocation process. Their greatest resource is their direct link to their legislative delegations, which in the case of a large city such as New York, Chicago, or Los Angeles can have enormous influence. With these descriptive concepts in mind, we can now delineate individual groups beginning with the broadly based interests.

The State Teachers Association. Teachers affiliated with the NEA remain a strong, if not the strongest, group in most states. Although weakened by the growth of the rival AFT and expulsion of school administrators, the local associations maintain a tremendous resource advantage over other groups. Because of sheer numbers, the money from dues used for political action, and their sophisticated staffing, they remain, according to one analysis, "giants by comparison."[40]

This glowing assessment of the associations' influence must be tempered by the fact that power cannot be measured by a simple aggregation of membership, money, and information. Internal cohesion is also crucial to effective mobilization of those resources. For example, Michigan Education Association (MEA), although far superior in numerical terms to many others, is so internally divided over local political strategies that it is unable to muster much influence at the state level. MEA's power is therefore more apparent than real; local rivalry with the AFT has certainly contributed to this ineffectiveness.

The State Teachers Federation. Although growing rapidly in most urban areas, the AFT affiliates have a tendency to bypass state level lobbying in favor of local militancy. However, this underdeveloped and inconsistent state influence does not apply in California. There, the federation's strong labor stances in the 1970s have compelled rival NEA locals to take more militant postures; the latter no longer characterizes itself as a purely professional association. Between 1965 and the late seventies the proportion of teachers in the AFT versus the NEA remained stable. NEA controls teachers in 87 percent of the LEAs of students over 1,000; the AFT controls 13 percent.

Classified School Employees Associations. The nonprofessionals who work in schools are usually ignored by commentators of state educational interest groups. That neglect can be explained by their relatively recent emergence in state politics and by their lack of a substantive focus. They are labor unions whose sole objective is the protection of their membership's financial interests. Classified employees include custodians, secretaries, and food service personnel. Until the recent jump in state authority, these people have been able to rely on local collective bargaining strength. Their sheer numbers and financial resources give them considerable potential clout at the state level; thus they became a factor in school finance policy making.

The State School Board Association. Members of the State School Boards Association find themselves pitted against the teachers in an effort to hold the lid on salaries. Increasingly in the 1970s, local school boards, confronted with the politically, economically, and legally complex realities of collective bargaining, came to rely in varying degrees upon the information and expertise that the state association could muster. At the state level, school board groups are viewed by policy makers as deserving of respect and empathy because they represent locally elected officials who, in turn, unselfishly represent the interest of the public.[41] This status and prima facie credibility is augmented by small but generally efficient lobbying staffs funded with the highest membership dues of all the education groups.

The State School Administrators Association. School administrators often try to be "a bridge over troubled waters" for school principals, business officials, superintendents, personnel managers, and other administrators. Once firmly entrenched at the peak of most state teachers associations, the administrators became exiled by teacher militancy, and administrator groups now find themselves allied with the school board groups in order to provide some semblance of balance vis-à-vis the teachers. Legislators accord administrator groups respect as representatives of educational leadership in their districts. In fact, face-to-face contact with legislators in their home districts is a prevalent political strategy. This is reversion, born of necessity, to tradition— locally based, disparate, interest-group politics. However, this predilection for going it alone can hamper the group's lobbying efforts. The administrators pay high dues, second only to the school board's, and maintain an effective lobbying staff.

Other Groups. In addition, there are categorical interests and associations of geographically based groups too numerous to mention. As noted in Duane and Bridgeland's discussion of the special focus groups, they can be powerful players in state educational politics. They have their champions in the legislatures, either individual members with pet interests or constituency links or, in the case of programs for the disadvantaged, Black and Chicano caucuses. Their bureaucratic home bases have a vested interest in sustaining and adding to the programs, and they often have recourse to the threat of judicial intervention. In short, many special-focus groups have clout disproportionate to their numbers.

The PTA. Associations representing nonprofessional or lay persons interested in education, while locally oriented, have both state and national organizations. The National Congress of Parents and Teachers is not only the largest of these groups but also the largest volunteer organization in the United States. Its strength is felt primarily at the local level where it actively pursues solutions to specific problems at specific schools. At the state level, its influence diminishes due to the heterogeneity of its membership and the lack of any method for maintaining internal discipline.

Labeled "good government groups," the PTA and its allies, the League of Women Voters (LWV) and the American Association of University Women (AAUW), are occasionally granted formal representation on advisory committees and asked to join educational coalitions. They generally restrict themselves to monitoring policy developments and provide lay support for the professionals' recommendations. The professionals who gain the most from PTA activism are the administrators. Others tend to regard them as useful friends when they agree but a not very bothersome enemy in the event of conflict. As we saw in chapter 4, though, many participants obtain psychological rewards from their involvement.

The LWV and AAUW exist to promote much broader social improvements. State branches may have a specialist in education, but they tend not to posit controversial views, preferring to provide general support for public education as an ongoing social good.

Lobbying Strategies

Whatever their type, groups are more than just structures of interests. They appear most clearly as dynamic parts of the policy process, from the emergence of issues through implementation and evaluation. We can grasp this dynamic quality in case studies of single-issue conflicts, such as that over the MACOS textbook, but little systematic knowledge emerges from this kind of understanding. We can portray the interaction more fully by focusing upon the lobbying strategies used by education interest groups.

Both personal experience and research suggest that lobbying strategies in the states parallel those at the national level. Partisanship is risky in competitive two-party situations except where party identification of interests is a foregone conclusion. Thus, management and labor tend to support the Republican and Democratic parties respectively. Timely campaign contributions sprinkled across party lines, however, is an effective means of obtaining access and occasionally of influencing a vote. However, individual lawmakers do not want to become obligated or "owned" over the long haul. In the aggregate, campaign contributions are of much lower volume in state politics than at the national level, "although a little money goes a longer way at the state level."[42] Contributions of volunteers and endorsements in association newsletters are also popular tactics, especially in large membership labor groups. In heavily unionized states, the labor organizations can take on the entire job of running a campaign. The mass public relations pressure tactic, more prevalent in national politics, is usually too expensive and too complicated for state education interest groups.

Direct contact with state legislators is easier, cheaper, and still more effective. So most education lobbying strategies are fundamentally low key; they emphasize expertise, professionalism, and honesty. Lobbyists prefer to work within the conventional mode; they are, after all, represenatives of the dominant social interests and have a corresponding commitment to the maintenance of the status quo. If the moderate approach does not work in a particular instance, contributions of money and election workers to specific legislators may help. Another step often adopted before "all-out-war" is cooperative lobbying and coalition building.

State Coalition Concepts

In large part, politics is fashioning coalitions of influence in an attempt to determine what values will be authoritatively implemented by government. Different individuals and groups bring different interests and objectives to state educational policy forums. Amid this tangle, an essential quality of a state education leader is to build political coalitions.

The coalition perspective on state decision making envisions any decision as possible if there is enough support for it among interest groups. In order to secure support, various trade-offs are undertaken. Policy proposals are modified to include (or exclude) items of concern to key potential supporters; agreements are made to trade support on other or future state policies for support on a current issue; third parties are encouraged to intervene. In short, coalitions are formed by horse trading until an acceptable policy is hammered out.

Riker has developed several theories on coalitions that can be validated in state education lobbying.[43] He contends that the growth of coalitions depends on the ability of leaders to attract followers by offering "side payments." These include anything that has value for possible coalition members, including money or promises on policy. Sometimes coalition leaders have a stock of side payments in their hands as working capital when they begin negotiations. As they dispense promises they use this capital, which presumably will be replenished from the future gains of a winning coalition. More typically, in our judgment, education leaders operate on credit; that is, they promise rewards with the understanding that they will honor their promises only if they are successful.

Leaders and followers are differentiated according to whether they offer or receive side payments. A leader rarely has enough resources to pay everybody. Moreover, excess members of a winning coalition cost something to acquire, and they lessen the gains. Therefore, at some point in the process of making side payments, the leader decides that all has been paid out that is worth winning; but as some factions are still left out, the attempts to form a coalition generate opposition that could result in an opposition coalition.

Riker enumerated various kinds of side payments, which can be illustrated from education lobbying.

1. *The threat of reprisal.* This side payment consists of a promise not to carry out the threat, and the follower simply gains escape from prospective misfortune. For example, a governor can threaten to campaign against an elected state superintendent of schools.

2. *Payment of objects that can be converted to money.* One example is appointment of a major financial backer of a key legislator to a position in the state education department.

3. *Promises on policy.* A leader accepts an amendment to his or her bill that brings the support of the state teachers' association but modifies the policy thrust of the bill.

4. *Promises about subsequent decisions.* For example, the Speaker of the Assembly can promise to support an agricultural bill if rural interests will vote for an income tax dedicated to education.

5. *Payments of emotional satisfaction.* Some legislators, for example, will follow the educational decisions of a charismatic governor.

These strategies involve subtle considerations by lobbyists, for the possibilities in any single policy conflict are numerous. The ways these considerations can be combined in practice are particularly complex. Such analysis requires making judgments and answering strategic questions.

Is there a winning coalition? Is the goal to be achieved by a winning coalition unique? Is anything (for example, a particular legislative provision) clearly excluded? Would the possibilities (for example, more school finance reform) be changed by expanding the coalition slightly? It follows that in some situations there are several potentially winning coalitions. Consequently, there is a role for leadership in constructing a particular coalition and thereby limiting the policy options and goals. It is this matrix of lobbies with which the state legislatures are faced.

State Legislatures

With exceptions, the following characterizes American state legislatures:[44]

1. Primarily political, not value-free, institutions.
2. Recently subject to more demands.
3. Recently taking on a more professional caste, for example, more and better staff.
4. Better apportioned as a result of Supreme Court actions that resulted in an increased voice for urban and suburban interests, an advantage to Democrats, and more responsiveness to new needs.
5. Often recruited to office by policial parties, but the turnover rate high and the influence of the party upon legislative votes varying widely with state tradition.
6. Electoral competition for seats limited.
7. The general public evaluating them negatively (mostly for wasting time), but they are very responsive ("conguent") to public wishes on controversial issues.
8. Some policies innovative (usually controversial), but many are incremental (for example, budgets).
9. Subject to influence from external and internal sources (committees, caucuses, governors, lobbies, experts, and so on), but the comparative effects of these sources have not been studied.

10. Pressure groups everywhere influential, but one group's influ-
    ence varies from state to state (most often mentioned: trade
    unions, teachers, manufacturers, farmers, truckers, and utilities).

Observers agree that the legislative role in school policy making
has changed recently. Education was once of limited interest to
legislators, but they have recently taken a strong hand in finance
reform and minimum competence testing.[45] In particular, lawmakers
are now more involved in the distribution of state revenue, both its
proportion and its uses. The reasons for this change reflect other
changes.[46] That is, because legislatures are now more representative
and better staffed, groups can turn to a body ready and willing to act;
as their sessions became longer, they were readier longer. Legislatures
are also developing closer ties with other state school agencies,
exchanging ideas about program possibilities.

Explanation of the legislature's role in school policy making is
confounded by three vigorous research traditions.[47] The *institutional*
approach (the oldest) focuses upon the internal structure of the
legislature. The *process* approach examines the dynamic interaction
between its structure and its outside environment, for example,
correlations among environmental characteristics of states, their policies, and legislative votes. The *behavioral* approach (the most recent)
explores legislators' interactions within the body itself. As a consequence of these different approaches, what is known is much like the
four blind persons who described an elephant in terms of the particular part each touched. However, great variation in both stable and
dynamic elements are found in legislatures from state to state.

American Governors

Head of state and of party, the American governor has had to
weave these two roles together to be effective.[48] But the recent increase
in demands upon all states has brought this office under greater cross-
pressures. Service demands continue to increase, but so do demands
to cut taxes that would pay for the services. The social welfare needs of
the central cities are countered by suburban and nonmetropolitan
legislators who are less responsive to those needs. Most observers
would agree that beneath the federal level, the governor is the most
important agent in American policy making. This fact emerges in
many individual studies of policy making, even though it runs counter

Table 8.6
Index of Governors' Involvement in Education Policy Making in Twelve States

	Number of States at Each Stage:			
Involvement Index	Issue Definition	Proposal Formulation	Support Mobilization	Decision Enactment
Low 1	2	3	1	5
2	2	2	4	1
3	1	–	2	–
4	1	4	4	3
High 5	6	3	1	3
Average score	3.6	3.2	3.0	2.8

Source: Calculated from Edward Hines, "Governors and Educational Policy Making," in Roald Campbell and Tim Mazzoni, eds., State Policy Making for the Public Schools: A Comparative Analysis, (Berkeley: McCutchan, 1976), p. 166.

to recent macrolevel analyses that stress the primacy of the state's environment (especially economic factors) rather than the political context in determining state policies.[49]

What is the significance of the governor for education policy? The limited research of this role prior to the 1970s generally found it minimal, "most often nonexistent, and when it does exist it appears sporadically, reflecting the idiosyncratic character of particular governors and/or educational crises in specific states."[50] When the first truly comparative analysis of this figure appeared in the early 1970s, it found a much wider range of behavior.[51] Table 8.6 summarizes the results from twelve states; the governor's influence varies across the states and across the stages of policy making. As policy making progresses, the governor's influence declines. Governors do their most in defining educational issues preparatory to their authorization and their least in having a decisive effect upon policy enactment. But again, the spread is in the usual American style—a wide range of possibilities.

The source for table 8.6 shows that strong gubernatorial leadership emerges in particular kinds of states. These are the larger industrialized states with very effective legislatures and a moralistic political culture that emphasizes policy reform. The governor is most likely involved and powerful in certain issues, particularly where there is a traditional policy climate of supporting education by creating much revenue—Wisconsin, Minnesota, Michigan, New York, and California.[52] The weaker governors appear in different policy cultures—Nebraska, Massachusetts, Colorado, and Georgia.

Further, this office is becoming more politicized over educational policy, as with other agencies of government. In 1970, three of four governors focused on education in their campaigns. Their particular interest was in school finance, some favoring contracting and some expanding it. This is a clear sign of the new pressures for more state aid to schools and the counter pressure against too high taxes discussed earlier. Even traditionally weak governors had initiated or vetoed such policies in 1972–73, and all had expanded their staffs of education experts.

Some governors led in expanding finances and improving schooling quality, for example, Nelson Rockefeller (New York), Edmund (Pat) Brown (California), and John Gilligan (Ohio). Some, caught between school finance retrenchers and expansionists, sought refuge by passing the issue elsewhere. They gave it to voters in statewide referenda, to study commissions that could defer action, or to courts (in New Jersey in 1974 the governor asked a federal judge to devise a more equitable school tax).

Like interest groups and legislatures, the governor's office fails to provide regular leadership for the development of educational policy in the American states. Some do so, of course, but episodically and only on limited issues. Like Sherlock Holmes's nonbarking dog, the systemic importance of this office is that it does not consistently do the expected.

THE IMPLEMENTORS OF STATE SCHOOL POLICY

The initiation and authorization of major school policy do not complete the policy process, for laws are not self-executing. The implementation state in state school policy involves three agencies: state school board (SBE), chief state school officer (CSSO), and state education agency (SEA). The diversity of these authorities has already been suggested in table 8.1, so again our focus is upon patterns of behavior.[53]

The State Board of Education and Chief State School Officer

School policy implementation has been spread among three agencies, with the SBE and CSSO responsible for oversight and innovation and the SEA for daily administration. The linkage between the SBE and CSSO is complex because their methods of appointment and authority are so diverse. They may be independent (elected, appointed, or a mix) or the SBE may choose the CSSO. Some SBEs only issue regulations, while others have operating responsibilities (vocational schools, state colleges, or universities). Rarely, however, are such broad responsibilities unified in a single office (except the New York Board of Regents).[54]

SBEs are usually appointed by the governor and the CSSO by the SBE, but the linkage is not ministerial. The selection methods of the SBEs seem to have consequences for their policy behavior. That is, elective bodies are designed to be open to more conflict, while appointed bodies respond only to their appointers. Such is the case with the SBEs, for 69 percent of those appointed reported little internal disagreement compared with 42 percent of those elected.[55]

Whatever their origins, these actors have differing influence. One observer reported that SBEs are "only marginal policy actors in the legislative arena and are largely overshadowed by the CSSO in state education."[56] Elected SBEs appear to have more influence with the CSSO and legislature, for they can speak with independent power. But recall that few SBEs are elected, and that their elections are rarely competitive, visible, or draw many voters; one observer called such elections "non-events." In the main, then, the SBE is a weak policy actor, primarily because of its inability to hire or remove the CSSO who has major constitutional oversight of state education. The SBE is also often poorly staffed or organized to operate effectively and often lacks political lines to the legislature and governor. They seem to wander about in the wilderness while the battle is being fought on a plain somewhere else.[57]

The CSSOs, however, know where the action is and are often in the thick of it. While they vary in authority, staff, and discretion, a recent review concluded that "almost without exception they exert great influence in the state education agency area." SBEs look to them for leadership and information in policy conflict and seldom oppose them. Their method of appointment is unrelated to their strength. But the CSSO is not a strong office with the legislature unless it is elected and has a big staff and formal powers and unless the party life of the state is weak and the economy poor. The same office can be used for quite different policy concerns by different occupants; thus in California in the 1970s, successive officials differed in sensitivities to minorities, curricula, and local control. By 1980 the CSSOs, through better interstate coordination and national networks, were becoming even stronger.[58]

The State Education Agency

The daily job of implementing state policy goals rests in the hands of anonymous bureaucrats in the SEA. These agencies were tiny when the century opened, but then succeeding waves of school reform were left with the SEAs to administer, and so they expanded greatly.

Today SEAs supervise a vast array of federal and state programs, either through direct administration (for example, state schools for the blind) or through overseeing state guidelines. Their compliance techniques include requiring and reviewing a torrent of reports from the LEAs; enforcing mandated levels of service (for example, curriculum); assisting LEAs in designing and staffing newly required programs; providing continuing career education of professionals; and so on.[59] In a larger perspective, they were given the task of institutionalizing the professional model of the schools states adopted over the last century. Programs fell to them that sought the "Americanization" of immigrants, vocational training for farm and city work, upgraded language and math training, improved resources for educating disadvantaged and minority children, and so on in an almost unending list.

A recent study provides a rare look at several hundred top members of this invisible bureaucracy in twelve states.[60] They appear primarily to be "locals," that is, born, educated, recruited, and serving mostly in their own states. These qualities generated in them a distinct parochialism in defining good education and proper state-local relations. Some were more rural in origin, others were more experienced and educated, and a few were mobile types who had worked in several states. There was, however, little discernible relationship between such types and their states' political, social, and economic environments. It seems as though the local political culture does not differentiate much among professional bureaucrats, who may well be instead more responsive to the nationwide norms of their profession.

Specialists in little niches of expertise, SEAs constitute a complex of daily spear carriers for curriculum, finance and accounting, administration, personnel, and many other matters. Their political influence may be the most subtle, that of inertia in defense of the status quo. Their role in innovation and its implementation is one of the many unstudied aspects of the educational policy system.

In democracies, numbers count as do organizations of voters. The chief organization is the political party, so its role in shaping any public policy must be seen. After all, the institutions reviewed above are products of electoral impulses diffracted through political parties in times past. And the epitome of individualism is not merely voting for officeholders but speaking directly on policy matters through the initiative and referendum.

A surprisingly little studied aspect of school policy making is the role of political party. The reports available show that parties differ on school policy making, although there is no consistent pattern in this difference. Some of these studies are of single states in which the party is seen as a significant agent affecting policy making.[61] Yet we still have no fifty-state comparison using such process-oriented studies. One four-state study of legislatures and school policy making, examining parties as only one factor, found the familiar variety. Thus, Republicans supported increasing state taxes for schooling more than Democrats did in Massachusetts and North Carolina (two quite different wings of the Democratic party, incidentally) but less than Democrats did in Oregon and Utah. Even this association between party and policy was influenced more if the legislator came from a competitive district and was a party leader.[62]

THE PRESENT STATE IN THE POLITICS OF EDUCATION

Common Streams of Turbulence

Several impressions remain from the survey just completed. Variety is of course the hallmark of state school policy making, but perhaps more important, there also emerge some commonalities. First, until recently, state school policy had been left mostly in the hands of professionals and their lay cohorts, what could be termed Low Conflict politics. Pressure groups concocted policy recommendations that legislatures accepted with little debate; governors were usually not involved in such a process; SBEs and their active managers, the CSSOs, made major policy and oversaw its administration, while the SEAs took charge of the daily operations of the states' schools. Political parties took little role in many states, and even where they did, recent events have made them act much alike. So in the Low Conflict mode of educational policy making, the policy making stages of initiation, formulation of alternatives, authorization, and implementation were primarily in the hands of the professionals themselves or their supporters. It was a game played by few with the rules set by the players.

A second commonality is that this general situation has altered dramatically over the last decade as the states entered a High Conflict mode. Political turbulence from different lay groups has stimulated elected state officials to take more direct interest in school policy making. Governors and legislators have been goaded by widespread popular discontent with school taxes and with purported teaching "failures." These officials everywhere have moved to take education under their budgetary control. School policy is no longer regarded as being apolitical by these policy makers or having little political return for them. Rather, it is now seen simply as one of a number of policies that must be held more accountable and administered on tighter funds to match the efficiency mood of the 1970s.

Another development underlying this recent turbulence is a third principle. This has been the challenges to traditional definitions of how school policy should be decided, policy services delivered, and schools financed and in what amounts. Much of this has involved a shift in defining and financing policy objectives to the state level, accompanied by the opening up of state policy making once closed to all but professionals. This means not only a larger role for laity— although that is still episodic and affects only a few issues—but it also points to the fragmentation of school professionals themselves. More-over, it points to the increased decisional roles of legislatures and governors.

A fourth commonality has only been hinted at: the degree to which a state's school policy making is shaped by distinctive beliefs based upon historical decisions or events. Thus it seems that contemporary forces are diffracted by the prisms of state political culture. If ESEA funded expanding state education bureaucracies, not all states dealt with this stimulus the same way.[63] All might use the money to add staff—some dynamics of bureaucracy are eternal—but whether and where they then led the state's educational program development depended very much upon the state's political culture. New York, already a national leader, simply got better; a second state might do nothing because it always had, but a third might seize the federal funds in order to improve the quality of its education. Whether for this or other programs for dispersing federal aid to education, states use traditional ways of operating to reallocate resources, and these reflect customary ways of defining such basic political values as individualism. We noted earlier that how state versus local control is defined depends upon a state's political culture, rather like dam gates built in earlier eras to regulate the flow of power between the two units. Thus the past provides a common influence among the fifty states, but like streams down a mountainside, the influence takes different courses.

What of the future? The 1980s will be a decade of school closings and an attendant drop in personnel. In addition, reforms aimed at making professionals accountable for producing measurable gains in children's learning will also continue. Other reforms aimed at expanding the role of lay representatives in LEA decision making will likely spread, as they have been pioneered in Florida and California. Here, then, is a picture of a shrinking service industry—fewer children, teachers, and administrators but more decision makers and less money for the service.

That is quite a different picture from the closed system noted by observers in previous years. Hence, the research must also share this tentative condition, echoing the professionals' cry that, "The times they are a-changing." In these respects, the American public school and school decision making are in a transition unknown since the reform effort to extricate schools from party control late in the nineteenth century. Everywhere there is talk about the crisis in education, about reduced public support for schools and its products, about reaching for new decision-making techniques, and about emerging redefinitions of professionals' roles vis-à-vis new political agents. These currents also characterized the reform era of a century ago, and from them emerged a much better system of education. At the time, however, few then could visualize the nature of the result, and there is also no agreement today.

NOTES

1. An excellent review of this regional variety and its political consequences is found in Daniel Elazar, *American Federalism: A View from the States* (New York: Crowell, 1972).

2. George Collins, "Constitutional and Legal Basis for State Action" in *Education in the States: Nationwide Development since 1900*, eds. Edgar Fuller and Jim Pearson (Washington: National Education Association, Washington, 1969), pp. 29–30.

3. For a review of five interpretations, see David Tyack, "Ways of Seeing: An Essay on the History of Compulsive Schooling," *Harvard Educational Review* 46 (1976): 355–89. Also useful is Michael S. Katz, *A History of Compulsory Education Laws* (Bloomington, Ind.: Phi Delta Kappa Educational Foundation, 1976).

4. See Michael S. Katz, *School Reforms: Past and Present* (Boston: Little, Brown & Co., 1971).

5. For a full description of this process, see Raymond E. Callahan, *Education in the Cult of Efficiency* (Chicago: University of Chicago Press, 1962).

6. Frederick M. Wirt, "Political Turbulence and Administrative Authority in the Schools" in *The New Urban Politics*, eds. Louis Masotti and Robert Lineberry (Cambridge, Mass.: Ballinger, 1976), chap. 3.

7. National Center for Education Statistics, *Digest of Education Statistics 1980* (Washington: Government Printing Office, 1980), p. 78.

8. Ellis Katz, *Education Policymaking 1977–1978: A Snapshot from the States* (Washington: Institute for Educational Leadership, 1978).

9. The definitive review of these events, policies, and results is Walter Garms, James Guthrie, and Lawrence Pierce, *School Finance: The Economics and Politics of Federalism* (Englewood Cliffs, N.J.: Prentice-Hall, 1978). For a valuable introduction to future issues, see James Guthrie, ed., *School Finance in the 1980's* (Cambridge, Mass.: Ballinger, 1980).

10. An authoritative review of the following constitutional aspects of schooling law is Tyll van Geel, *Authority to Control the School Program* (Lexington, Mass.: Lexington Books, 1976).

11. This development is analyzed in the influential Callahan, *Education Efficiency,* and in Lawrence Cremin, *The Transformation of the School: Progressivism in American Education, 1876–1957* (New York: Vintage Books, 1964).

12. A useful set of essays on many of these developments since 1900 is found in Fuller and Pearson, *Education in the States.* An updated catalogue of state education requirements for each of the fifty states is found in National Institute of Education, Department of Health, Education and Welfare, *State Legal Standards for the Provision of Public Education* (Washington D.C.: National Institute of Education, 1978).

13. Collins, "Constitutional Basis," p. 21.

14. Frederick M. Wirt, "State Policy Culture and State Decentralization" in *Politics of Education*, ed. Jay Scribner (Chicago: Yearbook of the National Society for the Study of Education, 1977), pp. 164–87. A brief statement is in Frederick M. Wirt, "What State Laws Say about Local Control," *Phi Delta Kappan* 59 (1978): 517–20.

15. See Michael Kirst, "The State Role in Regulation of Local School Districts" in *Government in the Classroom*, ed. Mary William (New York: Academy of Political Science, Columbia University, 1979), pp. 45–56.

16. Ibid, p. 11. A detailed source of regulation is Advisory Commission on Intergovernmental Relations, *State Mandating of Local Expenditures* (Washington D.C.: Government Printing Office, 1978).

17. This research tradition is well reviewed in Paul Peterson, "The Politics of American Education," in *Review of Research in Education II,* eds. Fred Kerlinger and John Carroll (Itasca, Ill.: Peacock, 1974), pp. 348–89.

18. Multivariate analysis shows that this association is shaped not by economic

resources but by a more basic factor, the "political culture" of these states. This cultural concept originates in Elazar, *American Federalism*, chap. 3; its SCS attributes are developed in Wirt, "State Policy Culture," pp. 176–79; the multivariate analysis is found in Frederick M. Wirt, "Does Control Follow the Dollar? School Policy, State-Local Linkage, and Political Culture," *Publius: The Journal of Federalism* (Spring 1980).

19. Stephen Bailey et al., *Schoolmen and Politics* (Syracuse: Syracuse University Press, 1962), p. 47; see this source at chap. III for the factors allied with localism.

20. Elazar, *American Federalism*, p. 202.

21. These data and the following account are drawn from Michael Kirst, "The New Politics of State Education Finance," *Phi Delta Kappan* 60, No. 6 (February 1979): 427–32.

22. For description of all seventy-four laws and state budgets thereunder, see NEA, pp. 22–36; for a history of state-federal relations, see Jay Scribner, "Impacts of Federal Programs on State Departments of Education" in Fuller and Pearson, *Education in the States*, chap. 11.

23. Paul Berman and Milbrey McLaughlin, *Federal Programs Supporting Education Change* (Santa Monica, Calif.: Rand, 1975) vol. IV, R-1584/4HEW; and the special issue of *Teachers College Record* 77, "Making Change Happen," (February 1976).

24. Joel Berke and Michael Kirst, *Federal Aid to Education,* (Lexington, Mass.: Heath, 1972).

25. The fullest analysis of these developments is Gary Orfield, *Must We Bus? Segregated Schools and National Policy* (Brookings Institution, Washington D.C., 1978).

26. Harrell Rodgers and Charles Bullock, *Coercion to Compliance,* (Lexington, Mass.: Heath, 1976).

27. Everett Cataldo et al., *School Desegregation Policy: Compliance, Avoidance, and the Metropolitan Remedy*, (Lexington, Mass.: Heath, 1978).

28. Michael Danielson, *The Politics of Exclusion* (New York: Columbia University Press, 1976).

29. On the former, see Ellis Katz, *Education Policymaking,* p. 23; on the latter, see Michael Kirst, "Strengthening Federal-Local Relationships Supporting Educational Change" in *The Dynamics of Planned Educational Change*, eds. Robert Herriott and Neal Gross (Berkeley: McCutchan, 1979), chap. 11.

30. The following is drawn from Harmon Zeigler and Henrick van Dalen, "Interest Groups in State Politics" in *Politics in the American States: A Comparative Analysis*, Herbert Jacob and Kenneth Vines (Boston: Little, Brown & Co., 1976), chap. 3.

31. Ibid, p. 134.

32. Ibid, pp. 95–109 so characterize and detail these types. For a fuller elaboration based on four states, see Harmon Zeigler and Michael Baer, *Lobbying: Interaction and Influence in American State Legislatures* (Belmont, Calif.: Wadsworth, 1969).

33. For a brief history, see J. Howard Goold, "The Organized Teaching Profession" in Pearson and Fuller, *Education in the States*, chap. 14, and Lorraine McDonnell and Anthony Pascal, "National Trends in Teaching Collective Bargaining," *Education and Urban Society* 11 (1979): 129–51.

34. The following is drawn from Laurence Iannaccone, *Politics in Education* (New York: Center for Applied Research in Education, 1967), chap. 3.

35. J. Alan Aufderheide, "Educational Interest Groups and the State Legislature," in *State Policy Making for the Public Schools: A Comparative Analysis*, Roald Campbell and Tim Mazzoni, Jr. (Berkeley: McCutchan, 1976), p. 201.

36. See the review of Iannaccone's typology using twelve-state data in Raphael Nystrand, "State Education Policy Systems," in Campbell and Mazzoni, *State Policy Making*, chap. 7. Nystrand's analysis may not have fully tested this typology according to some critics.

37. Michael Kirst and Stephen Sommers, "Collective Action Among California Educational Interest Groups: A Logical Response to Proposition 13," in *Education and Urban Society* 13, No. 2 (1981): 235–56.

38. Ibid.

39. Ibid.

40. Aufderheide, "Educational Interest Groups," p. 213.

41. Ibid, p. 209.

42. Zeigler and van Dalen, "Interest Groups," p. 147.

43. William H. Riker, *The Theory of Political Coalitions* (New Haven, Conn.: Yale University Press, 1962).

44. For a useful introduction to this literature, see Samuel Patterson, "American State Legislatures and Public Policy" in Jacob and Vines, chap. 4. The major survey is Malcolm Jewell and Samuel Patterson, *The Legislative Process in the United States*, 2d ed. (New York: Random House, 1973).

45. Nicholas Masters, Robert Salisbury, and Thomas Eliot, *State Politics and the Public Schools* (New York: Knopf, 1964); Jerome T. Murphy, "The Paradox of State Government Reform," in *Educational Policymaking*, Yearbook of the National Society for the Study of Education, 1978, ed. Milbrey McLaughlin (Chicago: University of Chicago Press, 1978).

46. Ellis Katz, *Education Policymaking*, pp. 40–41.

47. A major review and addition to this scholarship is Douglas E. Mitchell, *Shaping Legislative Decisions: Education Policy and the Social Sciences* (Lexington, Mass.: Lexington Books, 1978).

48. The following draws on Sarah Morehouse, "The Governor as Political Leader" in Jacob and Vines, *Politics in the American States*, chap. 5. An invaluable exploration of this office is Thad Beyle and J. Oliver Williams, *The American Governor in Behavioral Perspective* (New York: Harper & Row, 1972).

49. The seminal work is Thomas Dye, *Politics, Economics, and the Public*, (Chicago: Rand McNally, 1966).

50. Iannaccone, *Politics in Education*, p. 44.

51. Edward Hines, "Governors and Educational Policy Making" in Campbell and Mazzoni, *State Policy Making*, chap. 4.

52. An excellent analysis is Mike Milstein and Robert Jennings, *Educational Policy Making and the State Legislature: The New York Experience* (New York: Praeger, 1973).

53. A full catalogue of these authorities is Sam Harris, *State Departments of Education, State Boards of Education, and Chief State School Officers* (Washington, D.C.: United States Government Printing Office, 1973).

54. For their history and variety, see Lerus Winget, Edgar Fuller and Terrel Bell, "State Departments of Education" in Fuller and Pearson, *Education in the States*, chap. 2. For New York, see Milstein and Jennings, *Educational Policy Making*.

55. Winget et al., "State Departments of Education," p. 83.

56. Ibid, p. 84.

57. On the "non-event," see a major challenge to the once-popular notion of the SBE influence, Gerald Sroufe, "State School Board Members and the State Education Policy System," *Planning and Changing* 2 (April 1971): 16–17. For a twelve-state review of the SBE, see Roald Campbell, "The Chief State School Officer as a Policy Actor" in Campbell and Mazzoni, *State Policy Making*, chap. 3.

58. Drawn from Campbell, "Chief School Officer." On California, see Michael Kirst, "The Politics of Education in California," in Berke and Kirst, *Federal Aid to Education*, chap. 3.

59. Almost all the comparative chapters of Fuller and Pearson, *Education in the States*, detail these SEA functions. Especially useful for understanding the different kinds of authority under which SEAs operate may be found in chaps. 8, 10, and 13.

60. Drawn from Gary Branson, "The Characteristics of Upper Level Administrators in Departments of Education" (Unpublished part of the Campbell and Mazzoni study, mimeo).

61. Milstein and Jennings, *Educational Policy Making*; Bailey et al., *Schoolmen and Politics*.

62. Zeigler and Baer, *Lobbying*, pp. 143, 146, 149.

63. Jerome Murphy, *State Education Agencies and Discretionary Funds* (Lexington, Mass.: Lexington Books, 1974); Mike Milstein, *Impact and Response* (New York: Teachers College Press, 1976).

9

The State Role
in Education
Policy Innovation

HISTORICAL BACKGROUND

Under the United States Constitution, education is a power reserved to the states. In turn, state constitutions charge the state legislatures with responsibility for establishing and maintaining a system of free public schools that are operated locally. Local control of education has been a hallmark of American education, distinguishing us from most other Western nations. But an unprecedented growth of state influence over local education has taken place since the 1960s, which will be the focus of this chapter.

States display different historical patterns of control over local policies on such matters as curriculum, personnel, finances, and teaching, but all states established minimums below which local school operations could not fall. Presumably the state's general welfare required a basic educational opportunity for all children. Consequently, states require a minimum number of days at school, certain courses of study, and standards for teacher certification. There has been an urban-rural distinction to this state role. Most states also required localities to levy a minimum tax and guaranteed a base level of expenditures. Earlier in this century, states began upgrading the standards of rural schools, but the cities received less attention because their expenditures and property wealth were already the highest in the state. Indeed, Chicago, New York, and Philadelphia had special statutes that exempted them from major areas of state control. Decades later, in the 1970s, state school finance reforms created special provisions for the core cities, but then the rationale was based on unusually high fiscal stress.

A principal reason for state intervention is that only the state can ensure equality and standardization of instruction and resources. This rationale is contested by local control advocates, who contend that flexibility is needed to adjust to diverse circumstances and local preferences. Local control advocates stress that there is no proven educational technology that is optimal for all conditions. This dispute over state against local control is really over two values—equal treatment versus freedom of local choice. The traditional compromise has been a state minimum with local option to exceed the minimum, but this compromise was challenged by school finance reformers in the 1970s because state minimums provided an inadequate floor or were substantially exceeded by localities with extraordinary taxable property.

Before turning to the implementation of school finance reform, we will sketch the overall state role in education at the onset of the 1970s.

VARIATIONS IN STATE CONTROL AT THE BEGINNING OF THE 1970s

The best way to grasp the historical state role is to focus on specific policies from state to state. Variations in how much the state controls each policy causes the differences between the states. States spread out across a centrist-localist spectrum. In New England, local schools enjoy an autonomy from state control that may well be rooted in colonial hatred of the English governor. On the other hand, textbooks and courses of instruction in the southern states are often centrally determined. State-mandated curriculums have both historical and political roots. In many cases, it took state laws to ensure newer subjects, such as vocational education and driver training, a place in the curriculum. These subjects were introduced into the curriculum after 1920 amidst great controversy, whereas mathematics and English never required political power to justify their existence. The standard subjects are therefore less frequently mandated by state laws.

Underlying the interstate variation in local control is what has been called "political culture," that is, differing value structures that show up in the characteristic behavior and actions of states and regions.

Table 9.1

School Centralization Scores and Ranks by State, 1972

State	Score	Rank	State	Score	Rank	State	Score	Rank
Ala.	4.67	3	La.	3.19	37	Ohio	3.65	22
Alaska	3.38	31	Maine	3.09	41	Okla.	4.91	2
Ariz.	2.91	43	Md.	3.56	27	Oreg.	4.30	6
Ark.	3.57	26	Mass.	2.73	48	Pa.	3.75	21
Calif.	3.65	22	Mich.	3.85	15	R.I.	3.21	36
Colo.	3.79	19	Minn.	4.10	8	S.C.	4.61	4
Conn.	2.68	49	Miss.	3.93	10	S. Dak.	3.08	42
Del.	3.15	39	Mo.	2.84	46	Tenn.	3.48	28
Fla.	4.19	7	Mont.	3.47	29	Tex.	2.88	45
Ga.	3.24	35	Nebr.	3.81	16	Utah	3.42	30
Hawaii	6.00	1	Nev.	2.84	46	Vt.	3.17	38
Idaho	3.26	34	N.H.	3.13	40	Va.	3.88	13
Ill.	3.32	33	N.J.	3.87	14	Wash.	4.37	5
Ind.	3.90	11	N. Mex.	3.79	19	W. Va.	3.94	9
Iowa	3.80	17	N.Y.	3.63	24	Wis.	3.62	25
Kans.	3.38	31	N.C.	3.80	17	Wyo.	1.86	50
Ky.	3.90	11	N. Dak.	2.89	44			

Source for Tables 9.1–9.3: Frederick M. Wirt, "What State Laws Say About Local Control," *Phi Delta Kappan* 59 (April 1978): 517–20. Reprinted with permission.

Political culture ranges widely in its objects—political rules, party structures, government structures and processes, citizens' roles, and attitudes about all of these. In short, political culture is a value system that accounts for major differences between states in the degree of state control and policy feasibility. It also helps determine whether state control will expand and how inclined local officials are to evade state influence.[1]

A content analysis of the variety and extent of state control in thirty-six areas of school policy, using assembled statutes, constitutions, and court opinions, provides a view of these political cultures in educational policy.[2] A scale of state control was constructed from these authoritative statements. It suggested a range of state control: absence of state authority, 0; permissive local autonomy, 1; required local autonomy, 2; extensive local option under state-mandated requirement, 3; limited local option under state-mandated requirement, 4; no local option under state-mandated requirement, 5; and total state assumption, 6.

As table 9.1 indicates, in 1972 the states displayed a striking diversity, from Hawaii's total state assumption of schooling, stemming from its royal tradition, to rural Wyoming's local autonomy.

Table 9.2
Policies of Highest State Control, 1972

Policy	Fifty-State Score	Number of States with Total Assumption
Certification	5.50	33
Vocational education	4.89	15
Attendance	4.64	12
Accreditation	4.50	27
Financial records	4.27	16
Median score	*4.64*	

At the same time, there is a concentration between 3 and 4 on the centralization scale. Regional patterns are not clear-cut, but there is high local control in some states of the Northeast and high state control in some southeastern states. States clustering at each end are both rich and poor. Size, in terms of both population and total square miles, appears irrelevant. The "average state," scoring 3.56, has extensive state guidelines with many local options, and the variation in state control is more noteworthy than the statistical average. As subsequent sections demonstrate, the state role has expanded during the 1970s in several states that formerly had low centralization scores. Connecticut, Illinois, Maine, and Kansas have all enacted major school finance reforms that dramatically increase state control. Massachusetts, with one of the lowest centralization scores, passed a highly prescriptive program for special education. Some of the formerly centralized states such as Florida have become even more centralized through accountability and school finance initiatives enacted in the 1970s. This widespread phenomenon of states assuming local school policy prerogatives suggests that major political, social, and economic forces overrode historical constraints against centralization in several states. A table compiled today would show a higher average than that obtained in 1972.

This analysis distinguished areas of policy characterized by the greatest state control. Table 9.2 presents policies where there is virtually complete state control. The reforms of earlier eras are clearly highlighted—personnel, compulsory attendance, records, and accreditation. As we will see, during the 1970s, major increases in state control focused on accountability (testing, pupil achievement, parent participation), collective bargaining, and categorical programs.

Table 9.3
Policies of High State Control, 1972

Policy	Fifty-State Score
Special education	5.09
Curriculum	4.41
Safety-health	4.37
Textbooks	4.35
Transportation	4.34
Teacher employment	4.17
Calendar	4.09
Graduation	4.06
Admissions	3.82
Construction	3.76
Records	3.71
Adult education	3.63
Revenue	3.57
Median score	*4.09*

Table 9.3 presents areas of high state control. Some of these policies reflect the traditional state "gatekeeping" role (teacher employment, calendar, records, and revenue controls). Curriculum, student progress, and physical facility regulation are other major areas of high state control. There are also policies in which states are about evenly divided between state and local control, including new state programs for pupil enrichment, pupil-teacher ratios, and evaluation. Local responsibilities are being eroded incrementally in these policy areas. Indeed, these data demonstrate how the state domain of minimum specifications has gradually expanded, while local discretion has contracted since the early twentieth century.

Little is known about the operational impact of state mandates, but our experience suggests that state enforcement is sporadic and activated primarily in response to local complaints. Certainly, there is no systematic state inspection system. A survey of local perceptions and behavior is needed, particularly to answer the following significant political questions: Is practice consistent with policy; that is, are state statutes and regulations enforced fully and effectively? What inducements or sanctions are most effectively employed in this enforcement? There is, however, enough evidence at hand to analyze how this state control came to be.

SOME CAUSES FOR THE GROWTH OF STATE INFLUENCE

Some of the major policy areas that signify the dramatic increase of state influence within the last two decades are state administration of federal categorical grants, state role in education finance, state requirements for educational accountability, state specifications and programs for children with special needs, and state efforts to stimulate experimentation and innovation. These substantive changes have become possible in large part due to an increase in the institutional capacity of states to intervene in local affairs. Thus, most state legislatures have added staff and research capacity, and they also now meet annually or for more extended sessions than in earlier years. Thus legislators now have the resources to formulate and oversee educational policy. Governors now have their own education specialists and improved fiscal staffs too. Moreover, during the 1970s, the states diversified their tax sources and expanded their fiscal capacities.

The capacity of state education agencies (SEAs) to intercede in local school policy has also increased dramatically in the last twenty years. Ironically, the federal government provided the initial impetus for this expansion. The Elementary and Secondary Education Act of 1965 and its subsequent amendments required state agencies to approve local projects for federal funds in such areas as education for disadvantaged, handicapped, bilingual, and migrant children and for educational innovation. In each of these federal programs, 1 percent of the funds were earmarked for state administration. Moreover, Title V of ESEA provided general support for state administrative resources, with some priority given to state planning and evaluation. By 1972, three-fourths of the SEA staffs had been in their jobs for less than three years. All the expansion in California's SEA from 1964 to 1970 was financed by federal funds. In 1972, 70 percent of the funding for the state education agency in Texas came from federal aid. New staff capacity was available for SEA administrators or state boards that wanted to take a more activist role in local education.[3]

A further factor is the increased confusion among and decreased respect for traditional supporters of local control. Thus, local control advocates, such as teachers' unions, school boards, and school administrator associations feud among themselves and provide a vacuum that state control activists can exploit. As we have seen, these education

Table 9.4

Government Expenditures from Own Funds
Selected Years

Year	Total	Federal	State	Local
	Public Sector Expenditures in Billions of Current Dollars			
1969	$285.6	$188.4	$ 49.6	$ 47.6
1979	764.5	507.0	145.0	112.5
	Public Sector Expenditures as a Percent of GNP			
1969	30.5%	20.1%	5.3%	5.1%
1979	32.2	21.3	6.1	4.7
	Public Sector Expenditures as a Percent of Personal Income			
1969	38.0%	25.1%	6.6%	6.3%
1979	39.7	26.3	7.5	5.8

Source: Advisory Commission on Intergovernmental Relations, *Significant Features of Fiscal Federalism,* 1978–79 (Washington, D.C.: United States Government Printing Office, May 1979).

groups cannot agree on common policies with their old allies such as parent organizations. The loss of public confidence in professional educators and the decline of achievement scores also cause many legislators to feel that local school employees should no longer be given much discretion.

In addition to all of this, a key structural change in the growth and diversification of state tax sources has developed. From 1960 to 1979, eleven states adopted a personal income tax, nine a corporate income tax, and ten a general sales tax. Thirty-seven states used all three of these revenue sources in 1979, compared with just nineteen in 1960. State income taxes provided 35 percent of all tax revenue in 1978 compared to 19 percent in 1969. This diversification of the revenue systems provided the states with a capacity to increase services as evidenced by table 9.4.

STATE SCHOOL FINANCE REFORM IN THE 1970s

No policy arena better demonstrates the new activism of the states during the 1970s than the dramatic initiatives in school finance. This increased state role in school financing was accompanied by other forms of increased state influence over local policy in many cases. In most states, the concept of a minimum financial base was abandoned for a new state role. The federal impetus in this nonincremental policy change was minimal. The United States Supreme Court ruled in the 1973 *Rodriguez* case that while the Texas school finance system resulted in unequal expenditures, "we cannot say that such disparities are the products of a system that is so irrational as to be invidiously discriminatory."[4] Thus, the courts left the issue to be resolved by the states. While the Nixon administration studied taking a significant federal role in school finance equalization, it backed away from actually committing federal resources (except for research).

If the federal courts did not intervene, however, numerous state courts declared their own state's school finance system unconstitutional. Between 1970 and 1980, twenty to thirty states (depending on one's criteria) "reformed" their finance systems or were in the midst of carrying out court orders to do so. These states accounted for about two-thirds of the pupils in the United States. Moreover, reform in some states caused others to increase state aid without any actual reform in state distribution formulas. All this was happening in a decade when states were adding new tax sources and increasing their expenditures as a percent of GNP and of per capita income. As table 9.4 demonstrates, state spending increases outstripped federal or local increases.

During this same era, support for public education shifted from the local to the state level. As table 9.5 demonstrates, from 1969 to 1979 state sources of revenue for public education grew from $13.9 billion to $41.2 billion—up 44.5 percent in real terms. While state aid for public schools doubled during the last decade, table 9.6 shows that school reform states more than doubled their spending and dramatically increased their percentage of total state and local expenditures. We cannot be certain that school finance reform "caused" all these fiscal changes, but a relationship is unmistakable. This growth in state expenditures enabled total education expenditures to grow over 40 percent faster than inflation despite a dramatic downward trend in enrollments. Nationally, current operating expenditures increased 274 percent over the decade (from $657 per pupil to $1,798).

THE ELEMENTS OF SCHOOL FINANCE REFORM

Not surprisingly, the larger state fiscal role has been accompanied by greater state control of local education policies. Before turning to

Table 9.5
Sources of Revenue for Selected School Years, 1969–1979

School Year	Local	Federal	State	Total
	Amount (in Billions of Dollars) From			
Ending in				
1969	$18.3	$13.9	$2.6	$34.8
1979	38.0	41.2	7.6	96.8
Increment				
1969				
to 1979	$19.7	$27.3	$5.0	$52.0
	Amount as a Percent of Total			
1969	52.7%	39.9%	7.4%	
1979	43.7	47.4	8.8	

	Expenditures per Pupil, 1969 to 1979	
	Amount	Percentage Increase from 1969
1969	$ 657	–
1979	1,798	273.7

Source: National Education Association, *Estimates of School Statistics, 1978–79* (Washington, D.C.: NEA, 1979) pp. 20, 25.

this, we examine the elements and political roots of school finance reform.

Several common elements characterize the divergent school finance reforms enacted during the 1970s. There has been an evolution from state increases in local unrestricted spending to the inclusion of special state aid for disadvantaged youth (including the handicapped) and for the large core cities. Several key *state* court suits based on clauses in different state constitutions have caused variations in state approaches. Thus, the initial California suit (*Serrano*) relied solely on variations in local property tax capacity.[5] Subsequent suits in Washington (*Seattle* v. *Washington*) and New York (*Levittown* v. *Nyquist*) added considerations of special pupil needs and big city problems. There have been several consistent results of such reform. Below are the key reform elements.

1. Districts with low property wealth per pupil have received considerably more state aid. Their per-pupil spending has been "leveled up" to approach that of the higher-spending, property-rich districts. Some redistribution from high spending to low

Table 9.6
State Education Expenditures in 1970 and 1979
as Percentage of Total State/Local Education Expenditures
(Selected School Finance Reform States)

	1970		1979	
State	Amount (Millions of Dollars)	State Percent of Total State/Local Spending	Amount (Millions of Dollars)	State Percent of Total State/Local Spending
California	$1,536	(31.9)	$5,598	(64.9)
Colorado	119	(26.2)	450	(36.9)
Florida	631	(55.0)	1,666	(56.1)
Illinois	768	(31.1)	2,000	(39.6)
Iowa	158	(24.8)	504	(38.9)
Kansas	136	(31.2)	403	(46.7)
Maine	70	(37.4)	1,787	(47.1)
Michigan	856	(45.0)	1,831	(44.8)
Minnesota	444	(47.4)	1,057	(54.5)
Missouri	261	(31.3)	582	(36.2)
New Jersey	411	(26.9)	1,378	(40.6)
New Mexico	128	(61.3)	353	(67.0)
Ohio	515	(27.1)	1,625	(43.2)
Washington	425	(55.8)	942	(61.3)
Wisconsin	273	(30.1)	713	(36.5)

Source: National Center for Educational Statistics, *Digest of Educational Statistics, 1972* (Washington, D.C.: United States Government Printing Office, 1973), p. 59, for column 1; National Education Association, *Estimates of School Statistics, 1978–79* (Washington, D.C.: National Education Association, 1979), p. 20. As of 1980, states under court order include Connecticut and Wyoming.

spending was involved, but basically increased state money was used for this.

2. Property tax relief has been targeted to school districts with a high property tax effort, low assessed property value, and consequent below-state-average per-pupil expenditures. Indeed, school finance reform has been plagued with confusion as to whether it was aid for children or for taxpayers in school districts with below average assessed property values.

3. Funds for special pupil needs were added as it became apparent that disadvantaged and handicapped pupils did not always reside primarily in districts that had low assessed property values (a case in point was Levittown, New York). Another rationale was that these pupils needed *more* than an average expenditure. At

Table 9.7

District Disparities in the Serrano Decision

	Assessed Value Per Pupil	Tax Rate	Expenditures Per Pupil
Beverly Hills	$550,885	$2.38	$1,232
Baldwin Park	$ 3,707	$5.48	$ 577

the close of the decade, sixteen states had categorical programs of compensatory education serving 1.9 million economically or educationally disadvantaged children at a total cost of $647 million. Another eight states had special adjustments for compensatory education in their base allocation formulas.

4. Special provisions were made for unusually high-cost local situations including both rural and big city districts.

THE STATES AND THE CITIES: A FISCAL DILEMMA

The *Serrano* approach in California was a negative standard, requiring that the amount of expenditures per pupil could *not* be determined primarily by the property tax wealth of the school district. The 1971 *Serrano* decision cited the comparison of tax rates and expenditure levels seen in table 9.7. But many core cities have higher than average assessed values per pupil because of the immense valuation of downtown office or industrial properties. They also have large numbers of single parents or private-school-oriented parents. These two characteristics cause many cities to appear wealthy if one looks only at property tax per pupil. However, large numbers of special-needs children in eastern and midwestern cities generate above average demands for other public services and especially high costs for compensatory education.

A typical example is Seattle, whose voters turned down frequent requests for property tax increases. Subsequently, a court suit was brought by Seattle, even though finance reformers in the early 1970s considered the city a "wealthy property district." Seattle asserted that school finance had to be adjusted to the special needs of cities, and the Washington courts so ruled.

To meet such problems, several states have formula adjustments or categorical aids for cities.[6] Michigan allocates more state aid to districts in which the noneducation tax rate exceeds the statewide average by more than 25 percent. Florida uses a cost-of-living index to increase state aid to its urban areas. California has an urban impact aid program that earmarks funds for cities. In this way, state school finance reform continues to search for formulas that will recognize unique city needs without violating the general principle of equal treatment for all districts.

THE POLITICS OF STATE SCHOOL FINANCE REFORM

Public policy issues emerge on state political agendas for many reasons, but one of the most important and least understood is the role of interstate "policy issue networks" that sponsor and promote programs in a wide variety of forums. These interstate network elements include entrepreneurs, private nonprofit advocacy organizations, lawyers, interstate technical assistance groups, and often private foundations. Such networks spread ideas and create opportunities for state politicians to champion particular causes or programs. Many of the most interesting educational innovations, such as minimum competency testing, have been promoted by such networks.

Recently two of the largest state policy networks—school finance reform and spending/taxing limits—have begun to clash with each other. School finance reformers advocate large increases in state and local spending to meet the property tax "equity" criteria without leveling down and the special needs of bilingual, handicapped, and city children. At the same time, crusaders for tax limitation seek to stabilize or reverse the growth in state and local spending.[7] Both networks have been developed by entrepreneurs who generate the activity and structure the rewards. Both draw together membership from diverse organizations.

The entrepreneur with resources ample enough to launch the school finance reform network was the Ford Foundation working in close collaboration with HEW's National Institute of Education (NIE). The Ford Foundation provided publicity, grants, travel, and recognition as resources to motivate and bond together the network participants. Indeed, it funds, directly or indirectly, all the network's major elements, which include:

1. Lawyers to sue the state. Ford grants were made to the Western Center on Law and Poverty (California) and the Lawyers' Com-

mittee for Civil Rights under Law (Washington, D.C.) to coordinate interstate legal activities. These Ford-funded lawyers devised and litigated *Serrano* and *Levittown*, and the Lawyers' Committee has assisted in more than twenty subsequent state suits.

2. Private agencies to spread the concepts of finance reform around the nation, such as state branches of the League of Women Voters and National Urban Coalition. These agencies publicized general principles that the network supported.

3. Scholars to testify as expert court witnesses in favor of reform and then to advise the state on how to meet court orders. These scholars from prestigious universities adapted the network's principles to specific state contexts.

4. Interstate technical assistance groups such as the Education Commission of the States (ECS) and the National Conference of State Legislatures. These groups worked with the scholars and provided computer simulations of various solutions. They were hired by proreform state politicians that the network discovered or after court suits overturned the school finance system and made reform seem likely.

5. State politicians and political institutions, such as the Governor's Citizens Committee on Education in Florida and the Oregon Legislature's Committee on Equal Educational Opportunity. These temporary government units employed network scholars and groups like ECS as their chief advisors.

6. Research and action centers oriented to minority groups, including the International Development Research Association (Hispanic, located in San Antonio) and the New Jersey Urban Coalition (Black, headquartered in Newark). These Ford-funded organizations ensured that minority concerns were brought to the attention of the groups mentioned above.

7. Graduate students—from Stanford to Columbia—who received full scholarships to prepare themselves as the next generation of school finance advocates or technicians.

Ford and the National Institute of Education provided operating expenses, travel, consultants, research papers, and other appropriate incentives to make the network effective. Periodic meetings of key network participants were used to select target states for intervention.

States that were "ripe" found all seven elements descending on them. In all states, the symbolism emphasized the legal concepts of equity, fundamental rights, and nondiscrimination against the poor and other ethnic minorities.

THE EBB AND FLOW OF SCHOOL FINANCE REFORM

In 1974 the pace of school finance reform slowed. A national recession eroded state budget surpluses. Some states, such as Connecticut and South Dakota, passed finance reform laws without funding them. The United States Supreme Court ruled in *Rodriguez* that it was inappropriate for the federal government to intervene. There were also disheartening losses in state courts, such as in Oregon and Washington. The *Serrano* impetus for state equalization of the local property tax base behind each child seemed to run out of gas. Coalitions were harder to build, in part because of the erosion of budget surpluses but also due to splits within the education groups— arguments between school boards and teacher organizations, between cities, suburbs, and rural areas.

Beginning in the late 1970s, however, the pace of school finance reform quickened again. The school finance network started moving in new and different directions, especially in reformulation of their legal concepts; Ford-financed research and legal analysis had led to a midstream correction. The *Serrano* approach, relying solely on variations in local property tax capacity, had ignored variations in pupil needs, such as those of the disadvantaged and handicapped. The Ford/NIE network won two novel suits (in New York and Washington) that seem to portend the direction of things to come. Courts in New York ruled that a system with equal tax yield for equal property tax effort, for example, *Serrano*, in fact discriminated against the big cities. Cities have high assessed value per pupil, but they also have large numbers of disadvantaged children and high tax rates for social services other than education. Consequently, appeal courts in New York ordered more spending to be targeted to special pupil needs and to urban areas in addition to the *Serrano* property tax focus that required more state spending in low-property-wealth suburbs.

Through its flexible instruments, the Ford Foundation coordinated and spearheaded the network. Often a grant was not as effective as an informal conference to line up state activists, a commissioned report about a new legal strategy, a joint venture (with HEW or the Carnegie Foundation), the creation of a new citizens' organization, or scholarships for graduate students. The network's successes are impressive, with a consistent outcome of major state spending increases. Indeed, a recent Rand report emphasized that school finance reform had rarely eliminated differences between school districts but had led to more spending in all states.[8]

A recent analysis of eight state cases of such reform found there were several ingredients for successful reform besides the national reform network:[9]

1. Gubernatorial or legislative commissions did much of the compromising in advance of legislative action. These special commissions, such as the Florida Governor's Citizens Committee on Education, accommodated high-spending districts through "hold-harmless" provisions (no district received less money than the prior year) and rural interests with increased transportation aid.

2. Another key component was the availability of a state fiscal surplus. This well illustrates an old adage that "politicians can only equalize on a rising tide."

3. Court pressure was a necessary stimulus to reform. There was an effect of California's *Serrano* case on other states. State political leaders in many states felt that they faced litigation unless reform was instituted. Successful suits were based on constitutional equal protection clauses in some states, education sections in others.

4. Finally, school finance reform evolved over a long period of time. Reform reflects a logical progression from earlier consideration of previous proposals and formula changes, though it may appear to be radical in nature when it finally appears.

The importance of national policy issue networks in school finance reform provides new insights into how policies are diffused and raises doubts about prior political concepts and theories. Regionalism explained little. The eight-state study could find no strong impact of followers and leaders within distinct regions of the country as Walker posits.[10] Theories of the diffusion of innovation seemed to obscure what happened here. Thus, analysis of diffusion curves, whereby innovation is said to occur because of interaction effects between users and nonusers, obscures the actual political processes discussed above.[11] The environmental explanation of the Dye school came up empty. Thus, there was no significant relationship between school finance reform and allegedly predictive measures such as state per capita income and urbanization. Traditional interest-group theory stresses that policy change is driven by producer-oriented interest groups. The eight-state study found that producers in this issue—teacher and other employee organizations—were not crucial factors. Moreover, the concept of the power of the iron triangle of government agency heads, legislative committees, and producer interests with a fragmented, self-interested view was not evident in this reform. The iron triangle was in fact a reactive force that made marginal changes in network-inspired reforms.[12] There was no cheer either for the students of federalism who believe that states politics research may best be organized around the federal government as crucial innovator, with states merely reacting to this stimulus.[13] The federal role in school finance reform was not large and was limited to research and a subordinate network role.

STATE COURTS AND THE POLITICAL SYSTEM

A crucial factor in state innovation was court stimulus. The 1970s was a period of expansion in state court influence over state and local educators. In California, the state education authorities were sued only four times in 1968, but in 1980 the state was sued thirty-four times in the first ten months alone. If courts were a stimulus, school finance reform is an excellent case of implementation problems stemming from judicial intervention. The legislature often regards the courts' legal principles as abstract and not useful in formulating legislative solutions. If the courts do not provide a clear signal of their intent but keep pressuring the legislature for change, then tension between the branches intensifies.

For example, in *Serrano*, the California Supreme Court enunciated a negative standard termed "fiscal neutrality": support of the schools cannot be a function of wealth other than the wealth of the state as a whole. There would be no significant relationship between local property wealth and local per-pupil expenditures. The vagueness of the phrase *fiscal neutrality* created enduring confusion in the California legislature. Were taxpayers or schoolchildren the intended beneficiaries of school finance reform? Should the legislature be concerned primarily with equalizing school district tax effort or with eliminating substantial expenditure differences between school districts? How much inequality in either sphere (tax equity, expenditure equity) would the state supreme court tolerate? Elmore and McLaughlin spell out some political consequences for the legislature.

The issue created a difficult problem of coalition politics. It produced two broad divisions among legislators—those who stood to gain or lose from tax equity, and those who stood to gain or lose from expenditure equity. Because the two divisions did not relate to each other in any straightforward way, legislators had no simple decision rule for figuring out whether they should be for or against a given reform proposal.[14]

Serrano also contained other fundamental conflicts. Court-initiated reform often flows from a negative injunction (like fiscal neutrality) in response to a political minority, but legislative compliance requires a majoritarian outcome, a positive plan, and a coalition of many interests. There was no broad-based constituency for school finance reform but, as we have seen, an elite interlocking network advocating the concept. Consequently, implementation of school finance reform was more difficult than the creation of free public schools was in response to a broad social movement in the nineteenth century. Given these difficulties, it is surprising that California was able to implement as much school finance change as it did by 1980; approximately 88 percent of California's pupils were in school districts with per-pupil expenditures that varied by no more than two hundred dollars.

THE SCOPE OF STATE POLICY INNOVATION
IN THE 1970s

The newest state finance reform is the tax limitation movement. If such a limitation focuses on the local property tax, as it did in Massachusetts and in California's Proposition 13, then local choice will be eroded. The California property tax is limited to 1 percent of assessed valuation, and there is no way local voters can increase their school expenditures beyond that level. An unintended effect of Proposition 13 was full state assumption of education finance and the elimination of local fund raising. Given the California tradition of extensive intervention, it is inevitable that state control will increase.

Following the passage of Proposition 13, the state has already required local school districts to give priority to child care and adult education. Yet many local boards wanted to reduce these two areas significantly.

School finance reform and movements such as Proposition 13 may stimulate statewide teacher bargaining. If the state controls all funding increases, then teachers must negotiate with the state for salary raises. Consequently, a two-tier approach may develop. Some issues, such as salary schedules and fringe benefits, would be bargained for at the state level, but other areas of school policy would be reserved for local negotiations. Two-tier negotiations, however, would restrict the ability to reach compromise solutions because trade-offs would no longer be possible between economic salary issues and other considerations, such as teacher preparation periods.

The demand for equal educational opportunity has spawned new state programs for populations with special needs. States now classify children in several ways, and they mandate services and standards for the various special categories of students. Some of these pupil classifications are vocational education, career education, mentally gifted, disadvantaged, migrants, underachievers, non-English-speaking, American Indians, pregnant minors, foster children, delinquent children, and twenty or more different categories of handicapped children. An example is found in Massachusetts, a state noted for its strong belief in local control, which adopted a sweeping special education law mandating entirely new programs. As a result, new procedures for individualized evaluation that exceed federal requirements were to be established and parents involved; new working relationships are required for teachers, psychologists, and other specialists; new evaluation techniques are outlined to avoid misclassification of students.

New bilingual statutes, in twenty-four states by 1981, now regulate local teaching policies. For example, in California, any class with ten or more pupils whose English is limited must have a state specified program. Federal programs for the disadvantaged and handicapped require the states to impose additional requirements on local schools. The states must determine if the local proposals meet federal regulations. Sixteen states have started their own programs for the disadvantaged, building on the federal concept. In short, in the 1970s, states became suspicious of how much local initiative and commitment to disadvantaged and minority populations there actually was without state regulations.

State governments have also been skeptical of local willingness to adopt innovative programs. Consequently, states have started innovative categorical programs for which localities must compete. Massachusetts has an experimental school program that combines magnet schools for multiracial populations with community control. California has the School Improvement Program, which provides over one hundred dollars per pupil to school-based councils composed of parents, teachers, administrators, and students. These school-site councils are charged with devising new ways to individualize education and meet other state goals. Some of these state innovations provide greater local flexibility; for example, legislation permits lawyers, craftspersons, and artists to teach courses. In addition, some states permit waivers of requirements if the local district can provide a special justification.

Another development has been state mandating of "accountability." As stated, between 1966 and 1976, thirty-five states passed accountability statutes, and fourteen claim to have "comprehensive systems" with several components, and despite a lack of common definition and concepts, four thousand pieces of accountability literature were published.[15] In effect, accountability has focused state control on school outcomes in addition to state-defined minimum inputs. Such control covers matters such as new budget formats (including program budgeting), new teacher evaluation requirements, new state tests and assessment devices that reorient local curricula, procedures for setting educational objectives, parent advisory councils for school sites, and minimum competency standards for high school graduation.

In Florida, for example, these various accountability techniques interact to enhance state control. State assessment tests in certain subjects are publicized through parent councils. Statewide tests are also required for high school graduation; students must score in the seventieth percentile or higher statewide to obtain a diploma. Student test scores are related to teacher evaluations. School districts in general fear the adverse publicity that can come with publication of test scores lower than those of other districts.

IS STATE CONTROL EXCESSIVE?

While much of the federal and state legal and bureaucratic entanglement in local education comes from a legitimate need to correct past failings such as the neglect of minorities in public schools, some fear that the pendulum may have swung too far. Moreover, there is no counterforce to this growth of nonlocal control. Dominant political and social forces are all moving in the same direction, toward more and more court and state intervention in local policymaking.[16] There is no national or state leadership advocating a complete reorganization and pruning of state education codes that would eliminate traditional and now obsolete regulations requiring substantial amounts of money. For example, thirty-one states have statutes requiring some form of contractual agreement between school systems and employees, but this mandate was not accompanied by repeal of personnel restrictions in prior state codes. States continue to set standards for personnel much as they did when teachers were not permitted to bargain with local school boards. This means that unions can begin their demands with the state code as a guaranteed floor.

Education has received poor publicity in recent years due to a variety of reasons—declining enrollments and test scores, vandalism, lack of discipline, and soaring costs. These complaints provide a rationale for state officials who contend that districts will neglect the needs of disadvantaged, bilingual, and handicapped children or waste money. States have increased their aid for specific purposes because they believe local boards are not tough enough to resist teacher demands for exorbitant salary increases. As a result, local officials frequently cannot act unilaterally but must take state regulations or guidelines into account.

Although the founding fathers had described state government as the keystone of the American governmental arch, by the 1960s several critics claimed that state government acted more like a fallen arch. Since elementary and secondary education consumes 58 percent of total state aid to local governments, the enhanced state role discussed above is an important general indicator of state policy implementation. While the 1960s was a decade of federal education innovation, the 1970s will be recorded as an era when the states were at the forefront. The federal era of the 1960s was followed by massive research on its effects. The 1980s should see a spate of research on state impact.

While it is easy to enumerate many policy areas in which states have encroached on local prerogatives, we lack an empirical assessment of overall aggregate impact on local decisions and operations. For example, researchers need to focus on how implementation of state policies affects classroom teachers. There are so many policies that the cumulative and interactive nature of local impact will be difficult to assess.[17] We know very little about the various effects of state rules and incentives—direct, indirect, or secondary. In 1981, we are about in the research stage with respect to state impact as we were vis-à-vis the federal role in 1970.

THE FUTURE STATE ROLE IN EDUCATION

It is unlikely that the past decade's impressive growth in the state role can continue. A strengthened and diversified state tax structure will confont (1) public support for slower growth in state spending; (2) slow or no real growth in the national economy; (3) demographic change, with client groups ceasing to expand; and (4) decreased stimulus from federal aid.[18] These national trends, however, obscure the rapid economic growth in several Sunbelt states that could continue to support their 1970–1980 growth rates in school financing. For example, economic growth in Texas permitted a jump in education expenditures from $1.2 billion in 1969 to $5.1 billion in 1979.

A major factor limiting state spending could be a "tax revolt," whether carried out through initiative or state legislation. However, a study by the Education Commission of the States found that the tax revolt is not a monolithic movement sweeping the country.[19] Voters perceive crucial differences between the various types of tax and expenditure limitation measures (TEL) and act on those perceptions. TELs aimed at limiting future growth in government expenditures elicited a response based on the respondent's philosophy about the proper role of government. TELs that required large property-tax cuts, however, were highly related to socioeconomic status and demographic characteristics. Case studies of TEL state campaigns by the Education Commission of the States revealed that successful strategies must be tailored to a specific state's attitudes and political culture. Yet the TEL movement is having a major effect in restraining state revenue growth. Recent growth in state revenues is driven by inflation and inhibited by political tax limitation efforts.

Whatever the outcome of the TEL movement, however, education will rely on state governments to provide its major fiscal sustenance in the 1980s. As we saw in chapter 8, local voter approval of property-tax increases has never recaptured the ground lost in the mid-1960s.[20] Indeed, a case can be made that local tax support for education will decline further in the 1980s. The proportion of people with a direct stake in education (for example, parents) who are not alienated from schools is declining. The major population sectors in which enrollments are increasing, such as Hispanics and low-income citizens, have little political influence over budgets. Special programs of interest to these groups, including bilingual education and desegregation, will lower support more from the rest of the population. Also, the number of people with no direct interest in education who, for a variety of reasons, are probable "No" voters in local school finance elections is increasing.[21] There will be a dramatic increase in the total number of senior citizens, who are also the citizens most likely to vote but who have no direct stake in the schools. Inflation psychology will depress any willingness to increase local property taxes. Moreover, education will confront increased competition for funding at the federal level from advocates for increased spending on defense, energy, and senior citizens. Given the probable erosion of political support at the local and federal levels, increased political cohesion of education groups at the state level is crucial.

During the 1970s, schools increasingly came to rely on state revenues. Maintaining the impressive growth in state support for education will be difficult, however, for the reasons just enumerated. The school finance reform political movement has peaked, but some state courts may continue to apply pressure for leveling up the low-spending districts. The state revenue base is the key to future fiscal support. In an era of tax limitation, public education groups may have to use their political muscle to win the redistribution of scarce state dollars from other public services over to education. This will require repairing the tattered alliances between teachers, administrators, school board members, and parent groups. Overall, the outlook for the state role in education appears to be a steady state in the 1980s, with expenditures lagging slightly behind inflation. The TEL movement is a strong indicator of the probable future trend—no drastic cutbacks but much slower increases.[22] The 1980s will be a decade of consolidating and digesting the large number of innovations from the 1970s.

NOTES

1. See Samuel C. Patterson, "The Political Cultures of the American States," *The Journal of Politics* 30 (February 1968): 187–209; David Elazar, *American Federalism: A*

View from the States (New York: Crowell, 1972). For a mid-1970s view of state education politics, see Roald Campbell and Tim Mazzoni, *State Policy Making for the Public Schools* (Berkeley: McCutchan, 1976). A recent synthesis of the loss of local control is in Mary A. Williams, ed., *Government in the Classroom* (New York: Academy of Political Science, 1979).

2. See Frederick M. Wirt, "School Policy Culture and State Centralization," in *Yearbook on the Politics of Education*, ed. Jay Scribner (Chicago: University of Chicago Press, 1977), pp. 164–87. See also Frederick M. Wirt, "What State Laws Say About Local Control," *Phi Delta Kappan* 59 (April 1978): 517–20.

3. For an overview of federal impact on states, see Joel Berke and Michael Kirst, *Federal Aid to Education* (Lexington, Mass.: Heath, 1972). For a subsequent review, see Mike Millstein, *Impact and Response* (New York: Teachers College Press, 1977). See also, Jerome Murphy, *State Education Agencies and Discretionary Funds* (Lexington, Mass.: Lexington Books, 1974).

4. See Joel Berke, *Answers to Inequity* (Berkeley: McCutchan, 1974), p. 223. Berke gives an overview of the fiscal, political, and legal evolution of state school finance reform from 1969 to 1974 and reprints the text of the *Rodriguez* case on pp. 206–80.

5. For a review of the court suits, see Lawyers' Committee for Civil Rights Under Law, *Summary of State-Wide School Finance Cases Since 1973* (Washington, D.C.: Lawyers' Committee for Civil Rights Under Law, 1980).

6. For the details of these school finance measures, see John Augenblick, *School Finance Reform in the States: 1979* (Denver: Education Commission of the States, 1979).

7. For an elaboration of this conflict, see Michael Kirst, "A Tale of Two Networks," *Taxing and Spending* 3 (Winter 1980): 43–49. The author is conducting a large empirical analysis of these networks.

8. Stephen Carroll, *The Search for Equity in School Finance* (Santa Monica, Calif.: Rand, 1979).

9. Susan Fuhrman et al., *State Education Politics: The Case of School Finance Reform*, (Denver: Education Commission of the States, 1979).

10. Jack L. Walker. "The Diffusion of Innovations Among the American States," *American Political Science Review* 63 (September 1969): 880–99.

11. Virginia Gray, "Innovation in the States: A Diffusion Study," *American Political Science Review* 67 (December 1973): 1174–85.

12. For the producer-interest-generated policy approach, see Robert Agger, Daniel Goldrich, and Bert Swanson, *The Rulers and the Ruled* (New York: Wiley, 1964). For an analysis of policy issue networks at the federal level, see Hugh Heclo, "Issue Networks and the Executive Establishment," in *The New American Political System,* ed. Anthony King (Washington, D.C.: American Enterprise Institute, 1978), pp. 87–124.

13. Douglas Rose, "National and Local Forces in State Politics," *American Political Science Review* 67 (December 1973): 1162–74. For an overview of the political science debate on policy diffusion, see Robert Eyestone, "Confusion, Diffusion, and Innovation," *American Political Science Review* 71 (December 1977): 441–47.

14. Richard T. Elmore and Milbrey McLaughlin, *Reform and Retrenchment: The Politics of California School Finance Reform* (Santa Monica, Calif.: Rand, 1981). For an excellent case analysis of a similar problem in New Jersey, see Richard Lehne, *The Quest for Justice* (New York: Longman, 1978).

15. Michael Kirst and Gail Zellman, *Accountability: What Is the Federal Role?* (Santa

Monica, Calif.: Rand, 1976).

16. For case studies, see Mary F. Williams, *Government in the Classroom* (New York: Academy of Political Science, 1979).

17. For an elaboration on this point, see Jerome T. Murphy, "State Role in Education: Past Research and Future Directions," *Educational Evaluation and Policy Analysis* 2, no. 4 (1980): 34–51.

18. For details on these trends, see Michael W. Kirst and Walter J. Garms, "The Demographic, Fiscal, and Political Environment of Public School Finance in the 1980's" in *School Finance Policies and Practice: The 1980's a Decade of Conflict*, ed. James Guthrie (Cambridge, Mass.: Ballinger, 1981).

19. Robert Pulaich et al., *Tax and Expenditure Limitation Referendum* (Denver: Education Commission of the States, 1980).

20. John Hall and Phillip Piele, "Selected Determinants of Precinct Voting Decisions in School Budget Elections," *Western Political Quarterly* 24 (September 1976): 440–56.

21. Philip K. Piele, "Voting Behavior in Local School Financial Referenda: An Update of some Earlier Projections," (Address to the American Education Finance Association, San Diego, California, March 1980). See also, Susan Abramowitz and Stuart Rosenfeld, eds., *Declining Enrollment* (Washington, D.C.: National Institute for Education, 1978).

22. For an overview of the impact of TEL, see Marc Menchik and Anthony Pascal, *The Equity Effects of Restraints on Taxing and Spending* (Santa Monica, Calif.: Rand, 1980).

10

The Courts As Policy Innovator and Implementor

COURTS AS A NEW POLICY AGENCY

The enlarged roles of state and federal governments in the local schools come not only from legislation and administrative mandates. In the last quarter century, the judicial branch has also become a major participant in what local schools do or are prevented from doing. Group after group, frustrated by school policies, have turned to the state and federal courts for relief. The courts became involved not merely in settling disputes, which is traditional adjudication; circumstances also often compelled them to initiate departures in policy solutions to school problems and then to oversee their implementation. This chapter surveys this dual judicial role for several major school innovations that have affected all school districts in some ways.

Litigation as a Political Strategy

A crude but clear measure of this recent development is seen in a simple tally of the volume and kinds of litigation pending against just one school authority in 1979, the California State Board of Education. This information is set out in table 10.1. Ranging from individuals to classes of plaintiffs, these numbers highlight a major change in the politics of education. Not only the quantity but the kinds of cases

253

Table 10.1
Pending Litigation Against the California Board of Education,
December 1979

Discrimination	Money	Curriculum	District Reorganization	Miscellaneous	
11 race	10 contract	5 handicapped		3 nonpublic schools	
3 bilingual	disputes	programs		3 citizen participation	
2 testing	8 local	2 textbooks		2 personal injuries	
2 employment	finances	1 inadequate		2 accreditation	
1 sexual				1 strike	
19	18	8	6	11	= 62
31%	29%	13%	10%	18%	= 100%

listed in table 10.1 are in many cases new to the schools. All those involving discrimination, the handicapped, and citizen participation would probably not have been the basis for litigation a few years ago, but now they account for over 40 percent of this 1979 list. The table actually understates the situation, for it excludes teacher certification cases that are handled by a separate state agency.[1]

The Magna Carta in San Bernardino

Another place to see results of the expanded judicial role is in the local district. For example, note the consequences of a set of mid-1970s Supreme Court decisions on the suspension and expulsion of fractious students. The high court insisted that children, too, had claim to the constitutional protection of due process of law, a concept with roots in the Magna Carta of 1215. Thus pupils could not be punished without a hearing and notice of complaint. What this means in district terms can be seen in the San Bernardino, California, schools, which by 1979–80 had over six pages of rules covering the requirements needed to be met before expulsion.[1]

First, an expulsion hearing was required, involving among other things a written notice to the pupil's parents or guardians at least ten days beforehand. This notice had to include: the date and place of the hearing, a statement of specific facts, a statement of charges, and a copy of all the discipline rules in the district. Moreover, the pupil's parent or guardian had to be given the opportunity to: appear in person with counsel, obtain and inspect all relevant documents, confront and question all witnesses and all evidence presented, present evidence in written or documentary form, and present witnesses.

That is just the beginning of a process that results in a hearing before three certificated staff members who review the case, conduct the hearing, and make a recommendation. This, in turn, is reviewed by the superintendent, who can make one of several decisions, including expulsion. Each step has specified deadlines and documents, and there is also the possiblity of appeal from the decision. In the last year, .5 percent of the cases reviewed were expelled, equally black and white in numbers but proportionately more of the former. All these details are a response to the thrust of outside regulation and in particular to the role of the judiciary as distinct from governmental administrators.

COURTS AND POLITICS

At first thought, courts seem an unlikely adjunct of schools and, for the naive, an unlikely partner in politics. Yet the history of education has been shaped by important court decisions on the duties and responsibilities of school components; though trivial, the right of students not to have their hair cut is only the latest of many such contributions. At a more significant level, the United States Supreme Court has been directly involved in the question of religion in our schools—Bible reading, required prayers, flag salutes, the transportation and other expenses of parochial students. Court involvement can be as direct—but narrow—as whether schools can be prohibited from teaching German or as indirect—and extensive—as whether schools can be segregated by race. School officials may react by massive noncompliance, as with the Bible and prayer decisions, but to be indifferent is very difficult.[2]

Court involvement in such matters surprises only those who view the bench as a political eunuch. Contemporary analysts of the judiciary emphasize not merely its behavior but the values that this behavior reflects. Judges are political because they must choose between competing values brought before them in conflict. As early as 1840, Alexis de Tocqueville was noting that "scarcely any political question arises in the United States that is not resolved, sooner or later, into a judicial question." The reason for this is that when citizens differ in the political arena, a recourse for resolution of that contest may be the courtroom. The form and rules of judicial contests may differ from those in other sites, but they are still essentially political. That is because contenders are seeking the authority of the political system to justify and command the distribution of resources—such as rights and property—that each deems desirable. The allocation of resources that follows from a court mandate can be as effective as that which issues from a legislature.[3]

What, then, are the relationships between the judiciary as part of the political system of the state and the political system of the school? What are the constraints and strengths in this relationship? What are the accommodations and conflicts in the input, conversion, feedback, and outcome phases of the political process here? How does federalism filter the outcome? What values are reflected among participants? These are the questions we pursue to illuminate the role of judges as policy initiators and implementors.

THE JUDICIARY AS A POLITICAL SUBSYSTEM

The judiciary is also a subsystem of the larger political system. Like other subsystems—legislatures, agencies, and executives—the judiciary's environment presents it with demands that it could convert into outputs. These interact with the environment to become outcomes in time and thus can generate later inputs to the court. This assumes that there are no distinct boundaries of the judicial subsystem separating it off from the others. Instead, it interacts with legislative and executive subsystems continuously, as well as with private systems in the social environment. Judges may not personally interact, but their decisions and opinions certainly do.

The environment judges operate in marches constantly into their chambers, sometimes unobtrusively and sometimes loudly seeking the protection or enhancement of certain values. The judge is not free to decide such matters alone. A historical constitutional framework imposes certain constraints, and these traditional forces also shape who is made a judge and what he or she does. Professional canons have their effect on who is selected or even considered; institutional traditions require procedures that shape the pace and division of labor. Further, the partisanship of extramural party life, which has affected a judge's recruitment and deliberations in our past, is not without influence even today.[4] Changes in the social order outside judicial chambers bring changes inside to the courts' domain, to its issues, structures, and attitudes.[5]

The value conflict thrust into the court seeks authoritative allocation of resources to implement those values. For this reason, courts have a *manifest* function of resolving conflict in accordance with special rules. Such decisions have an impact—not always favorable—on all branches of the national government and at all levels of the federal system. This task of conflict resolution also performs *latent* functions for the values underlying the conflict. Thus, the Supreme Court legitimizes national policies and the values they reflect and, conversely, illegitimatizes others. The difficulty, of course, is for the Court to do this in such a way that support for the courts as an institution does not decrease while their decisions are assured of acceptance.

Further, the Supreme Court must maintain some kind of balance with other national subsystems in order to reduce potential conflict among their respective policy decisions. In the process, the judiciary provides signals to litigants, general public, and political subsystems and their actors (including their own local courts) as to the policy-value outputs it will reinforce. The issuance of such signals is not the same as their acceptance, however. The Court throughout its history has had to balance itself carefully at key intersections of a nationally separated government, a federally divided nation, and a diverse population. Yet judicial policy making has shown more consistency than the preceding might imply. Whether at the trial or appellate level, distinguishable processes are commonly at work: initiation of controversies, accommodation via out-of-court settlement, persuasion of judge or jury, decision making, implementation of decisions, and their reconsideration.

All of this is understandable as a facet of systems analysis. Inputs for the judicial subsystem are evident as reflections of environmental demands. Their form and presentation differ for this subsystem, however. The lobbyist gives way to the lawyer, buttonholing becomes law review articles, and publicity campaigns are exchanged for litigants' briefs.[6] The demands are presented formally, dealing with matters of logic and legal precedent, although recent research has stressed the independent role of a judge's values in the decisional process. Outputs are seen as a function of the interplay of judicial values within the court procedures, all of this with political conse-

quences for the environment.[7] It is particularly when the issue is new
or has new applications that the psychological values held by the
bench exert an independent force as an explanation of judicial
outcomes.

However such decisions are derived, they constitute outputs for
society. They are something more than a statement of which litigant
won and lost. Rather, they instruct a larger circle as to the value norms
that the judicial subsystem seeks to impose upon the environment. At
different periods in our history, the norms of political, social, and
economic freedom have assumed different judicial priorities. We will
shortly turn to one of these.

The final need is to understand the impact of judicial outputs on
society. While the Court may signal authoritative norms, what if no
one notices or, if noticing, defies them or, if obeying, misinterprets
them? When the Court confirms what is widely accepted already, as
with its nineteenth-century opposition to polygamy, output and
outcome are similar, for compliance is very high. When, however, the
Court innovates in accepted norms, some gap between output and
outcome is to be expected, and compliance will be less than complete.

The conditions under which the judiciary can innovate are very
constraining. Given a majority of justices favoring a change, a national
majority in similar agreement, and the chances that the Court's
decision would not hurt it in other policy areas, innovation would be
forthcoming. But these combinations have not often existed in our
history; indeed, they have not in other political subsystems. Such an
absence accounts for much of the inertia and procrastination facing
emergent demands in the American political system. If the Court
moves when the maximum conditions do not exist, considerable
dissonance arises from other political subsystems. Then the Court is
said to lack "self-restraint" and is accused of being "activist."

More important, when the the output does generate dissonance,
the feedback will show evasion of the original decisions. So it was in
the school desegregation decisions of recent years. Not until the Court
was joined by a national majority and other elements of the national
political system was there compliance with the Court's insistence
on the social norm of racial equality in the education of children. In
the 1970s, however, this consensus fell apart, and the Court was
separated from the public and the other agencies of national government. Then it took on new roles of implementation.

INPUT AND CONVERSION IN SOUTHERN DESEGREGATION

The 1954 case of *Brown* v. *the Board of Education of Topeka* represents both an ending and a beginning of the Court's view of the linkage between race and schools.[8] The tumultuous events since then are too detailed for more than a sketch, but enough can be shown to suggest much about the Court as a political agency in the innovation and implementation of school policy.

The 1954 case was a dramatic turning away from six previous decades when the judiciary accepted "separate but equal" education in the South. Indicators of this judicial change of mind were seen during cases in the 1930s and 1940s, as the Court insisted that "equal" must mean truly equal for the education of Blacks—and it rarely did, of course. The *Brown* case was a challenge to de jure segregation of public education in four states and the District of Columbia, but all of the South was also challenged.

The cases arose as a direct result of a private party, the National Association for the Advancement of Colored People (NAACP), acting for its members' children. The NAACP sought a declaration that segregation violated the "equal protection of the laws" clause of the Fourteenth Amendment, no matter how equal the facilities provided were. Joining the NAACP were nineteen other groups in supporting arguments to the Court (for example, the ACLU, CIO, and the U.S. Solicitor General), speaking for the administrations of a Democratic president (Harry S. Truman) and later a Republican president (Dwight D. Eisenhower). The Supreme Court delayed its decision during the accession to power of the latter president, while many states insisted that the tradition of legalized school segregation (found in twenty-one states, seventeen requiring it) be maintained.

In May 1954, the lengthy deliberation finally yielded the historic opinion that the doctrine of "separate but equal" has no place in the field of public education. "Separate educational facilities are inherently unequal," the justices proclaimed unanimously. Yet how was this turnaround to be implemented? On this question, the Court heard arguments for yet another year, finally deciding only that "all deliberate speed" should be employed to abolish the dual school system. Private accounts indicate that the Court members were badly torn over remedies for this now-defined constitutional ill. Some wanted immediate compliance, some wanted it done a grade at a time, and some wanted it left totally to the states. The resulting vague formula was the only compromise Chief Justic Earl Warren could contrive to present a unanimous face to the nation.

In the absence of exact judicial guidelines for implementation, the southern states did very little except to throw up a variety of resistances into the feedback process. The first edition of this book detailed this elaborate barrage. The outcome was almost no change in the deep South but some in the border states. A decade after the *Brown* decision, there was still not a single desegregated district in Mississippi. During this first decade, public opinion had moved to a greater acceptance of the concept in the North but not in the South.

This stalemate changed dramatically in the Great Society era due to a combination of new laws on civil rights and education and the strong enforcement of desegregation by President Lyndon Johnson's administration.[9] The Supreme Court also came out of a decade of silence following the *Brown* decision with a set of decisions voiding the evasive tactics of southern states and, eventually, upholding the use of busing if it were the only policy that made desegregation possible. From the mid-1960s through the 1970s, then, even when later presidents withdrew active support of this change, the courts in Washington and the local districts heard individual suits against many southern school systems and with rare exception upheld Black plaintiffs.

By 1980 in the South, despite a trickle of white children into private "Christian" academies to avoid desegregation, the totally segregated school district or school site was a rarity. Even as early as 1972, the percentage of Black students in predominately white schools had risen from 18 percent in 1968 to 44 percent, while in the North actual segregation rose. When federal administrative action was joined to judicial pressure, the results were impressive. One study of thirty-three Georgia districts found that the only successful federal strategy for desegregation was "coercion to compliance," that is, the threat to withhold ESEA school funds.[10]

By the end of the 1970s, there were many changes evident in the South. For example, there was a dramatic change in the opinion polls from whites who had once objected to integrated education. In the South, where most desegregation had taken place, white opposition to integrating their children in schools with even a *few* Blacks had been 72 percent in 1959 but was only 15 percent in 1975; if the schools were *half* Black, the opposition still fell in those years, from 83 to 38 percent. In the North, the white opposition was always less, whatever the proportion of Black students in schools.[11] But repeatedly, whites, by as large as 75 to 80 percent, objected to busing as a way to do the job. Typically, in the same election Florida voters opposed busing but supported desegregation, both by large majorities. Yet in seven county-wide, desegregated school systems in Florida about the same time, parents were found grudgingly to comply with desegregation if they stayed with public schools (most did); their general attitudes, for or against desegregation, shaped their judgment of whether it was working.[12]

DESEGREGATION IN THE NORTH

The Resistance Continues

Outside the South in recent years there has been another picture, often repeating the earlier southern efforts. As segregation diminished in the South, it increased elsewhere. By 1976, the United States Commission on Civil Rights, using complex demographic measures, found segregation for Blacks and Hispanics to be least in the Southeast, or the old Confederacy, but greatest in the Northeast and North Central regions.[13] Central cities in the North increasingly became islands of minorities in a sea of white suburbanites. City after city in the northeastern quadrant of the country became majority Black, first in school population and then in total population. The courts were an active agent in this part of the nation too. Through changes in presidential administrations and new membership, the Supreme Court unanimously overturned vestiges of de jure desegregation, although they wavered increasingly in the late 1970s on how to define other forms of this separation.[14]

Just as after the *Brown* decision when southern school systems delayed and obstructed, so in the North, middle-sized and large cities used a variety of devices to resist compliance. When such matters entered federal courts on challenge, however, the school systems were found to be using a variety of methods to maintain separate school systems. Table 10.2 presents the court findings in twenty-six northern sites, revealing how far the courts had moved from simply striking down laws explicitly and racially desegregating schools.

Table 10.2
Discrimination Found by Federal Courts in Northern School Desegregation Cases, 1956–76

School District

Type of discrimination found by courts	Benton Harbor	Boston	Buffalo	Cincinnati	Cleveland	Dayton	Denver	Detroit	Gary	Grand Rapids	Hillsboro	Indianapolis	Kalamazoo	Kansas City	Las Vegas	Manhasset	Minneapolis	New Rochelle	Omaha	Oxnard	Pasadena	Pittsburg	Pontiac	San Francisco	South Holland—Phoenix	Springfield
Discriminatory drawing or alteration of attendance zones	—	×	×	—	×	—	×	×	—	—	×	×	×	—	—	×	×	×	×	×	×	—	×	×	×	—
Discriminatory location of new schools	—	×	×	—	×	—	×	—	—	—	—	×	×	—	×	—	×	—	×	×	×	—	×	×	×	—
Discriminatory expansion of existing schools (such as enlarging minority schools rather than transferring minority students to nearby white schools with available space)	—	×	—	—	×	—	×	—	—	—	—	×	—	—	×	—	×	—	—	×	×	—	—	×	—	—
School board's failure to relieve overcrowding at white schools by transferring white students to nearby minority schools with available space	—	×	×	—	×	—	—	×	—	—	—	×	—	—	—	—	—	—	—	×	×	—	—	×	—	—
Discriminatory hiring of teachers and administrators	—	×	×	—	—	—	×	—	—	×	—	—	—	—	×	—	—	—	—	—	×	—	×	—	×	—
Discriminatory assignment of teachers and administrators	×	×	×	—	×	—	—	—	—	—	—	×	×	—	—	—	×	—	×	×	×	—	×	×	—	—
Discriminatory promotion of teachers and administrators	—	×	—	—	—	—	×	—	—	—	—	—	—	—	—	—	—	—	—	—	×	—	—	—	×	—
School board's perpetuation or exacerbation of school segregation by its strict adherence to neighborhood school policy *after* segregated school system had developed	—	—	×	—	×	—	—	—	—	—	—	—	—	—	×	×	×	×	—	×	×	—	—	—	—	×

School board's failure to adopt a proposed integration plan or to implement previously adopted plans

— — X — — — — — — X X — —

School board's adoption of "open enrollment" or "free transfer" policies, with the effect of allowing whites to transfer out of black schools without producing a significant movement of blacks to white schools or whites to black schools

— X X X — — — — — X X — — X X X — — — —

School segregation de facto rather than the result of state action

— — X — — — — X X — — X

Source: Center for National Policy Review, Catholic University Law School, "Why Must Northern School Systems Desegregate? A Summary of Federal Court Findings in Recent Cases" (Washington, D.C., January 1977; processed); cited in Gary Orfield, *Must We Bus?* (Washington, D.C.: Brookings Institution, 1978).

There is much variation around the country in the amount of effort necessary to desegregate. Most school districts have such small minority populations that desegregation would be a small task; most of the Northwestern states are of this kind. Elsewhere, some states have problems with only a single city, and some of these have been desegregated relatively easily—Denver, Omaha, Minneapolis-Saint Paul, Las Vegas. In a review of this variation, Orfield concluded that "Most of the thirty-three states outside the southern and border state regions have either negligible segregation problems or ones that are manageable without basic change."[15] Finally, it is in the largest northern cities that the conditions for desegregation have become worse and will continue to do so in the 1980s. "White flight" has depleted many of these cities of whites, and even "Black flight" is noted in Newark, Chicago, and San Francisco; the great middle-class hegira to the suburbs has no respect for color.

Desegregation Methods: Busing and Metropolitan Plans

There has been a flood of litigation surrounding the northern struggles, as suggested in table 10.2. Several principles had emerged out of that complex legal situation by 1981.[16] Unconstitutional segregation must indeed be removed by district authorities; it is their inescapable responsibility. Also, segregation existing in a significant area of a city establishes the presumption that the entire school system is unconstitutionally segregated. Further, plaintiffs and judges can use such information as site selection, boundary lines, and other matters that have been board policy as means to determine racial effects. Moreover, besides Blacks, Hispanic children must also be desegregated. Finally, metropolitan desegregation remedies are not suitable to deal with the problems of a single district (like the central city). Although desegregation of both the central city and its suburbs has been offered by many as a solution to the problem of white flight from central cities—and the Florida evidence strongly shows it can be effective[17]—the Supreme Court rejected it by a five to four vote in 1974; later it was upheld for special reasons in Wilmington, Delaware. As the composition of the Court changed with the more conservative appointments made by President Nixon, a majority came to accept the view that it was not necessarily evidence of discrimination when school board policies *resulted* in segregation. Rather, it had to be shown that this result was the *intent* of school officials—a much more difficult proposition to prove, although not impossible.

Yet much to the disappointment of conservatives on this matter—including recent presidents—the Court upheld the busing remedy when intent was demonstrated. "Busing" had become a symbol of deeply held opposing views among the general public. It was a symbol unrelated to a reality in which half of all American students bus to school, segregated academies actually bus most of their own children, many pupils can be moved with only minor adjustments in the busing schedule, and other evidences that busing is not what the contention is about. Opponents see it as an invasion of the traditional "neighborhood school" attendance zones, which they defend as a part of developing children's sense of social self. Busing supporters see opponents as more concerned about racial fears than about educational results ("It's not the bus, it's us!")[18] A 1980 study found a curious little-noted effect of busing in metropolitan desegregation plans. Unlike other cities of comparable size, central cities involved in desegregation with their suburbs show that more residential integration takes place *after* busing and that the busing itself decreases in amount. Charlotte, North Carolina, became a third more integrated racially and therefore bused less over a ten-year period.[19]

This brief review of court-initiated desegregation demonstrates the judiciary's potential for societal influence and the resulting differences in group response. Despite the possibility for resolving the conflict in busing and metropolitan plans, the changing demography of American cities and continuing white resistance make further progress unlikely in the biggest cities during the 1980s. We will consider the role of courts futher in order to review another judicial policy innovation occurring under different circumstances.

THE COURTS AND FINANCE REFORM

Earlier in this book we pointed out that a major aspect of the new school turbulence is found in efforts to reform the basis of school financing. As with desegregation, the judiciary played a key role in stimulating this effort, and it did so by formulating a general constitutional evil and calling for a change in school policy. Unlike desegregation, however, most of this effort has been a product of the states' highest courts, not of the United States Supreme Court. By a narrow five to four majority in 1974, the Supreme Court refused to claim a constitutional safeguard against finance schemes that discriminated between rich and poor.

Finance reform of the schools began in California as a result of the stimulus of the reform network cited earlier.[20] That state's supreme court declared a new principle, in *Serrano* v. *Priest*, that the "quality of public education may not be a function of the wealth of . . . a pupil's parents and neighbors." Because financing schemes had to possess "fiscal neutrality" and California's did not, therefore it offended the equal protection clause of the federal and state constitutions, and so reform would have to be undertaken by the state legislature. And so it was to be, as across the land challenges to over half the state school financing systems sprang up like daffodils in the spring. By the early 1980s, several dozen states had made some changes, some minor but some major, to meet this new standard. In some states, the route of the referendum was attempted, but it was much less effective than a legislative alternative. While the Supreme Court's refusal to join their state brethren in this reform halted matters for awhile during the mid-1970s, the pace picked up again shortly thereafter.

More inequities than just those traceable to taxable wealth came under attack. Complex state financial support formulas were introduced to adjust for city service overburdens and for special kinds of educational needs afflicting handicapped, vocational, and other educationally needy children.[21] The degree of technicality now contemplated generates serious problems. The courts are moving into areas that scholars may know less about—how to adjust for pupil needs in some precise way, to control for uncontrollable costs of education, or to compensate for municipal overburden. It was much easier when the task was only to devise formulas by which equal property tax effort resulted in equal amounts of local school revenue.

As noted in an earlier chapter, such changes also require additional state funds to raise low-wealth districts, but such new fund demands come in at a time when state surpluses have been drained by inflation or else there are tax or expenditure limitation movements (the "Proposition 13" syndrome). Political limitations also emerge out of the effort to sustain a reform coalition through economic straits, where each partner worries about getting its own slice of limited resources.[22] That need became even more pressing when the federal government under presidents of both parties was reluctant to increase its share of local school costs.

The initiative of the state courts thus generated a flurry of legislative actions, and both court and legislature were further stimulated by an elite of scholars and educational reformers. The latter met with much success in many states at both arenas of power, providing authorities with new knowledge and policy options, as noted earlier. If success is measured by the number of states addressing the problem of resource inequity, then the reform did well; at least half of the states made changes. But if success is measured by how much money actually got redistributed to improve the poor's schooling, the evidence is less certain. An intensive 1979 study of five states indeed found changes in the tax imbalances, but some of the poorest districts had not benefited; they may in fact have lost ground.[23] But the effects of the great stagflation of the late 1970s and early 1980s confounded this question of effects. Certainly the reform left behind a strong cohort of school finance reform specialists, possessed of inventive minds, and the knowledge resources needed to fight on another day.

ROLE OF THE JUDICIARY IN TRADITIONAL AND REFORM LITIGATION

These descriptive accounts of two major educational reforms in which the judiciary played a major part do not exhaust either the impact of this process or the reforms; the latter are much too extensive for any but the most superficial review. Rather, it is to the meaning of the courts in the political process that we now turn, to its role in the origins and implementing of public policy, and to its place in the political process.

Judicial and Legislative Policy Functions Compared

It would help to understand first that there are far more similarities between what courts and legislatures do than is popularly known.[24] Traditional litigation may seem very different from the action in sweaty legislative committee rooms or boisterous chambers, but the differences are in some part matters of form. Also, some have argued that reform litigation differs from the traditional litigation, partaking more of legislation than do court decisions.[25] Table 10.3 brings these three policy processes together in comparative fashion to demonstrate their policy equivalents.

The distinctions emerge clearly between, on the one hand, traditional litigation and, on the other, public law litigation and legislation.

Table 10.3

**Structural Aspects of Traditional Litigation,
Public Law Litigation, and Legislation**

Structural Aspect	Traditional Litigation	Public Law Litigation	Legislation
Parties	Two, with mutually exclusive interests	Many with diverse interests— for example, amici in *Robinson v. Cahill*	Intervention by multiple interest groups is the rule
Fact-Finding	Retrospective and adjudicative (what happened, and so on)	Prospective and "functional"— what will work	Problem-solving approach is the norm
Relief	Coextensive with violation— nature of violation determines relief	Violation tells little about relief. New factors, like cost, enter in	Total pragmatism
	Relief closes transaction	Continuing jurisdiction, relief modifiable	Corrective amendments common
	Relief "nonintrusive," especially damages	Relief often entails running local governments	More detailed plans common
	Relief imposed and adjudicated (defendant has no role)	Formulation of decree involves negotiation, compromise	Social reform usually accommodates opposing interests
Decision Maker's Role	Judge is passive as to fact-finding, uninvolved with relief, no public identity	Judge must form court's position on facts, work out relief, and become identified with cause	Legislative fact-finding committees, work on specifics of bill, legislator identification with bill.

Source: William H. Clune with Robert E. Lindquist, "Understanding and Researching the Implementation of Education Laws: The Essential Characteristics of Implementation," Law, Governance, and Education Seminar, Institute for Research on Educational Finance and Governance, Stanford, February 1980, p. 31.

Table 10.4
Judicial and Legislative Implementation Tasks

Courts	Legislatures
Decree formulation: negotiations between plaintiffs and defendants, use of experts, concern with such factors as fiscal burden and personnel resentment, setting intelligible standards.	*Formation of legislation:* input from interested parties, expert testimony, budgetary role, setting intelligible standards.
Monitoring: retention of jurisdiction and compliance reports, need for master or special experts to serve as unbiased ally of courts.	*Administrative monitoring:* compliance data, field offices, inspections, and so on.
Dispute resolution: application of standards to new facts, differing interpretations of standards.	*Administrative dispute resolution:* negotiation when standards are unreasonable, appeal to administrative law judge, and so forth.
Enforcement: use of contempt power, brinkmanship, clarification of responsibilities, obtaining new resources, graduated sanctions.	*Enforcement:* continuum of harassment (extra reports, inspections), threatened fund cutoffs, actual cutoffs, and so on.

Source: Note, "Implementation Problems in Institutional Reform Litigation," *Harvard Law Review* 91 (December 1977): 428–63.

The first deals with only two interests, looks backward, provides relief for a revealed violation that is sharply defined and, finally, involves a policy actor (judge) who is passively unpartisan in the matter. But the other two possess quite different qualities. They deal with multiple interests and look to the future for a "solution" that will work; the relief sought is modifiable and involves others; and the policy actors (judge, legislature) are partisan in the sense of being advocates. Of course, table 10.3 skims over much that is complex, but it directs attention to what many see as the new role of courts in matters of public policy.

The implementation of decisions made by these bodies also takes on other similarities. Table 10.4 sets out different tasks that courts and legislatures undertake when they seek to reform an institution, as in the cases of racial discrimination and finance noted above. In either case, implementation breaks down any time even one of these tasks is undone. Note the problems that arise in just one of the tasks, for example, "setting intelligible standards." We have seen in the discrimination and finance cases sketched above that the highest courts—federal and state—failed in this task in their initial decrees. When there was no supportive coalition to seek fuller compliance in the state legislatures—as with desegregation—parties had to go back to courts for standard setting drawn from specific cases. Yet where there was support for the court decision, as with financial reform, parties in each state still had to work their way through the labyrinth of the legislative process, in which each member was vitally interested in the outcome for his or her district. But in the latter case a much more precise set of standards—various formulas of tax reform—resulted in the early stages than was the case with desegregation.

Judicial Strategies in the Policy Process

Why, then, should courts or legislatures be so vague? There are some major strategic advantages to ambiguity under some circumstances. As van Geel noted about the Supreme Court on the desegregation cases:

Ambiguity may be, in part, a tactic to minimize the anger caused by the opinion. An unclear opinion leaves people puzzled and, consequently, less angry. Ambiguity also leaves the Court more room to maneuver in the future, to change directions as practical requirements arise which recommend such a change. Finally, ambiguity might be marked up to judicial uncertaintly regarding its proper role without scheme of government. . . . When doctrine is less clear, this leaves more room for the political process to have its way . . . choices can be left to the discretion of others.[26]

If there are change agents willing to seize on one aspect of the ambiguous goal that the court sets, such as with finance reform, then the political process can be carried out, but what if judicial vagueness lacks any decisive public support so that normal political processes are blocked? That occurred in the South for a decade after the *Brown* decision and increasingly in the North as Congress and presidents backed off from enforcement of both court orders and national law.[27] Then the other tasks of implementation noted in table 10.4—monitoring, dispute resolution, enforcement—fall into the laps of the judges. The result is that the highest court at first seeks to provide only broad guidelines, but these change as more and more specific situations are brought to it on appeal. This means that the lower level judges

become increasingly embroiled in the implementation of desegregation. As Buell's close study of the Boston case reveals, the monitoring
judge can get into innumerable minor details of school administration—boundary changes, personnel replacements, and so on—
either because the local school system ignores the original order to
desegregate or because it thoroughly resists the order.[28] As judges
become increasingly faced by noncompliance with what to them is a
constitutionally based order, they are compelled to take on more of
the implementation tasks usually associated with administrative oversight for legislation.

AN EVALUATION OF JUDICIAL ACTION

There are clearly limits to what judges can do. It is not the case that
judges should do nothing when there is no political support for
correcting an unconstitutional situation. If this were the case, we
could leave the interpretation of every law up to each citizen, an
excellent formula for social anarchy and a major reason why we have
rules of law in the first place. But in over two decades of judicial
involvement in major policy reform and institutional changes, courts
have been able to do some things better than others. As a scholar
concerned about the "limits of legalism," Kirp has noted that the
federal government can provide national standards of service and
behavior and can provide funds to implement these, but settlement of
the standards' details is better attained by political agencies at all levels
of government.[29] Yet, as southern and northern cases demonstrate,
what if those agencies not only do not act but actually obstruct the
national standard?

Judicial Activism and Its Effects

How can judicial activism be characterized as to its consequences?
Besides having direct effects upon groups of citizens, it can affect
other governmental institutions as well. Note this chapter's opening
references to the San Bernardino structural reforms, pursuant to state
law and Supreme Court requirements, in due process for potential
expellees. Or, in desegregation, there is what Orfield terms a "ratchet-
ing" effect, in which one court's determination that a particular school
practice is discriminatory becomes an input to federal agencies; they

incorporate it into their regulations, which can then be used in other courts as litigation arises. Or courts may affect one another more directly. State supreme courts have been found to influence one another mutually in public policy initiatives, a form of "horizontal federalism," for example, in school finance reform.[30]

Convoluted events in New Jersey over financial reform brought the state supreme court into conflict with the state legislature.[31] The latter's lack of guidelines for policy direction, as well as its mandate to correct the unconstitutional financing law, threw the politics of that state into great conflict for eighteen months in 1974–1976. However, the results did establish standards for generating challenge to such laws in other states, just as the California decision in the *Serrano* case in the late 1960s set off a round of challenges.[32] A close analysis of the New Jersey controversy by Lehne concluded that the results demonstrated that the judiciary's main role must be "agenda setting," not "decision making." That is, courts do their utmost when they present policy issues that other government agencies must resolve without designating the actual process of solution.

Others have noted the broader policy roles of state supreme courts in our history. They have innovated in policy making, complemented state legislative goals, elaborated the meaning of Supreme Court opinions, restricted the latter's opinions to protect their state's laws from invalidation, and lobbied in legislature to maintain and develop their own judicial institution.[33] All of these actions have consequences for public policy—causing new policy issues to emerge, stimulating discussion of policy alternatives, authoritatively deciding the direction of new policies, and overseeing policy administration.

When undertaking implementation, the judiciary is in the position of possessing considerable authority, trust, and information. A judge is thus in a strategic position in policy conflict to assure that decisions are emphatically enforced. The judicial presence changes the power quotient of the plaintiffs, for if court sanctions and information can be added to their side, law can much more easily be woven into the fabric of social life. Policy goals thus become more easily put into effect. However, courts can also lag in such matters; they can misconceive and misapply knowledge, and they can use sanctions that are too clumsy and are actually counterproductive. Then, as is true of other governmental agencies who fail in their political tasks, the policy results will not meet plaintiffs' needs and so will generate lack of trust in the courts.[34]

The Judiciary in the World of School Policy

The judiciary has made its inescapable role in the arena of educational and other policies much more evident in the last two decades. When it *does not* act to define problems and needs that are policy relevant, other agencies do so. When it *does* act, new distributions of resources and values usually emerge. If both judicial inaction and action have policy consequences, both conditions make the courts policy actors. When the United States Supreme Court sidesteps making a decision on a constitutional value in the finance reform case presented it, then other levels of government feel free to seek their own solutions. However, when that same Court voids de jure segregation, it sets the scene for political combinations that effectively eliminate the practice a decade later. If, however, the Court is curiously evasive in defining northern segregation problems, then the federal appellate and district courts take on a much more active and determinative role.[35]

The judiciary, however, cannot do everything, as initial southern rejection of the *Brown* decision demonstrated. Intervening between what the court seeks (outputs) and what eventuates (outcomes) are barriers of group resistance, popular ignorance, communication failure, information overload, and other confounding aspects of social and policy conflict. Even with a court mandate, much must be done to move people. A mandate does not bring total or quick acceptance; it does not provide sufficient resources for the resourceless; or it does not teach how to resolve conflict or to live with ambiguity. Additional persons and events must perform these tasks, even with a supportive judiciary. On the one hand, the judiciary has been a major stimulus for educational innovation in the last quarter century, yet it has also met with obstruction, misunderstanding, and uncertainty. The court is thus in the position that Shakespeare described in *Henry IV*, when one character proclaims, "I can call spirits from the vasty deeps," and Hotspur responds, "Why, so can I, or so can any man, but will they come when you do call for them?"

The supreme courts of state and nation have been called upon from their "vasty deeps" by citizens afflicted by racial and fiscal discrimination. Despite some reservations about how much courts can do in policy innovation, both judicial friend and foe would agree that little would have been changed without positive judicial response to such calls. That agreement marks the significant potential for educational policy innovation and implementation that inheres in these judicial "spirits." Even on its own, the judiciary can at least create a national dialogue about the standards of education that we will provide our children. In this way, the unthinkable of yesterday becomes the convention of today. Creating this flexibility of mind is a function that the judiciary and good teachers share equally.

NOTES

1. Youth Services Office, "Administrative Hearing Panel: Procedural Guidelines for Expulsion," San Bernardino City Unified School District, n.d., mimeographed. Expulsion figures are from annual report, Oct. 27, 1980. We thank Douglas E. Mitchell for bringing this to our attention and providing materials.

2. For review of these cases, see Milton R. Konvitz, *First Amendment Freedoms* (Ithaca: Cornell University Press, 1963), pt. 1. For reactions to these decisions, see Frank J. Souraf, "*Zorach* v. *Clauson*: The Impact of a Supreme Court Decision," *American Political Science Review* 53 (1959): 777–91; Robert H. Birkby, "The Supreme Court and the Bible Belt: Tennessee Reaction to the 'Schempp' Decision," *Midwest Journal of Political Science* 10 (1966): 304–15; H. Frank Way, Jr., "Survey Research on Judicial Decisions: The Prayer and Bible Reading Cases," *Western Political Quarterly* 21 (1968): 189–205; and William K. Muir, Jr., *Prayer in the Public Schools* (Chicago: University of Chicago Press, 1967).

3. Seminal statements of this thesis are Benjamin Cardozo, *The Nature of the Judicial Process* (New Haven: Yale University Press, 1921); and, in the contemporary period, Jack W. Peltason, *Federal Courts in the Political Process* (New York: Random House, 1955).

4. David J. Danelski, *A Supreme Court Justice Is Appointed* (New York: Random House, 1964); for a bibliography, see Loren P. Beth, *Politics, the Constitution, and the Supreme Court* (Evanston, Ill.: Row Peterson, 1962), p. 108–10.

5. Wallace Mendelson, *Capitalism, Democracy, and the Supreme Court* (New York: Appleton-Century-Crofts, 1960).

6. Clement R. Vose, *Caucasians Only* (Berkeley: University of California Press, 1959); and "Litigation as a Form of Pressure Group Activity," *Annals of the American Academy of Political and Social Science* 319 (1958): 22–25.

7. The behavioral school embodying this concept of values is illustrated in Glendon Schubert, *Constitutional Politics* (New York: Holt, Rinehart & Winston, 1960); and Glendon Schubert, ed., *Judicial Decision-Making* (New York: Free Press, 1963).

8. Robert Kluger, *Simple Justice* (New York: Knopf, 1975) is an exhaustive account of this human drama.

9. For a thorough coverage of the 1960s, see Gary Orfield, *The Reconstruction of Southern Education* (New York: Wiley, 1969). For the most comprehensive analysis of all phases of desegregation up to 1978, see Gary Orfield, *Must We Bus? Segregated Schools and National Policy* (Washington: Brookings Institution, 1978). The following account relies heavily upon these sources.

10. Harrell R. Rodgers, Jr., and Charles S. Bullock III, *Coercion to Compliance* (Lexington, Mass.: Lexington Books, 1976).

11. Orfield, *Must We Bus?*, p. 109.

12. Everett F. Cataldo, Michael W. Giles, and Douglas S. Gatlin, *School Desegregation Policy: Compliance, Avoidance, and the Metropolitan Remedy* (Lexington, Mass.: Lexington Books, 1978); "Policy Support within a Target Group: The Case of School Desegregation," *American Political Science Review* 72 (1978): 985–95.

13. United States Commission on Civil Rights, *Desegregation of the Nation's Public Schools: A Status Report* (Washington: Government Printing Office, 1979), pp. 20–21.

14. Tyll van Geel, "Racial Discrimination from Little Rock to Harvard," *University of Cincinnati Law Review* 49 (1980), and "School Desegregation Doctrine and the Performance of the Judiciary," *Educational Administration Quarterly* 16, no. 3 (1980): 60–81.

15. Orfield, *Must We Bus?*, pp. 66–67.

16. The fullest review is Tyll van Geel, *Authority to Control the School Program* (Lexington, Mass.: Lexington Books, 1976).

17. Cataldo et al, *School Desegregation Policy.*

18. See the attitudinal evidence in John B. McConahay and Willis D. Hawley, "Is It the Buses or the Blacks?: Self-Interest versus Symbolic Racism as Predictors of Opposition to Busing in Louisville," Center for Policy Analysis, Duke University, 1977, and David O. Spears, Carl P. Hensler, and Leslie K. Speer, "Opposition to 'Busing': Self-Interest or Symbolic Racism?" *American Political Science Review* 73 (1979): 369–84.

19. A National Institute of Education study by Diana Pearce, Center for National Policy Review, Catholic University, November 1980. Two sets of seven paired cities were compared.

20. The following draws on: Donna E. Shalala and Mary F. Williams, "Political Perspectives on Recent Efforts to Reform School Finance," in *Political Science and School Politics*, eds. Samuel K. Gove and Frederick M. Wirt (Lexington, Mass.: Lexington Books, 1976), chap. 3; Joel S. Berke, *Answers to Inequity: An Analysis of the New School Finance* (Berkeley: McCutchan, 1974); Michael W. Kirst, "The New Politics of State Education Finance," *Phi Delta Kappan* 60 (1979): 427–32; Stephen J. Carroll and Rolla E. Park, *The Search for Equity in School Finance*, (Santa Monica, Calif.: Rand, 1979); Norman C. Thomas, "Equalizing Educational Opportunity Through School Finance Reform: A Review Assessment," *University of Cincinnati Law Review* 48 (1979): 255–319.

21. A thorough examination is found in Walter Garms, James Guthrie, and Lawrence Pierce, *School Finance: The Economics and Politics of Education* (Englewood Cliffs, N.J.: Prentice-Hall, 1978).

22. Michael W. Kirst, "Coalition Building for School Finance Reform: The Case of California," *Journal of Educational Finance* 4 (Summer 1978): 29–45; Berke, *Answers to Inequity.*

23. Carroll and Park, *Search for Equity;* David L. Kirp, "School Desegregation and the Limits of Legalism," *Public Interest* 47 (1977): 122–28.

24. For different basic views on the policy function of courts, see Alexander Bickel, *The Supreme Court and the Idea of Progress* (New York: Harper & Row, 1970); Archibald Cox, *The Role of the Supreme Court in American Government.* For an understanding of the judiciary as an active policy agent, see Stephen Wasby et al.,

Desegregation from Brown to Alexander: An Exploration of Supreme Court Strategies (Carbondale, Ill.: Southern Illinois University Press, 1977).

25. Abrahm Chayes, "The Role of the Judge in Public Law Litigation," *Harvard Law Review* 89 (May 1976): 1281–1316. For actual commentary by judges involved in desegregation, see *Law and Contemporary Problems*, 39 (1975), 135–63.

26. van Geel, "School Desegregation Doctrine," p. 78.

27. Orfield, *Must We Bus?*, pt. two.

28. See the details in Emmett H. Buell, Jr., *School Desegregation and Defended Neighborhoods: The Boston Controversy* (Lexington, Mass.: Lexington Books, 1981).

29. David L. Kirp, *Elusive Equality: The Evolution of American Race and Schooling Policy* (Berkeley: University of California Press, forthcoming); Donald L. Horowitz, *The Courts and Social Policy* (Washington: Brookings Institution, 1977).

The role of social science in such litigation is a new facet of the politics of litigation. See the articles in Ray C. Rist and Ronald J. Anson, eds., *Education, Social Science, and the Judicial Process* (New York: Teachers College Press, 1977), and empirical studies by Mark A. Chesler et al., "Interactions among Scientists, Attorneys and Judges in School Desegregation Litigation," Center for Research on Social Organization, University of Michigan, 1981.

30. A wide review of these roles is found in G. Alan Tarr and Mary C. Porter, "State Supreme Court Policymaking and Federalism" (Paper presented to the American Political Science convention, August 1980).

31. Richard Lehne, *The Quest for Justice* (New York: Longman, 1978).

32. For a review of these interstate reactions, see Thomas, "Equalizing Educational Opportunity."

33. Tarr and Porter, "State Supreme Court Policymaking."

34. William H. Clune with Robert E. Lindquist, "Understanding and Researching the Implementation of Education Laws: The Essential Characteristics of Implementation" (Paper presented at the Stanford Berkeley Seminar on Law, Governance, and Education, 1980), pp. 33–34. Compare the judge's role with that of the "fixer" in administration in Eugene Bardach, *The Implementation Game* (Berkeley: University of California Press, 1977).

35. On the active role of other federal courts, see Michael W. Combs, "Courts of Appeals and Northern School Desegregation: Questions, Answers, and Public Policy" (Paper presented to the Midwest Political Science convention, April 1981).

11

The Growth of Federal Influence in Education

In the last two decades the federal government has expanded its monetary commitment to elementary and secondary education in a striking manner, as indicated by the growth of the Office of Education's budget from $477 million in 1960 to $8 billion in 1981. The federal share of overall education expenditures at all levels, however, has undergone only a slight increase from 4.4 percent to 9 percent. However, federal funds for elementary and secondary education are primarily earmarked for specific categories, such as vocational education, special compensatory programs, and environmental education. Consequently, they have a more precise impact than unrestricted aid does. This targeting of federal resources has given federal funds more stimulating potential and leverage than the small amount of total education expenditures would normally permit had federal officials merely "put money on the stump and run."

Many recent studies, however, have tended to deflate claims made for the impact of the increased federal categorical funds.[1] In aggregate terms, most annual increases in education expenditures from 1970 to 1980 have been provided by state and local funds, particularly the latter. Over this decade federal expenditures increased by $5 billion, state expenditures by $27.2 billion, and local expenditures by $20 billion. More important, state and local funds have often been distributed in such an inequitable manner that the relatively modest amount of federal aid has not been able to overcome the expenditure disadvantage of poor districts. Indeed, federal aid itself works at cross purposes—the bulk of it is equalizing (Title I, Elementary and Secondary Education Act)—but some programs operate to give wealthier school districts or schools a larger share than poorer ones. Finally, the categorical intent of federal funds is blunted by the various mechanisms of substituting local priorities for federal ones as the money flows from Washington to the local classrooms. For example, the impressive growth of federally supported research has been offset in part by the difficulty of installing the research products in local schools.

At first glance federal aid appears to be a major factor influencing school policies, but a closer inspection reveals that funds have frequently not hit their targets or have been overwhelmed by larger state and local developments. Where federal efforts succeeded in creating new educational institutions—child care centers, CETA skill centers, and regional research laboratories—the impact has been more visible and enduring than in working through the existing K through 12 systems. On the other hand, it is very difficult to build viable new institutions with uncertain, fluctuating, and "soft" money from Washington. It is these offsetting trends that will be a major focus of this chapter.

Any analysis of federal influence must emphasize the crucial role of the federal judiciary. In the field of education, no single public decision has had more impact than the 1954 Supreme Court decisions to desegregate the schools. Whatever one's views on the murky impact of federal financial aid, federal judicial rulings have caused very large extensions of federal influence.[2] The recent spate of court decisions on students' rights has resulted in large part from suits brought by federally funded lawyers. Consequently, federal influence now extends to such areas of local operations as student dress and discipline. The role of the courts has been treated specifically in chapter 10.

Modes of Federal Influence

There have been basically six alternative modes of federal action for public schools:

1. General aid: Provide no-strings aid to state and local education agencies or minimal earmarks such as teacher salaries. A modi-

fied form of general aid was proposed by President Reagan in 1981. He would consolidate numerous categories into a single block grant for local education purposes. No general aid bill has ever been approved by the Congress.

2. Stimulate through differential funding: Earmark categories of aid, provide financial incentives through matching grants, fund demonstration projects, and purchase specific services. This is the approach of ESEA.

3. Regulate: Legally specify behavior, impose standards, certify and license, enforce accountability procedures. The bilingual regulations proposed by the Carter administration (and rescinded by President Reagan) are a good example.

4. Discover knowledge and make it available: Have research performed; gather and make other statistical data available. The National Institute of Education performs the first function and the National Center for Education Statistics the second.

5. Provide services: Furnish technical assistance and consultants in specialized areas or subjects. The Office of Civil Rights will advise school districts who design voluntary desegregation plans.

6. Exert moral suasion: Develop vision and question assumptions through publications, speeches by top officials. Thus, Secretary of Education Shirley Hofstedler, in the Carter administration, stressed the shortage of science teachers.

In 1981 the Reagan administration endorsed a tuition tax credit to reimburse parents who send their children to private schools. Although various congressmen have pushed this idea for decades, this is the first time a president has endorsed it. Tuition tax credits will be a major issue in federal aid during the 1980s. It will be vociferously and unanimously opposed by public education interest groups. The Reagan administration will promote the following basic changes in the federal educational policy of the past twenty years:

1. from minimal support of private education to significant support;
2. from a prime concern with equity to more concern with efficiency and state and local freedom to choose;
3. from a larger and more influential federal role to a mitigated federal role;
4. from mistrust of the motives and capacity of state and local

educators to a renewed faith in governing units outside of Washington;

5. from categorical grants to more unrestricted types of financial aid;
6. from detailed and prescriptive regulations to deregulation.

The poorly defined value of promoting equal educational opportunity has been the most pervasive theme of federal education policy. Its most obvious expression is through numerous categorical grants targeted to students not adequately served by state and local programs (for example, disadvantaged, handicapped). The federal government has also attempted to stimulate educational reform through the Teacher Corps or demonstration programs such as women's equity and career education. The Reagan administration will attempt to scale back aggressive federal activity in such areas. The interest groups that are the recipients of federal policy will resist, but the key will be whether they can form coalitions as discussed in chapter 4. The findings by Mosher et al. are not optimistic for such alliances among these categorical groups.

... there is little evidence of common effort among the groups; the voracious categories of need tend to be strictly compartmented when demands are made for political remedies. ...
    The interest groups are also quite typical in their efforts to concentrate as much influence as possible, at the appropriate time, in a variety of policy arenas—the courts, particular state legislatures, the Congress, federal agencies, and so on. The accomplishments of the past decade indicate that they have all acquired a large degree of sophistication in political maneuvering.[3]

The last comment indicates that the objectives of categorical interests such as the handicapped may lose out at one level of government only to succeed at another.

The Evolution of the Federal Role

In 1950, when the U.S. Office of Education (USOE) was transferred to the Federal Security Agency, forerunner to the Department of Health, Education, and Welfare (HEW), it had a staff of three hundred to spend $40 million. Growth was slow and largely unrecognized. In 1963, forty-two departments, agencies, and bureaus of the government were involved in education to some degree. The Department of

Defense and the Veterans Administration spent more on educational programs than the USOE and National Science Foundation combined. The Office of Education appointed personnel who were specialists and consultants in such areas as mathematics, libraries, school buses; these specialists identified primarily with the National Education Association (NEA). Grant programs operated through deference to state priorities and judgments. State administrators were regarded by USOE as colleagues who should have the maximum decision-making discretion permitted by categorical laws.

While the era of 1963–1972 brought dramatic increases in federal activity, the essential mode of delivering services for USOE remained the same. The differential funding route was the key mode, seeking bigger and bolder categorical programs and demonstration programs. The delivery system for these categories continued to stress the superior ability of state departments of education to review local projects. Indeed, the current collection of overlapping and complex categorical aids evolved as a mode of federal action that a number of otherwise dissenting educational interests could agree on.[4] It was not the result of any rational plan for federal intervention but rather an outcome of political bargaining and coalition formation. Former USOE head Harold Howe expressed its essence this way:

Whatever its limitations, the categorical aid approach gives the states and local communities a great deal of leeway in designing educational programs to meet various needs. In essence, the Federal government says to the states (and cities) "Here is some money to solve this particular program; you figure out how to do it. . . ." But whatever the criticisms which can in justice be leveled against categorical aid to education, I believe that we must stick with it, rather than electing general aid as an alternative. The postwar period has radically altered the demands we place on our schools; a purely local and state viewpoint of education cannot produce an educational system that will serve national interest in addition to more localized concerns.[5]

An incremental shift in the style of USOE administration also came with expanded categories. The traditional provision of specialized consultants and the employment of subject-matter specialists were ended in favor of managers and generalists who had public administration rather than professional education backgrounds. These newer federal administrators have been more aggressive and have created a political backlash against federal regulation that Ronald Reagan was able to highlight in his 1980 campaign.

AN OVERVIEW OF FEDERAL FUNDING

Along with the USOE program growth from 1964 to 1980, there was a new aggressive strategy of federal-local categorical grants, bypassing the states, through such federal agencies as the Office of Economic Opportunity (Head Start, migrant education, Follow Through) and Department of Labor (Jobs Corps, CETA). These federal-local grants could be accompanied by more explicit federal controls than those that employed general guidelines for states to reinterpret. The Office of Economic Opportunity (OEO) and the Labor Department funded or created agencies supplementing the K–12 educational system such as Head Start, child care centers, and CETA skill centers. These programs were operated by mayors and city councils rather than by the school systems. It has been traditional for educators to acknowledge the curriculum outside the K–12 system and then to ignore it in their analyses.[6] Indeed, federally funded public TV broadcasting has a potential for an even more profound and pervasive impact than the programs of any federal agency to date.

A breakdown of overall federal funds for education including higher education is presented in table 11.1. However, President Reagan proposed a 25 percent cutback in almost all these areas for 1982 and abolished the remnants of OEO.

Table 11.2 provides a breakdown of federal aid for all levels of education and demonstrates the numerous agencies involved. The 1980 formation of the Department of Education *did not* result in fewer federal agencies funding education.

This unconsolidated budget obscures the numerous separate categorical programs. Since no one was sure what type of federal intervention would be effective, the congressional view was to try almost any politically palatable program. President Reagan would reverse this trend through massive consolidation into two block grants—one for LEAs and another for SEAs.

The growth of federal education expenditures has made the secretary of education a highly visible and important leader. The predecessors, the USOE commissioners from 1867 to 1963, are known by only a few historians. The secretary can use his or her Cabinet position to command widespread media attention. However, President Reagan's plan to downgrade the Department of Education to sub-Cabinet status may lower the visibility of the chief federal education officer.

Table 11.1

Federal Expenditures for Educational Programs by the Office of Education, 1960–1982

Program	Fiscal Year						Carter Proposals 1982	Reagan Proposals 1982
	1960	1964	1968	1972	1976	1980		
	(in millions of dollars)							
1. Vocational education	45.2	54.5	255.2	416.9	590.9	622.4	779.2	623.2
2. Federally impacted areas	258.2	334.3	506.4	648.6	598.9	619.5	401.0	408.0
3. NDEA	52.8	42.5	75.8	47.8	29.0	31.2	—	—*
4. Educationally disadvantaged children (ESEA Title I)	—	—	1,049.1	1,570.4	1,760.8	3,010.6	3,873.2	43.2*
5. Bilingual education	—	—	—	26.0	79.5	148.6	209.0	144.0
6. Education for the handicapped	.4	5.0	41.0	93.1	191.4	814.1	1,225.0	0.0*
7. Emergency school aid assistance	—	—	7.4	92.2	204.0	321.2	306.0	0.0*
8. Other consolidated programs	10.7	29.0	311.8	224.9	297.0	323.1	449.9	155.9
9. Other programs	17.7	19.9	138.3	232.6	361.7	446.0	344.1	81.8
10. Local block grants	—	—	—	—	—	—	—	3,647.0
11. State block grants	—	—	—	—	—	—	—	715.0
TOTAL	385.0	485.2	2,385.0	3,352.5	4,113.2	6,336.7	7,587.4	5,818.1

* Included in local block grant (item 11).

Table 11.2
Federal Outlays for Education and Related Purposes

Agency	1980 actual	1981 estimate
	(in millions of dollars)	
Education	13,783	14,931
Related outlays supporting other major missions:		
Elementary and secondary education:		
Health and human services	1,790	1,837
Defense	42	46
Veterans Administration	248	205
Agriculture	4,190	4,256
Interior	17	18
State	11	13
Other	18	23
Subtotal, elementary and secondary education	6,316	6,398
Higher education:		
Health and human services	1,922	1,933
Defense	515	577
Veterans Administration	182	161
Agriculture	12	12
Interior	3	3
State	1	1
Transportation	1	1
Other	53	53
Subtotal, higher education	2,689	2,741
Other		
Health and human services	197	209
Defense	751	845
Veterans Administration	186	163
Housing and urban development	23	21
Agriculture	268	299
Transportation	33	35
Justice	29	28
Labor	662	767
Other	1	1
Subtotal, other	2,150	2,368
Total related outlays	11,155	11,507
Total federal outlays for education and related purposes	24,938	26,438

Source: United States Bureau of the Budget, 1981.

FEDERAL INFLUENCE ON LOCAL SCHOOL OPERATIONS

The impressive growth of federal funds has not been automatically translated into influence on local education. Except for the impacted areas program, large-scale federal programs stress the promotion of innovation or change in state and local programs, priorities, and improvements in classroom practice. For instance, the National Defense Education Act of 1967 stimulated more science and math courses, a new science curriculum, and more guidance counselors. The Vocational Education Acts since 1917 emphasize reorienting local vocational education programs so that they match the large-scale transformation in labor force needs—for example, from agriculture to computer technology. ESEA Title I was not to provide "more of the same" educational approaches for disadvantaged children but special programs for special needs.

Despite uncertainty and frequent policy changes, the federal government has been the only public agency supporting a large-scale demonstration effort. Very few local districts have the discretionary money to support demonstrations, and states have only minor programs. Local funds are often programmed into standard operating procedures and routine efforts that are characterized by theories or organizational rigidity and choice.[7]

For our purposes here, it is important to realize that federal aid is change-oriented money that is being filtered through rather rigid local educational organizations.[8] Indeed, federal leverage should extend to the locus of where the child comes in contact with educational services—at the classroom level. Given our definition of *influence*, the relevant questions become: Has federal aid altered the process of education in a large number of classrooms? Have the services purchased with federal aid reached the classroom level, or have they been diverted?

The federal efforts most likely to have a lasting effect in the schools contain three characteristics: (1) they are structural or organizational—often adding layers or new functions such as vocational education or school breakfasts; (2) they create a specialized constituency; and (3) they are easily monitored. The federal change efforts least likely to leave a residue are those that require changes in classroom teacher effort or methods.[9]

The numerous constraints on effective and focused implementation (at each level of the political system) are indeed disconcerting. It is a long delivery chain from Washington, D.C., to a classroom in Houston, Texas. When one adds up the various structures and individuals at all three levels that must be changed or overcome by categorical aid (that asserts the primacy of federal goals), implementation becomes an awesome task. Federal aid essentially relies on a top-down delivery mechanism to insure that its objectives are accomplished. This top-down strategy (operating largely through administrators wielding federal-state regulations and guidelines) requires sanctions and incentives to insure that the aid reaches the intended targets or reorients classroom practice. A review of the largest federal program, Title I ESEA, will demonstrate the importance of feedback in the federal system for accomplishing federal objectives.

Feedback in the Political System

An output of the political system—whether statute, administrative order, or school board resolution—is rarely permanent. Nor is any output self-executing, for how or even whether it is executed is a function of numerous intervening variables—the attitudes and resources of its opponents and supporters, the energy with which political authorities seek compliance, and so on. Thus an output arrives in the cold world like an infant, alive with infinite possibilities; the law is a memo to the future.

A theme of this chapter is put well in these words, for we seek to show how policy outputs from Congress take on flesh and blood in the process of their administration. In the main, we bypass the input and conversion phases on which, as we shall show, the literature is already abundant. Instead we seek to learn what happens after Congress makes a law or the courts issue an order.

Each of these is taken as a political decision at one point in time— "Yesterday we agreed so and so." That decision will differentially affect the values and resources of its supporters and opponents, who, interacting with the decision, will advance different interpretations of its administration. These interpretations create stress, which in turn leads to new wants and demands that impinge upon administrators' efforts and to which they must respond. These demands provide information to political authorities, which is used to judge the need for new adaptations to stress. At one point in time, then, stands the output and, somewhere ahead in the dim future, lies the final disposition—the outcome. This, however, may well necessitate a recycling of the conversion process.

In this concept of the policy process, this input-conversion-output-outcome is generated by that part of the feedback loop running between output and income (see figure 11.1). That loop is powerful in its consequences, providing information for authorities and citizens alike, provoking discontent about the law's effect, promoting support either for output or the total political system—and it thus makes the regeneration of the cycle possible. Feedback requires a communications system that allows for a two-way flow of information, wants, and demands. These channels take such forms as telephone calls, letters, investigations, media coverage, confrontation between administrators and the administrated—and all those manifest ways Americans have for enhancing or inhibiting the role of law in their individual lives.

The dynamics of this process in the United States is made greater by the fact that we operate within a *federal* system. This is no distinct compartmentalization of sovereignties and powers among the three governmental levels of nation, state, and locality but rather an interlocking pattern of cooperation and conflict. In Grodzin's phrase, it is not a three-layered cake but a marble cake. When a systems framework is imposed upon the mosaic of subsystems constituting federalism, the policy flow may be represented symbolically as in figure 11.1.

At the beginning, arbitrarily labeled Time 1A, a sequence of stress-conversion-output is conceived as occurring through the national political system. *School outputs I* refers to the resulting policy set that is transmitted for administration at Time 1B to the *State school system.* This forms a somewhat different *Stress pattern 2*, the difference as well as similarities indicated by the 1, 2 designation of demands and supports. The result is *School outputs 1, 2,* the numerals indicating that the national policy has been transmuted by state inputs and withinputs into a somewhat different form.

At Time 1C, state outputs are administered upon the *Local school system* (direct federal-local system relations can exist also), constituting the altered *Stress pattern 3* and another combination of transmuted and yet similar demands and supports (1,2,3). These may be decisions on curriculum, attendance, zoning, salary improvements, racial composition of faculties, budget allocations, and so on. This policy set is then administered so as to achieve some kind of *Educational outcome* for those who interact with local schools—students, teachers, and so forth.

Figure 11.1
Intergovernmental Relations in a Systems Framework

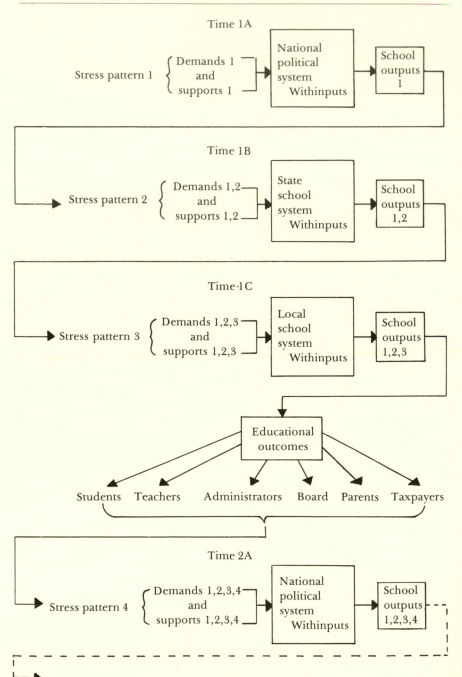

The outcomes may change the educational stress that originally precipitated the policy-making process greatly or not at all. For example, does the output of federal aid, when it finally gets down to those it is designed to affect, actually achieve the desired outcome—for instance, more qualified teachers of science or language, more students better prepared to start school or express their ideas? These outcomes may in turn generate another set of stresses, for example, defects in administrative techniques, insufficient resources being employed, or unattainable goals. As a consequence of this feedback, (Time 2A) the whole process is recycled at some future time.

While systems analysis contributes to our understanding of this complex process, its utility does not end there. If sufficient data can be provided to describe what happens for many of the jurisdictions symbolized in figure 11.1, it may become possible to develop some predictive theoretical statements for testing. Both vertically within the federal system and horizontally within any of its levels, sets of resisters and transmitters exist. Many of these have been indicated in earlier chapters; they block or bolster the transformation of outputs into what policy makers originally had in mind. Almost visible here is the underlying pulse of American individualism operating at the multiple access points of federalism to protect and promote individual and group interests. Most of the concepts raised in this section will now be illuminated by the history of ESEA, Title I.

ESEA AFTER FIFTEEN YEARS OF FEEDBACK

ESEA 1965 became a wide-ranging piece of legislation that now—fifteen years after passage—requires a book for its comprehensive treatment. Indeed, several volumes have been written on its passage and implementation.[10] Our objectives here, however, are to analyze the act in terms of (1) the feedback conflict over its objectives and (2) the political interactions involved in a federal-state-local system for delivering educational programs to the classroom level.

A substantial amount of feedback over subsequent policy adjustment was assured by the special conditions of ESEA's hurried passage. Participants at its birth still vividly recall the periodic waves of near panic that accompanied the precedent-shattering eighty-nine-day passage, as rumors persisted that some key educational group would depart the coalition or that the church-state compromise was breaking up. Its quick passage led to a congressional quip that ESEA should be renamed the "Railroad Act of 1965." Doubts about the effectiveness of its provisions had to be deferred until the principle of federal aid to education was established.

Main Provisions of ESEA

Title I of ESEA is by far the largest financial component (over $3.5 billion in 1981) and the one surrounded by the most political controversy and feedback.[11] The purpose of this program (as outlined in Public Law 89-10) is "to provide financial assistance . . . to local educational agencies serving areas with concentrations of children from low-income families to expand and improve their educational programs to meet the special educational needs of educationally deprived children.[12] The central thrust of the law is to aid low-income children. When first signed, it required the use of two poverty indicators in its fund-distribution formula: (1) the number of children aged five through seventeen from families with an annual income of less than $3,000 (updated by the 1980 census); (2) the number of children aged five through seventeen from families with incomes exceeding $3,000 in the form of aid to families with dependent children (AFDC) under Title IV of the Social Security Act.

The United States secretary of education, as well as state and local education agencies, have responsibilities for administering the Title I program. We will summarize these.

The Department of Education:

1. develops and disseminates regulations, guidelines, and other materials regarding the approval of Title I projects;
2. reviews and assesses the progress under Title I throughout the nation.

State education agencies:

1. approve proposed local projects in accordance with federal regulations and guidelines;
2. assist local educational agencies in the development of projects;
3. submit state evaluative reports to USOE.

Local education agencies:

1. identify the educationally deprived children in the areas where there are concentrations of low-income families and determine

their special educational needs;
2. develop and implement approved projects to fulfill the intent of Title I.

ESEA did not deal only with children, however. Title I also provided 1 percent of its $3.4 billion (1981) for state agencies to administer the program, and Title V allocated $30 million to strengthen the general administrative capacity of state agencies. In effect, as noted earlier, ESEA included a deliberate policy of underwriting the growth and reorientation of state departments of education, which had traditionally been independent of and, in part, antagonistic to an increase in federal administrative control of education. As we shall see, Title I was based on a creative tension between federal administrators, who wield general guidelines for local categorical programs, and SDEs with sole power to approve specific local project proposals.

The feedback after Title I's passage reflects the broad mandate of legislation that engendered a wide range of expectations. Unlike 1970, when about $1.4 billion was appropriated for Title I, the problem facing the bill's authors in 1964 was how to get *any* kind of major school aid bill enacted. An analysis of the failure of numerous school aid bills over the years concluded that federal aid "had been beaten down in every way known to parliamentary man." Although after World War II large education bills passed the Senate seven times and the House twice, as late as 1964 the president had never received a large federal aid bill.

Title I was and still is by far the largest financial component of the ESEA package, with an appropriation of over $3.4 billion for 1981. The purpose of the program, as stated in the bill's "Declaration of Intent" is ". . . to provide financial assistance to local educational agencies serving areas with concentrations of children from low-income families to expand and improve their educational programs by various means. . . ."[13]

Some read this language to mean that the program's top priority was to begin reform of the entire fabric of American education. Reform in this context meant restructuring of state and local educational agencies' allocation priorities, which traditionally spent more per child in those schools with high concentrations of students from *high-income* families.[14] Others saw Title I as a cleverly disguised general aid program. These individuals recognized the political expediency of using the "disadvantaged child" as a symbolic rallying point to get the bill passed and believed that Title I was designed to provide general aid to districts with limited property tax bases. Unlike the reform interpretation, the assumption here was that the present institutions are functioning as well as can be expected and they just need more money to better address the problem of educating poor children.

These two interpretations called for two very different implementation scenarios in the feedback process. The reformists would accept a strong federal involvement in the development, implementation, and evaluation of state and local projects, whereas the other interpretation would limit federal involvement to determining the size of entitlements and signing checks.[15] The two priorities, (1) the reform agenda of some of the program's original designers and (2) the maintenance of state and local control over federal funds, form the underlying ideological tension for the implementation of Title I over time.

Implementation Theory and the Federal System

A decade ago, implementation research pioneers such as Pressman and Wildavsky complained that "except for a few pieces mentioned in the body of this book, we have been unable to find any significant analytic work dealing with implementation.[16] That statement was debatable in 1973; it certainly is not the case today.

Within the last ten years, implementation research on federal domestic programs has passed through two distinct, although overlapping, periods. The first period began in the late 1960s and peaked in the mid 1970s. It was characterized by a flurry of case studies describing the initial few years of implementation for a variety of specific Great Society social service and regulatory programs in education, civil rights, urban development, employment opportunity, health services, and environmental protection.[17] In aggregate these initial, predominantly descriptive, case studies represented the first stage of theory development, a stage Eckstein has termed "probability probes."[18]

The most widely cited of these "first generation" short-run case studies:

1. were factually dense accounts, usually lacking explicit theory or conceptual frameworks;
2. found more failure than success during the initial phases of implementation;

3. underscored the wide scope of political, organizational, and socioeconomic factors that influenced the implementation process.

Certainly, the most comprehensive of the implementation perspectives to date is Sabatier's and Mazmanian's attempt to integrate several previous conceptualizations into a broad-scoped systems model that emphasizes the legal, political, and socioeconomic variables structuring the implementation process. They postulate that four variables most affect a program's first three to five years of implementation:

1. the "strength of the statutes and ensuing regulations

(a) how precisely and consistently the objectives are specified and ranked and (b) how clearly authority is delegated to organizational subunits

2. the presence of a "fixer"

a key legislator or administrator ideologically attuned to program requirements who controls resources important to crucial actors and who has the status, desire, and staff to closely monitor the implementation process

3. the resources of various constituency groups

the salience of an issue, its solidarity, the access to policy channels and information, and availability of side payments for representatives from implementing agencies and intended target group recipients

4. the commitment and leadership of agency officials

(a) the direction and ranking of statutory objectives in officials' preference ordering; (b) the skills in realizing these preferences

Yet the authors concede implicitly for the first three factors and explicitly for their most important explanatory factor—the commitment and leadership skills of implementing officials—that these variables are essentially "elusive concepts."[19]

They hypothesize two factors as having the most significant effect in the long run (after five years): (1) changing socioeconomic conditions, and (2) the ability of supportive constituencies to intervene effectively. Both are equally difficult to quantify.

ESEA and Implementation Problems and Successes

The evaluations of Title I's administration during the first five years splashed stories of weak federal administration and even malfeasance; early impact studies consistently found negligible educational impacts of the Program on Title I students.[20] After four years of the program's operation (1965–1969), the first comprehensive evaluation of Title I's administration by an external research group concluded that "many of the misuses of Title I funds were so gross that even non-experts can readily spot them."[21] All other early studies of Title I administration by external research agencies or individuals have reinforced this first negative assessment of wide-scale misallocation of Title I funds during the first four years of its implementation.

The major analysis of Title I administration conducted by a contracted research agency during the middle years of the program, from 1972 to 1973, used extensive interviews with USOE area desk personnel responsible for the monitoring practices of the SEAs, site visits to five states, and questionnaire data from a sample of ten states and thirty-six LEAs. Their general conclusion was that "the administration of the program in the Division of Compensatory Education is far more effective than the critics would have one believe."[22] However, they described the administrative efficiency and effectiveness as "quite depressing." Their major findings were that: (1) regulations published by USOE were inadequate for LEAs and basically worthless for SEAs; (2) criteria used by the HEW Audit Agency to determine noncompliance were drawn directly from the statutes since the regulations were inadequate; (3) USOE did not take into account LEA reporting burdens; (4) evaluations of Title I educational impact were not satisfactory; and (5) enforcement of sanctions for noncompliant behavior identified in HEW audits were virtually nonexistent.

More recent assessments of Title I management by external research organizations depict a strikingly different scenario. Using essentially the same major data source as the first compliance study of Title I in

HEW audit reports but covering eleven years rather than just the first four, Stanford Research Institute noted among its "most important trends" that "most states have developed adequate to good procedures for reviewing LEA applications for Title I funds. These systems have greatly reduced many of the initial problems. However, more subtle problems remain. . . ." and "at the LEA level, blatant misallocation of funds which clearly violated the intent of Title I have been subtantially reduced."[23] Based primarily on the findings of three other external analyses of Title I administration using data from 1972 to 1977, a longtime analyst of Title I contended in 1978 that:

The common view of Title I administration may be overly pessimistic and unjustified. A more current "end of the decade" view of the federal-state-local partnership could provide a good deal more confidence in the ability of the federal government to influence the operation of categorical programs in local school systems.[24]

Over time, for example, research reveals that federal efforts to *target* more Title I dollars to each participating student have been particularly successful. The ambiguous statutory language requires that Title I projects must be "of sufficient size, scope, and quality" to ensure that moneys are not spread too thinly and thereby threaten to diminish the effectiveness of the projects. In the early years of the program, there was a strong tendency for districts to use Title I as general aid by allowing more students to participate than were actually eligible to receive Title I funds. Table 11.3 indicates, for instance, that in 1966 approximately 5.5 million students met Title I's eligibility criteria for poverty. Yet more than an estimated 8.2 million students actually participated in the program, almost one and one-half times the eligible number. In contrast, in 1978, while about 9 million students were counted for local entitlements, only 5 million students, or less than 60 percent of the eligible students, actually participated in the program. This contributed to an increase in per-pupil expenditures from $116 in 1966 to $378 in 1979. Discounting for the effects of inflation (row V), this translates into a 62 percent increase in per-pupil expenditures over these thirteen years.

It is important to note that during this same time when per-pupil expenditures were increasing by 62 percent in real dollars, the total appropriations for Title I in dollars adjusted for inflation actually *declined* by 5 percent (row VII). Therefore, larger per-pupil expenditures were due to increased targeting of funds by local districts rather than additional appropriations.

Table 11.3
Targeting Figures for Title I from 1966 to 1978[a]

	1966	1970	1974	1978
I. Children (in millions) counted for LEA entitlements[b]	5,531	6,952	6,247	9,045
II. Participating (actual)	8,235	7,526	6,100	5,155
III. Percent participating of counted	1.49	1.08	.98	.57
IV. Per-pupil expenditures (unadjusted)	$116.46	$161.98	$247.75	$378.52
V. Per-pupil expenditures (adjusted for inflation)[c]	119.81	139.92	167.73	193.71
VI. Total Title I appropriations (in millions)	1,193	1,339	1,653	2,247
VII. Total Title I appropriations (in millions, adjusted for inflation)	1,217	1,151	1,232	1,162

[a] Figures derived from tables provided by Department of Health, Education, and Welfare, Office of Education.
[b] Figures for Rows I and II include only "educationally disadvantaged" children but do not include handicapped, juvenile delinquents, migrants, or children in agencies for the neglected.
[c] All adjusted figures are derived from the Bureau of Labor Statistics "Consumer Price Index for All Urban Consumers U.S. City Average" with 1967 as base year.

The Long View of ESEA Effects

One pervasive feature of implementation case studies is that they concentrated almost exclusively on the first three to five years of implementation. This preoccupation with short-run time lines continues in the face of growing empirical and theoretical evidence that a long-run perspective may reveal quite different patterns. Although the methodology for longitudinal analyses is not particularly exact, it appears that such an approach will at least broach the right questions.

Organizational theorists and researchers have observed that when power is widely distributed among a variety of administrative units, legislative factions, and interest groups, one center of power can rarely impose its policies on others.[25] In such a situation, policies that are the outcomes of bargaining among these actors are likely to reflect only a small degree of change over previous procedures. For example, incrementalism typically dominates the federal bugetary process,[26] and although perhaps more difficult to measure precisely, regulatory outputs are also likely only to change marginally over the short haul. Cyert and March, for instance, have noted in their study of various large private and governmental organizations that (1) goals are often initially vaguely stated in order to attain consensus; (2) incrementally these goals are made operational in standard operating procedures through bargaining and compromise; and (3) over time, *minor changes can lead to more fundamental changes.*[27]

Other research findings in the implementation of Title I ESEA from a fifteen-year perspective reinforce the theoretical arguments for using a longitudinal time line.[28] Specifically we have found:

1. Given the pluralistic nature of the groups responsible for policy setting and implementation of Title I within a highly political and bureaucratic setting of decentralized power, changes in established administrative policies and procedures have been dominated by incremental change.
2. When aggregated, these gradual changes have resulted in significant structural and substantive changes in implementation policies and practices.
3. The direction of these changes over time has been toward a more aggressive federal rule-setting, monitoring, and enforcement role in implementing some of the program's crucial categorical requirements and more congruence with key provisions of the law.
4. The following set of interrelated factors has most affected the pace and directions of these changes: (a) a shifting interest-group scenario from one that was initially dominated by professional education lobbies to one with an orientation toward compliance with federal mandates, including categorical program personnel, beneficiaries of Title I services, and lobby groups championing the recipients' causes; (b) broad social movements; (c) the political dynamics of a three-tiered (federal-state-local) structure of administration.

In order to maintain a manageable analytic scope for a longitudinal analysis, we compared changes in two of the fourteen major program requirements (or program administrative outputs): targeting and program design requirements. If a program is to be successful, moneys must first reach the intended beneficiaries. *Targeting requirements* detail the criteria for selecting eligible schools and the children who are to participate in the program within these schools. Once the moneys reach the targeted schools and students, some reporting mechanisms are necessary for federal officials to determine how the schools are spending Title I funds. *Program design requirements* set forth that each Title I school must identify its project's objectives and detail the activities and services used to achieve these stated goals. We have chosen these two requirements for cross-time comparisons as representatives of the two major categories of Title I requirements: funds-allocation requirements and program development requirements (these are later discussed in more detail). Although in the short run, improvements in the operation, monitoring, and enforcement of the requirements have occurred slowly and intermittently, when viewed from a perspective of fifteen years, one observes a dramatic shift in the implementation of these two program regulations. In effect, the standard operating procedures are much closer to federal intent in 1981 than they were in 1965.

Explanatory Forces: The Pressure Matrix

We have found that an interest-group framework integrated with a social-movement perspective provides a useful model of explanation for longitudinal implementation research. In the context of Title I, an interest-group perspective couches explanations in the political interplay among what has been called the iron triangle, consisting of:

1. Congress and, more specifically, the congressional subcommittees responsible for educational legislation;
2. implementing agencies; and
3. professional educators and special interest lobbies.

In the tradition of educational federalism, the symbolic language of the legislation accorded a potential for substantial power to each level of administration. The law gave to the commissioner of education the responsibility to develop "basic criteria" that the states were to use in their review of local applications. The states were reserved the power to approve or disapprove these projects. The local districts had wide latitude in planning, implementing, and evaluating the actual programs, be they for school construction or remedial programs for a highly selective group of students.

Overall, incremental change in the direction of more federal control has been characterized by an ongoing series of sallies, retreats, and parlays by (1) growing internal and external constituencies who see ESEA as a vehicle for changing schools and who favored or at least accepted a strict interpretation of the categorical intent of Title I, and (2) traditional education lobbies, most congressmen, and local and state administrators as well as a large number of federal administrators who preferred general aid and minimum federal involvement. Early in Title I's history, the lobby group scenario was almost exclusively dominated by interest groups representing established *professional* educational constituencies. These lobbies included, for instance: the National Education Association, the Council of Chief State School Officers, the National School Board Association, the American Association of School Administrators, the National Association of State Boards of Education, and the National Congress of Parents and Teachers. These six major educational lobbying blocs, known in Washington circles as "The Big Six," have rarely joined forces to form a unified lobbying front; however, they share a general ideological preference for protecting local and state control of education and minimizing federal regulations. Other active lobbies that usually have strong general aid preferences are the producers of educational material and supplies. Another general aid educational lobby group more active in the later part of the Title I implementation history is the Council of Great City Schools.

Over the years, the one lobby group promoting categorical restrictions on Title I funds during the initial enactment of Title I, the National Catholic Welfare Board, has been joined by a number of other groups concerned with resisting efforts to turn Title I into a general aid program. These interest groups generally represent special or focused interests of the providers or recipients of Title I funds and include: National Advisory Council for the Education of Disadvantaged Children, the National Welfare Rights Organization, the Legal Standards and Education Project of the NAACP, the Lawyers' Committee for Civil Rights under Law, and the National Association of Administrators of State and Federally-Assisted Education Programs. Some of the lobbying, technical assistance, and other advocacy processes of the special-focused pressure groups have received financial or consultative support from organizations such as the Ford Foundation and the Harvard Center for Law and Education.

In 1965, before those interest groups coalesced, Commissioner Keppel attempted to withhold all Title I funds from the Chicago schools until a civil rights investigation was completed. Illinois State School Superintendent Page informed Chicago's Mayor Daley of the impending loss of funds, and Daley in turn complained to President Johnson of unlawful federal intrusion into the local domain of providing public education. Under pressure from Johnson, Keppel rescinded the withholding ruling within five days. Thus USOE's first attempt to flex its jurisdictional muscle resulted in a precedent that for a time reduced its autonomy in the implementation of Title I.[29] The battle, however, had just begun.

Lobby Strategies in Implementation

A handful of new middle-level staff members gave initial impetus to attempts from several quarters to translate ambiguous statutory language into a more tightly monitored program. This small band of reformers in effect formed an internal constituency group within the largely traditional USOE bureaucracy. They had two basic strategies.

First, they persisted in pushing for an expansion of the "basic criteria" powers delegated to the commissioner by making the regulations guiding states' approval of local applications more explicit. The criteria they initially developed were to a large degree successfully resisted by more traditional elements within USOE and opposed by state and local administrators. After the widely publicized release of a highly critical report sponsored by a coalition of advocacy groups in 1969, other task forces again recommended tougher restrictions on the allocation of Title I funds, increased monitoring, and improvements in the procedure for resolving complaints by outside groups. As might be expected, traditional forces were partially successful in watering down these recommendations, but compared to the initial requirements and monitoring practices, substantial changes had accumulated through year-by-year incremental movement toward a more active federal involvement in the program's administration.

Second, these reformers took several steps to build constituencies at the state and local levels that would advocate or at least accept a stricter categorical interpretation. For instance, they encouraged the use of funds set aside for the state administration of Title I to establish special compensatory education units in each state department of education in order to circumvent the chief state school officers who generally were strong supporters of general aid. They actually invented the title of "State Title I Coordinator" and began bombarding these mythical figures with letters and bulletins and inviting them to regional meetings where Title I regulations and program materials were discussed, modified, and disseminated.[30] These figures are not so mythical today. In 1977 all states had categorical units headed by special directors of compensatory education.[31]

The $32 billion spent on Title I from 1965 to 1981 has spawned a national-to-local professional hierarchy with careers dependent upon and commitments more aligned to providing special services to disadvantaged children.[32] With state and federal categorical programs assuming a larger percent of public school expenditures, most urban and large suburban districts have not only local categorical program directors but also special program units operating at the district level. These staffs are versed in the technical skills required to cope with the bureaucratic minutiae seemingly endemic to federal social programs. In California, the special program coordinators from the state's thirty-three largest school districts, to which more than 80 percent of the state's Title I funds are targeted, have formed an informal consortium that holds monthly meetings and provides a vehicle for frequent and rapid exchange of information about technical aspects of implementation. These statewide consortiums are linked in a national network through regular regional meetings, yearly gatherings in Washington, and frequent newsletters and special bulletins under the auspices of the National Association of State and Federally-Assisted Education Programs. These formal and informal organizations foster strong informal norms to watch-dog district decisions so that they are consonant with categorical program requirements.

Parents of Title I children and of several state compensatory education programs are also organized from the school to the federal level in district, state, and federal advisory councils. At the federal level, the National Advisory Council for Education of Disadvantaged Children and several civil rights groups have proven to be increasingly effective lobby groups.

In chapter 8 we note that in Michigan's educational politics (a) special and compensatory education lobbies were among the most powerful education lobbies in the state, and (b) directors of special education and compensatory education were among the most influential individuals in the state educational policy process.[33] A Washington-based public interest law firm, the Lawyers' Committee for Civil Rights under Law (LCCRUL) has played a substantial role in improving enforcement of Title I categorical requirements. Its activities have included the preparation of manuals for bringing suits against districts believed to be in violation of Title I statutes and comprehensive analyses of the program's legal framework.[34] Several of their recommendations for strengthening the program requirements are quite evident in the 1978 amendments. In fact, the final 1978 Title I amendments bear a striking resemblance to the draft statute prepared by Robert Silverstein, formerly of LCCRUL.

The character of interest groups participating in implementation decision-making processes has slowly moved from a virtual monopoly by traditional professional interest groups (such as the National Education Association and the National Association of Chief State School Officers) with a strong general aid preference to a more diverse interest group situation. Numerous constituencies are now articulating an emphasis on enforcing the categorical goals for the program. Further, from a longitudinal perspective, these incremental changes when combined have resulted in a substantive shift in the nature of the interest group agendas toward targeted aid as intended by the Congress and USOE. These enforcement-oriented interest groups found allies in the Congress such as Senator Mondale, Senator Edward Kennedy, and the powerful chairman of the House Education and Labor Committee, Carl Perkins. They were reinforced by aggressive Office of Education Title I administrators.

Recently, political scientists have recognized that beyond relying on a more readily observable but perhaps somewhat myopic iron-triangle explanation for public policy formation and implementation, some consideration should also be given to the impact of broad-based social movements such as civil rights and govenmental accountability.[35] Explaining longitudinal changes in Title I's implementation involves more than just documenting how one or several ideologically consonant interest groups have coopted other lobbying constituencies serving their own private interests. Increased monitoring and oversight of Title I operations need to be seen in the light of a broader public demand for accountability in government and business during the late 1960s and early 1970s. "Creeping federalism" has spread its tentacles into city halls as well as local school districts.

The decade of the 1980s, however, will be a period of intense reconsideration of the federal role and national regulatory policy. The changes in Title I administration discussed above may be reversed and more state-local discretion permitted. The Reagan administration has radically changed the policy dialogue. The bargaining is no longer about refining and tightening federal control; the Reagan policy is total deregulation, and Congress will be pressured to trust the judgments and values of state and local administrators. Consequently, another feedback loop has started with a new dimension added to the pressure matrix. Indeed, in 1981 the Reagan administration eliminated some of the Title I regulations discussed above through an amendment to the Budget Act; it also succeeded in consolidating thirty separate education programs into one block grant costing $600 million.

ALTERNATIVE FUTURES FOR THE FEDERAL ROLE

In our view, the 1980s will differ from the previous two decades in terms of the political forces that are active and the response of the federal government to these forces. Consequently, we conclude with an analysis of the anticipated effects of the political changes prophesied for the 1980s on the federal role in education. Upon reflection, it is obvious that there are only three possible federal roles in the future. The role of the government will increase significantly, decrease significantly, or remain much the same as it has over the last two decades.

It should be possible to broadly characterize these alternative future dimensions of expansion, contraction, and maintenance and speculate as to the effects of each on Washington's role in education. In each alternative, however, the same set of contextual factors just analyzed will be applied but with a different emphasis.

The Expansive Alternative Future

Central to any significant expansion by the federal government would be a crisis in education that local and state forces could not handle. Historically, crisis has been the stimulus for all of Washington's entrances or expansion of policy in other areas. Two conditions must operate for this future to be realized: a crisis must exist, and state-local systems of education would not have the capacity to meet it. In the past, these conditions have brought state-local officials and concerned constituents to beat on the doors of Congress for relief. The explosive power of the postwar baby boom created just such a crisis for education two decades ago (preceded by a minicrisis over Sputnik, which produced the NDEA), and the spate of special-focus, national legislation after 1965 flowed from this.

What crisis could constitute a similar spur in the 1980s? Inflation seems a likely candidate, for it could mean that financially strapped LEAs and states might turn to Washington for an increased share of their school costs. Yet no such pressure has appeared to date, despite the worst recession since the 1930s. Certainly the Reagan administration's thrust to reduce national expenditures—including education— is not inducement to such pressure. There will clearly be no national repetition of the baby boom to generate a similar crisis, although the baby boomlet of the mid-1980s and thereafter will generate some local crises. Also, an improvement in the national economy (with regional variations) would enable LEAs to raise sufficient money without increasing their tax rates to meet local demands.

There is a "worst case" crisis that could expand Washington's role—a near total collapse of local public school systems, particularly in center cities of the Northeast. Boston comes closest to this example today with a federal judge controlling many aspects of education administration and financing in an effort to desegregate.[36] After all, Washington has propped up collapsing institutions in the past. It has done this for business, from the Wall Street panics of the last century to Chrysler quite recently. It has done so for agriculture in the Great Depression and for railroads and highways in the last quarter century.

The possibility is not farfetched for education in the future. Some northeastern big-city school systems are currently straining the capacity of not only their local revenue sources but also those of their states. Declining tax bases, fiscal mismanagement, desegregation, and other events suggest the possibility of institutional incapacity as the crisis that could lead to an expansion of Washington's role. Just that has happened when states were recently appealed to for bail-out funds in Chicago, Cleveland, Detroit, and Boston. But such a crisis would not be nationwide; it would probably affect only one major region and not even all the schools there.

The growing concerns over "failures" in teaching our young could also generate a crisis. Combined here are the complaints about not teaching literacy, science, and mathematics or languages well. In the past, Washington has funded comprehensive national programs to improve instruction and curriculum (MACOS, new math) as well as categorical grants to states for other innovations. A heated politicization of curriculum decision making has drawn in laity, professionals, publishers, schools of education, and all levels of government.[37] However, an expanded national role to meet the alleged failures seems unlikely, given the resistance to some of these past programs, the limited evidence (if any) that the public sees external governments as a remedy, and the divided advice from specialists on how to deal effectively with the problems.

Absent these extreme situations, it is difficult to see in either the first or last half of this decade crisis-generated national legislation. In making this judgment, there is an assumption that a crisis is not self-defining but rather is a matter of consensus.

It is difficult to detect an educational crisis possessing these crystallizing elements in emerging social trends. Possibly the increasing failure of LEA voters to support bonds, tax levies, and school budget referenda, unless checked, could eviscerate the local financial basis of many schools. Yet note that where this has occurred most severely, the state has been available to provide more funds. If this trend continues, we might see a movement toward a greater share of local costs coming from the state in the regions with the most depressed economies. When Proposition 13 passed in California, that state moved within one year from providing 44 percent to over 70 percent of LEA costs. The state tax-expenditure and limitation movement slowed in the 1980s, possibly as citizens realize that cuts will come not only in welfare but in public safety and other desired programs. Yet the same movement has grown at the federal level with the advent of the Reagan administration.

However, if such a crisis were to emerge—from the baby boomlet, the Northeast's big-city school problems, poor instruction, or tight school financing—what would be Washington's role? There should be great resistance from policy makers at rushing to meet the issues, mindful of the problems that have accompanied haste in the last two decades of national policy. That same history would also work in favor of categorical programs in the four cases mentioned. Because the needs generating these crises are quite different, they would foster, if not be stimulated by, functional interest groups such as attended the compensatory and handicapped programs. For Congress, it would be easier to appropriate funds for special uses in each case. Moreover, as noted earlier, general aid grants without formulas or guidelines end up not meeting national goals, while categorical grants, despite their slippage, do get more money on target and report better results.[38]

But the central finding of this speculation about an expansive alternative future is that the dynamic needed to create it—a systemic crisis—is not visible in 1981. Given possible crises, which primarily need larger funds, Washington's response would most likely be to give categorical grants to relieve special problems. A major exception to the lack of a Washington role in a contraction period is the judicial potential. The judiciary could open up new areas for Washington, for example, in a newly appointed Supreme Court that overturns the *Rodriguez* decision; but then, the court is always the wild card in national policy making.

The Contracting Alternative Future

An educational policy world in which Washington heavily cuts its controls and funds is the future most frequently discussed. These speculations also fit the comments of Washington observers: a new president who wants to dismantle the Department of Education and block Washington's "interference" with local governance; the June 1981 budget cuts, including drastically cutting even the popular federal impact and school lunch programs; abundant polls on the public's disenchantment with schools and their results, and so on. This is a time of "gloom and doom" for supporters of Washington's role in American education.

What would be the consequences for the contextual influences upon education policy set out earlier if this alternative future becomes a reality? Parental demand for schooling would be unaffected because there is probably little widespread public awareness of exactly what Washington does in one's local school. Special-focus groups would be distressed at the loss of federal aid in getting their interests realized in traditional schools. But as noted in chapter 9, they could turn their attention more to the state in order to maintain their share of allocations under a block grant condition. Broad-based interest groups of local school boards and teachers may feel this contraction as enabling their voices to be heard once again. As noted, their lobbies would likely concentrate even more on the state agencies, and it is possible that teacher groups would move in some places to statewide bargaining. The dimensions of this contracting future suggest a shift to a greatly strengthened *state* politics of education.

Nationwide interests historically shift to the political arena where they can be best accommodated. When Blacks found their concerns for equality ignored everywhere but the judiciary, they fought success-fully in the courts. Now when the Supreme Court seems less sup-portive, they turn to other more supportive centers of political power—increasingly hard to find, incidentally. If this shifting of the battleground is repetitive in American policy history, it is likely to appear again in a contracting future. It is as if the American policy system were a set of hydraulic linkages, so that blocking of needs in one link diverts the pressure to another. Given the immense needs that educational groups—professional or lay—currently reflect in the complex of programs, personnel, and objectives, that complex will not disappear merely because Washington shunts them away from the national level.

Washington's role in a contracting future could take a number of forms: nullifying the legislation of the last two decades; cutting back national funding, much or little, while continuing that legislation; eliminating everything except auditing controls on federal funds for education; arguing in the Supreme Court against enforcement of national legislation, as with desegregation; directing bureaucracies not to oversee the states and LEAs in the administration of national programs; shaping the public perception of Washington's role by presidential statements in the media, and so on. All of these have already emerged in the opening months of the Reagan administration.

The Maintaining Alternative Future

It is a Newton-like law of social dynamics that programs set in motion tend to continue on course unless external force is applied. That is why there is a law of incrementalism: mostly what will be is mostly what has been. Many policy changes in American history have been small, paralleling past programs, while major changes have come from ouside this world of actors. So, a maintaining alternative future is one in which only minor changes from the present educational programs occur.

In this maintaining future, despite the current talk of devolution, much of the change that occurs is symbolic, not substantive. This ineffectiveness can occur if the forces seeking devolution find themselves blocked because they did not really want change in the first place; the methods of achieving change got so complicated they could not be worked out; the volume of pressures against change was strong from state-local agencies and private groups who preferred that the cup of authority should not pass to them; or other policy areas demanded prior attention and allies, not to be diverted by a less salient issue such as education. In such cases, symbolic responses to situations by leaders who cannot make substantial changes are a traditional political tactic when one cannot win all the battles. To judge from previous administrations, these symbolic responses might include changing the names of ongoing programs and claiming that this change affects reality when it does not; reorganizing policy programs that one cannot alter in substance; introducing small programs with great publicity in the direction desired and then abandoning them later or letting them be amended to accommodate the existing policy system; accusing another branch of government or some pressure group of frustrating substantive change, then campaigning against them for reelection, and so on.

The contexts that point to the likelihood of a maintaining future include the complex of special-focus groups, including their allies among state-local school authorities, with a vested interest in program maintenance; the deepening financial crisis in state and local budgets with the cut in federal grants being difficult to absorb in some regions and no guarantee that even deeper cuts might not appear in subsequent years; the political liabilities that state agencies could accrue from the strain of allocating devolved block grants; the support that the Supreme Court has shown for the rights of beneficiaries of national programs; a more supportive public attitude about public schools if the economy improves or test scores drop no further; private sector substitutes for public schooling that are incapable of absorbing the demand for them or prove ineffective, and so on.

What would be the federal role in educational policy in such a maintaining alternative future? In keeping with the law of incrementalism, it would consist of light housekeeping, tinkering here or there with a bit more money or minor administrative change, including experimental devolution like the revised ESEA I discussed earlier. In such a future, a national program for purchasing or developing individualized instruction formats such as microprocessor technology might have a special attraction for Washington. A program like this could serve to test such developments, as it has other instructional materials, but more important it could help underwrite schools' purchase of them.

Note that this technology imposes no particular learning mode, subject matter, or moral lessons on a differentiated student body and school system. Given an array of such varied computer materials to diverse LEAs, combinations could be selected and purchased that are amenable to each district's preferences in educational matters. This technology is not unlike a blackboard; it thrusts no particular information or value on the user but rather can be employed for a variety of educational practices and values. Therefore, a federal government advocating such technology is much different than one pushing MACOS or new math curricula or phonics or other reading pedagogies. The private sector benefit from such sales is another attraction, especially to conservatives. There may be a hint of this possibility in the recent report that the army is contracting to private companies for electronic games that would teach tank and artillery gunners how to shoot.

There is no "the future" at any one moment of time but rather possibilities and probabilities. Gauging the likelihood of these alternatives requires a feeling for the mixing of influences in the past, numerous political and social forces in the present, and new events in the future. The latter suggests a frame of mind that sees policy as not set in concrete for all time. Rather it alters as the interplay of democratic politics moves policy from the present to a future with shifts from the possible to certainty. There is little in the concepts or training of those in social science that enables scholars to do more than analyze the outer edges of this matrix of historical and contemporary influences. We are excellent at postdictive analysis, fair on current analysis, but only amateurs on predictive analysis of public policy. We are certainly better than gypsy fortune-tellers and probably better than the Delphic oracles, but the best we can offer, as with these papers, is a reduction of the possibilities to a number of probabilities.

Beyond that, it is our hopes and fears that are being projected onto the analysis for a period as long as a decade. That is valid though because of such emotions dreams are made, and from dreams the future is molded into a subsequent present.

NOTES

1. For an overview, see Michael Timpane, ed., *The Federal Interest in Financing Education* (Cambridge, Mass.: Ballinger, 1979).

2. David L. Kirp and Mark G. Yudof, *Educational Policy and the Law* (Berkeley: McCutchan, 1982).

3. Edith K. Mosher, Anne Hastings, and Jennings Wagoner, "Beyond the Breaking Point," *Educational Evaluation and Policy Analysis* 3, no. 1 (1981): 47.

4. James Sundquist, *Politics and Policy* (Washington, D.C.: Brookings Institution, 1968), pp. 155–221.

5. Harold Howe, "National Policy for American Education," (Speech to the Seventy-first Annual Convention of the National Congress of Parents and Teachers, Minneapolis, Minn., May 22, 1967).

6. Lawrence Cremin, "Curriculum-Making in the United States," *Teachers College Record* 83 (1971): 207–20.

7. Willis D. Hawley, "Dealing with Organizational Rigidity in Public Schools: A Theoretical Perspective" in *The Polity of the School*, Frederick M. Wirt (Lexington, Mass.: Lexington Books, 1975), p. 187.

8. See James March and Herbert Simon, *Organizations* (Chicago: Wiley, 1958). A summary of the research in this area is in Graham Allison, *Essence of Devision* (Boston: Little, Brown & Co., 1971).

9. See David Tyack, Michael Kirst, and Elizabeth Hansot, "Education Reform: Retrospect and Prospect," *Teachers College Record* 81, no. 3 (Spring 1980): 253–69.

10. See Stephen K. Bailey and Edith Mosher, *ESEA: The Office of Education Administers a Law* (Syracuse, N.Y.: Syracuse University Press, 1966).

11. Samuel Halperin, "The Elementary and Secondary Education Act: Five Years Later," *House Congressional Record,* September 9, 1970, H. 8493.

12. The original ESEA legislation had five titles. In addition to Title I, which receives the largest share of the ESEA appropriation, the other four titles included: Title II, which provided funds for local library service expansion; Title III, which funneled financial aid and technical assistance for "innovative programs" and supplementary centers; Title IV, which supports federal research grants and contracts; and Title V, which invested federal dollars into the strengthening of state departments of education.

13. P.L. 89–10.

14. See, for instance, Allan S. Mundel, *Resource Distribution inside School Districts* (Lexington, Mass.: Lexington Books, 1975); John Owen, "The Distribution of Educational Resources in Large American Cities," *Journal of Human Resources* 7 (Winter 1972): 171–90; and Stephen Barrow, "The Impact of Intergovernmental Aid on Public School Spending," (Diss., Stanford University, 1974), pp. 59–66.

15. Floyd Stoner, "The Implementation of Ambiguous Legislative Language:

Title I of the Elementary and Secondary Education Act," (Diss., University of Wisconsin-Madison, 1976), pp. 84–89.

16. Jeffrey Pressman and Aaron Wildavsky, *Implementation* (Berkeley: University of California Press, 1973), p. 166.

17. For a summary of the most frequently cited of these first-generation case studies, see Paul Sabatier and David Mazmanian, "The Implementation of Regulatory Policy: A Framework of Analysis," No. 39 of Research Reports of Institute for Governmental Affairs (Davis, Calif.: University of California, 1979), f.m. 2–7; and James March, "Footnotes to Organizational Change" (Paper prepared for 1980 National Assembly sponsored by the National Center for Higher Education Management System, January 17, 1980, Denver, Colo.), f.m. 1–5.

18. Harry Eckstein, "Case Studies in Political Science," in *Handbook of Political Science,* vol. 7, eds. F. I. Greenstein and N. W. Polsby (Reading, Mass.: Addison-Wesley, 1975), pp. 79–138. See, for example, Eugene Bardach, *The Implementation Game: What Happens After a Bill Becomes a Law* (Cambridge, Mass.: MIT Press, 1977); Richard Elmore, "Organizational Models of Social Program Impementation" in *Making Change Happen?*, ed. Dale Mann (New York: Teachers College Press, 1978), pp. 185–223; Sabatier and Mazmanian, "Implementation of Regulatory Policy"; and Carl Van Horn and Donald Van Meter, "The Implementation of Intergovernmental Policy" in *Public Policy Making in a Federal System*, ed. Charles O. Jones and Robert D. Thomas (Beverly Hills, Calif.: Sage, 1976), pp. 39–62. Also see, John Meyer, "The Impact of the Centralization of Educational Funding on State and Local Organizational Governance," Draft report No. 79–C5, Institute for Research on Educational Finance and Governance (Stanford, Calif.: Stanford University, 1979); Walter Williams, "Implementation Analysis and Assessment" in *Social Program Implementation,* eds. Walter Williams and Richard Elmore, (New York: Academic Press, 1976), pp. 267–92; and Robert Yin, "Studying the Implementation of Public Programs" in *Studying Implementation*, ed. Walter Williams (Chatham, N.Y.: Chatham House, 1982).

19. Sabatier and Mazmanian, "Implementation of Regulatory Policy," pp. 21–22.

20. Early administration evaluations of Title I include: Ruby Martin and Phyllis McClure, *Title I of ESEA: Is It Helping Poor Children?* (A report by the Washington Research Project of the Southern Center for Studies in Public Policy and the NAACP Legal Defense of Education Fund, Inc., 1969); Jerome Murphy, "The Education Bureaucracies Implement Novel Policy: The Politics of Title ESEA, 1965–72" in *Policy and Politics in America*, ed. Allen Sindler (Boston: Little, Brown & Co., 1973), pp. 160–98; and Michael Wargo et al., *ESEA Title I, A Reanalysis and Synthesis of the Evidence* (Palo Alto, Calif.: American Institute for Research, 1972).

Major impact studies of Title I projects between 1965 and 1969 are: Gene Glass et al., *Education of the Disadvantaged: An Evaluation Report on Title I, Elementary and Secondary Education Act of Fiscal Year 1969* (Boulder, Colo.: University of Colorado, 1970); David Hawkridge et al., "A Study of Selected Exemplary Programs for the Education of Disadvantaged Children," pts. I and II, Final Report No. 08 9013 for United States Office of Education (Palo Alto, Calif.: American Institute for Research, 1968, mimeographed); and Harry Picariello, "Evaluation of Title I," United States Office of Program, Planning, and Evaluation (1969, mimeographed).

21. Martin and McClure, *Title I of ESEA*, p. 104.

22. *The Silken Purse: Legislative Recommendations for Title I of the Elementary and*

Secondary Education Act (Washington, D.C.: The Planar Corporation, 1973), HEW OS-72-224, pp. 16–18.

23. Stanford Research Institute International, *Trends in Management of ESEA Title I: A Perspective from Compliance Reviews*, vol. 1, "Overview, Findings, and Conclusions," prepared by Harold Winslow for the Office of the Assistant Secretary for Education (Menlo Park, Calif., 1977), p. iii.

24. Robert Goettel, "Financial Assistance to National Target Groups: The ESEA Tidal [sic] I Experience" in *The Federal Interest in Financing Schooling*, ed. Michael Timpane (Cambridge, Mass.: Ballinger, 1978), p. 156. The results of the findings of Title I administration studies conducted by Booz, Allen and Hamilton, Inc., Syracuse Research Corporation, and Policy Research Corporation are summarized in: National Institute of Education, *Administration of Compensatory Education* (Washington, D.C.: NIE, 1977), chap. IV.

25. Charles Lindblom, "The Science of Muddling Through," *Public Administration Review* 19 (Spring 1959): 79–88; Charles Lindblom and D. Braybrooke, *A Strategy of Decisions* (New York: Free Press, 1963); Ira Sharkansky, *Routines of Politics* (New York: Van Nostrand, 1970); and Aaron Wildavsky, *Budgeting: A Comparative Theory of the Budgeting Process* (Boston: Little, Brown & Co., 1975).

26. Aaron Wildavsky, *The Politics of the Budgetary Process* (Boston: Little, Brown & Co., 1964), chap. 3.

27. See Richard Cyert and James March, *A Behavioral Theory of the Firm* (Englewood Cliffs, N.J.: Prentice-Hall, 1963) (emphasis added).

28. Lester Salamon, "The Time Dimension in Policy Evaluation: The Case of New Deal Land-Reform Experiments," *Public Policy* 27, no. 2 (Spring 1979): 178–80.

29. John Hughes and Anne Hughes, *Equal Education: A New National Strategy*. (Bloomington, Ind.: Indiana University Press, 1972), pp. 63–66.

30. Ibid., pp. 41–42.

31. As reported in *United States Government Manual, 1979-1980*. (Washington, D.C.: United States Government Printing Office, 1979).

32. Based on interviews with Charlie Cooke, Director of Federal Education Programs for California (1/30/80) and Lillian Barna, Special Programs Coordinator, San Jose, California (1/28/79).

33. Edward Duane and William Bridgeland, "Power Differentiation among Educational Interest Groups," (East Lansing, Mich.: Michigan State University, 1979), unpublished paper.

34. Robert Silverstein, *A Policy Maker's Guide to Title I of the Elementary and Secondary Education Act and Its Relationship to State and Local Special Programs* (Denver, Colo.: Education Commission of the States, 1979), pp. 1–2; and interview with Charlie Cooke (1/20/80).

35. Louis J. Zurcher and R. George Kirkpatrick, *Citizens for Decency* (Austin, Tex.: University of Texas, 1976).

36. Emmett H. Buell, *School Desegregation and Defended Neighborhoods: The Boston Controversy* (Lexington, Mass.: Lexington Books, 1981).

37. Paul Goldstein, *Changing the American Schoolbook* (Lexington, Mass.: Lexington Books, 1978).

38. Advisory Commission on Intergovernmental Relations, *The Intergovernmental Grant System: An Assessment and Proposed Policies* (Washington, D.C.: ACIR, 1980).

Author Index

Subject Index